Wingshooter's Guide to
South Dakota
Upland Birds and Waterfowl

TITLES AVAILABLE IN THIS SERIES

Wingshooter's Guide to Montana

Wingshooter's Guide to South Dakota

Wingshooter's Guide to Arizona

Wingshooter's Guide to North Dakota
(Spring 1997)

Wingshooter's Guide to Idaho
(Spring 1997)

Wingshooter's Guide to
South Dakota
Upland Birds and Waterfowl

Ben O. Williams and Chuck Johnson
photos by Ben O. Williams

Wilderness Adventures Press

This book was made with an easy opening, lay flat binding.

Published by Wilderness Adventures Press
P.O. Box 627
Gallatin Gateway, MT 59730
800-925-3339

10 9 8 7 6 5 4 3 2 1

Printed in the United States of America

Library of Congress Catalog Card Number: 96-060290

ISBN 1-885106-22-X

To our daughters:
Robin Lovec
Susan Baker
Tracy and Jennifer Johnson

TABLE OF CONTENTS

Dakota Heritage Region & Maps

South Dakota Indian Reservations

National Wildlife Refuges and Waterfowl Production Areas

FOREWORD

by Mark Kayser

Most six-year-olds find escape in super heroes and cartoon characters. Not me. My fascination for South Dakota's colorful ring-necked pheasant started while learning my penmanship in a rural eastern South Dakota farm town. Begging to go hunting with dad and grandpa was expected from me and each hunt spurred my upland interest. My trophy collection of pheasant wings and tails would regularly have to be disposed of because of the medley of bugs they drew to my bedroom.

I guess it came as no surprise that as a six-year-old, I did not ask for Christmas toys like GI Joe dolls or sports paraphernalia. No, I wanted one thing for Christmas, a mounted ringneck for my wall. Fortunately and without faltering, my folks gave me that mounted pheasant…or I should say Santa gave it to me. I know deep down they gave me that pheasant because of my interest and appreciation for wild things, but it was also a clever ploy to eliminate the trail of bugs leading to my bedroom.

Upon reaching the legal hunting age of 12, my interests had definitely expanded beyond the loud cackling roosters. Evening hunts with grandpa exposed me to the tiny gray partridge that explode in a feathery fury, providing targets for only the calmest of hunters. Doves, ducks and geese all became animals to pursue in my after school hours.

It was when I reached 16 that I truly discovered the best of South Dakota, because I could legally hunt on my own. Not that I didn't want to hunt with grandpa, but his health prevented him from trekking into the back sloughs and the furthest, overgown fence rows. Oftentimes, when we did go together, grandpa would let me out and he would road hunt to the other side of the section to pick up a tired youngster. Having the luxury of hunting alone taught me the wily ways of the ringneck. It taught me to pick a target during the explosion of a partridge flush. And, it taught me the amount of decoys to place in a small creek…not to mention to shoot only drakes and not hens, which would end a duck hunt all too quickly.

On a snowy December evening in the eastern part of the state, I came in contact with the "other" upland birds of South Dakota. Working down a fence row with snowflakes blocking my view, a whirling of wings ahead automatically brought my gun to aim. Subconsciously, I knew the bird wasn't a pheasant and it looked too big to be a partridge…but what else could it be? At that age, I ended the quick thought with a shot from my grandpa's nickel-plated Winchester model 12. The bird had a short, rounded tail and banded featherss across its chest. Later, I would learn the bird's true identity, a greater prairie chicken. How that bird ended up nearly 150 miles from its range, I don't now, but it was my first taste of the prairie birds of future hunts.

Fourteen years later, my career took me to western South Dakota, a land steeped in history and bird hunting opportunities. It was here, on a rainy, September morning in the capital city of Pierre, that I met up with Ben Williams. Ben was on a mission from Montana, and it had prairie chicken written all over it. Introducing me to the infamous Winston, his beloved Britt, we quickly headed to the home of the prairie "ghosts."

Upon reaching the hunting location, despite the restricting gumbo mud, we dropped shells in the guns. Then, something strange happened. You see, Ben had a truckload of Britts which I thought were merely extras to replace a soon-to-be-tired Winston. I was incredibly wrong.

In one flurry, Ben released the "herd" of dogs upon the prairie, and they swept the grasslands before us like an uncontrollable prairie fire. I thought to myself, "What a mess this is going to turn out to be." Within the hour, I would be thinking otherwise.

The image of uncontrollability took on the look of a Super Bowl game strategy. The dogs were obviously a team and when they scented the first wisps of grouse, the entire clan honored each other, nearly circling a ridge-top location. The dogs did their job, but my 20 gauge didn't perform nearly as well. From then on, Ben's "herd" would be a welcome sight on any prairie grouse adventure.

South Dakota's rich bird hunting history predates written records as Native Americans utilized sharp-tailed grouse and prairie chickens for consumption and even incorporated spring mating rituals of these birds into their culture. Records of early explorers describe the waterfowl on the Dakota prairies as being nothing but incredible.

In 1908, a new immigrant entered the scene, the Chinese ring-necked pheasant. Pheasants quickly filled every niche of habitat like the homesteaders had done following the homestead act of 1862. Since then, South Dakota's waterfowl and upland birds have been on a roller coaster ride with peaking and diving population trends. Regardless of their numbers, game bird hunting in South Dakota continues to offer some of the finest opportunities in North America. Sharp-tailed grouse, greater prairie chicken, gray partridge, mallards, pintails, Canada geese and numerous other species, provide wingshooters a smorgasbord of opportunities. The *Wingshooter's Guide to South Dakota* will assist you in making those opportunities a lasting memory. Enjoy!

Mark Kayser
Media Relations
Department of Tourism
State of South Dakota

INTRODUCTION

Ben and I have hunted South Dakota extensively for the past twenty years. We have found the hunting exceptional and the people of South Dakota very warm and friendly. On my first hunt in South Dakota, Blanche and I hunted pheasants and deer over Thanksgiving. One of the deputy game wardens checked with us to make sure that we had found a place to hunt and when he found that we were staying over Thanksgiving weekend, he invited us to his house for dinner. Since all of the restaurants in town were closed, his invitation was greatly appreciated.

South Dakota has some of the finest upland bird and waterfowl hunting in the country. The South Dakota Game, Fish, and Parks Department has developed an extensive program to promote habitat and places to hunt. The Department of Tourism actively promotes hunting and encourages the towns and people of South Dakota to develop their hunting resources. We want to thank Mark Kayser, Media Relations, South Dakota Department of Tourism; Chamber of Commerce, Winner, South Dakota; Kelly Phillips; Ken Maun, South Dakota Game, Fish, & Parks; Steve Nelson; and the fine people of Winner, South Dakota.

Chuck Johnson, 1996

Chuck with Annie and Cody.

TIPS ON USING THIS BOOK

• The area code for the entire state of South Dakota is 605. When no area code precedes a phone number, you can assume it is a South Dakota number. You must dial 1 + 605 for all in-state long distance calls.

• Although we have tried to be as accurate as possible, please note that this information is current only for 1996. Ownership of hotels, restaurants, etc., may change, and we cannot guarantee the quality of the services they provide.

• Always check with the Game, Fish and Parks Department for the most recent hunting regulations. Prices, season dates, and regulations can change from year to year.

• Don't forget to ask permission before you hunt on private land.

• Finding a Place to Hunt: South Dakota has a lot of hunting pressure especially during the first two or three weeks of pheasant season. Plan your hunt early. Most of the towns have a list of land owners that allow hunting and also farms that take hunters and provide lodging. We suggest that you write to the towns where you intend to hunt and obtain their lists of places to stay and hunt.

Motel cost key:
$ — less than $30.00 per night
$$ — between $30 - 50.00 per night
$$$ — between $50.00 per night & up

SOUTH DAKOTA FACTS

75,896 square miles
Ranks 17 in size in the nation
220 miles north to south
375 miles east to west

Population: 715,400
    Ranks 45 in nation in population
    9.37 people per square mile
Counties: 67
Time zones: Central & Mountain

Attractions:
    Mount Rushmore
    Badlands National Parks
    2 National Forests: Black Hills & Custer
    8 Sioux Indian Reservations

Nicknames: Coyote State, Mount Rushmore State
Primary Industries: Agriculture, services
Capital: Pierre
Bird: ringneck pheasant
State Flower: pasque
Animal: coyote
Fish: walleye
Tree: Black Hills spruce

MAJOR ROADS & RIVERS OF SOUTH DAKOTA

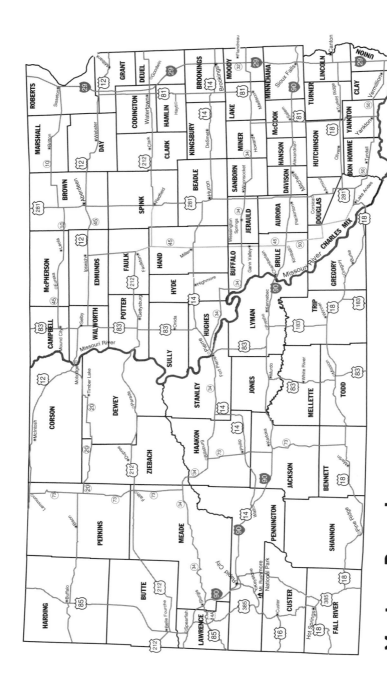

Major Roadways

◉ County Seats

◎ Area Activity Hub

SOUTH DAKOTA HUNTING REGULATIONS

UPLAND GAMEBIRDS

GENERAL REGULATIONS

Licenses — The following licenses are available through licensing agents throughout the state. Licenses are valid January 1 through December 31. Nonresident Waterfowl Licenses are only available from the Licensing Office in Pierre, 605-773--3393, 412 West Missouri, Pierre 57501; World Wide Web homepage URL: http://www/state.sd.us/gfp/. For locations and phone numbers of Wildlife Division Offices, see *Federal and State Lands Access.*

CURRENT 1996 FEES

	Res.	Nonres.
Sportsman's License	$30.00	$ —
Resident Basic Game and Fish License	$ 5.00	$ —
Small Game Stamp/License	$ 6.00	$65.00
Wildlife Habitat Stamp	$ 8.00	$ —
Nonresident Waterfowl License	$ —	$90.00
Waterfowl Restoration Stamp	$ 2.00	$ —

Trespass — No person may hunt or trap on private land without permission from the owner or lessee (see page 18, South Dakota Hunting Handbook).

Validating Stamps — Stamps, including the Federal Waterfowl Stamp, must be affixed to the back of the applicable license and signed in ink on the face to validate them. No state stamps are required by nonresidents.

Boundary Waters — Deeded islands in the Missouri River require the license of the state in which they are deeded. Hunters licensed by either South Dakota or Nebraska may hunt anywhere in the flowing Missouri River as long as water separates the hunter from the mainland of the other state.

Indian Trust Lands — State licenses are not valid on Indian trust lands unless authorized by the tribal council.

Small Game License — The Small Game License is valid for two periods of five consecutive days. The nonresident must choose the starting dates of both periods when the license is bought. Nonresidents may buy more than one Small Game License. The second five-day period can be changed, however, if done before the second five-day period begins.

Waterfowl License — The state Waterfowl License is required for nonresidents who hunt migratory waterfowl. Nonresidents must apply to the License Office for licenses. The Waterfowl License is valid for 10 consecutive days in Units 100B and 100D, and is valid the entire waterfowl season for hunters licensed for Unit 100A, comprised of Union, Clay, Bon Homme, Yankton and Charles Mix counties. Licensee must choose when the 10 days begin when applying, but the dates can be changed if done before the license period begins. The change must be made by the License Office in Pierre. Nonresidents may have up to two Waterfowl Licenses.

Hunting on Public Road Rights-of-Way — Public road rights-of-way are open for small game hunting without landowner permission except within 660 feet of schools, churches, occupied buildings or livestock. *NOTE: Fences are sometimes not on a right-of-way boundary and sometimes there is no fence. Most section line rights-of-way are 66 feet wide. Some acquired rights-of-way are wider. For more information, see page 9 of the* South Dakota 1996 Hunting Handbook.

Transporting, Shipping and Storing Small Game and Waterfowl — Game birds possessed, transported, placed in public storage, or accepted for shipment must have ONE FOOT or THE HEAD or SUFFICIENT PLUMAGE ATTACHED (waterfowl, feathered wing attached) to allow prompt identification of species and sex.

If the game is packaged, the package must have a statement attached signed by the packager showing the name of the licensee and the number and kind of game enclosed. Persons may carry or transport only THEIR OWN lawfully possessed game birds as personal baggage unless they have obtained a free Shipping and Transportation Permit.

To transport another person's small game to that person's residence for them or to ship small game by common carrier either within or outside the state, a free Shipping and Transportation Permit must be obtained from a Conservation Officer.

Shipping and Transportation Permits are not given as a means of allowing a person to exceed his or her possession limit. Follow these steps to obtain a permit:

1. Contact a Conservation Officer to arrange a meeting place and time.
2. All persons involved must meet with the officer and bring their hunting licenses and game to be transported.
3. Permits will not be issued before they are needed.

Individuals wanting transportation permits should be aware that hunting seasons are busy times for Conservation Officers and there may be a waiting period to get a permit. It's recommended each person arrange to carry or transport only his or her own game birds as personal baggage.

TURKEY
SPRING

All Spring Turkey Seasons — April 13–May 19

Prairie Turkey: Residents eligible for all units; nonresidents eligible for all units west of the Missouri River.
Custer State Park Turkey: Only South Dakota residents eligible.
Archery Turkey: Residents and nonresidents eligible.
Black Hills Turkey: Residents and nonresidents eligible.

Spring Turkey Deadlines

Season	Deadline
Resident Prairie Turkey	March 8
Nonresident Prairie Turkey	March 8
Resident Custer State Park Turkey	March 8
Resident Archery Turkey	No Deadline
Nonresident Archery Turkey	No Deadline
Resident Black Hills Turkey	No Deadline
Nonresident Black Hills Turkey	No Deadline

Prairie Turkey Leftover Licenses — Second deadline postmarked no later than **March 20**. Those who do not have a license may submit one application. Third deadline postmarked no later than **March 27**. Anyone may apply for additional licenses (3 maximum for season). Leftover licenses will be pooled and be available to either a resident or a nonresident beginning with this drawing.

FALL

Fall Prairie Turkey Season — October 1–31 (Bon Homme, Yankton and Union counties); all other units — **October 1–December 17**

Prairie Turkey: Residents eligible for all units; nonresidents eligible for all units west of the Missouri River.
Custer State Park Turkey: Season closed.
Black Hills Turkey: Season closed.

Fall Turkey Deadlines

Season	Deadline
Resident Prairie Turkey	July 7
Nonresident Prairie Turkey	July 7
Resident Custer State Park Turkey	March 8
Nonresident Archery Turkey	No Season
Resident Black Hills Turkey	No Season
Nonresident Black Hills Turkey	No Season

Prairie Turkey Leftover Licenses — Second deadline postmarked no later than **July 21**. Those who do not have a license may submit one application. Third deadline postmarked no later than **August 11**. Anyone may apply for additional licenses (3 maximum for season). Leftover licenses will be pooled and be available to either a resident or a nonresident beginning with this drawing.

GUIDES, OUTFITTERS AND LODGES

South Dakota has a number of guides, lodges, and outfitters that cater to bird hunters. They offer a variety of services and accommodations that range from deluxe clubhouses with all the amenities, to operators who prefer large groups of hunters, to an individual guide who will put you up in his farmhouse and who will take only small groups or individual hunters.

We have listed a number of these guides. You can find their listings in each of the four regions of the state. The greatest number of guides are located in the central part of the state in the Great Lakes region. The western part of the state, the Black Hills region, has the fewest guides for bird hunters.

We have listed the types of services offered by state guides based on information we received from them. We suggest that you call and talk to the guide service you are interested in before you book your hunt. The type of hunt offered varies with each guide. Many guides are looking for large parties and hunt with a large number of people, while some guides only take one group at a time. By talking to the guide, you can determine which one offers the type of hunt and services that you desire.

Many South Dakota small towns actively promote bird hunting and often have a list of local ranchers and farmers that offer hunting. I suggest that you write to several of the towns in the area that you wish to hunt and ask them for a list of guides and farms that take in hunters or allow hunting. The best place to write is the chamber of commerce in the town. Addresses for the chambers are listed at the end of each section in the region.

The South Dakota Professional Guides & Outfitters Association has a free list of all of its members. You can obtain this list by writing to:

South Dakota Professional Guides & Outfitters Association
P.O. Box 703
Pierre, SD 57501
605-945-2928

PHEASANT
Phasianus colchicus

QUICK FACTS

Local Names:
ring-necked pheasant, ringneck, Chinese pheasant, chink

Size:
Adult cocks are 30-36" in length—unlike other gamebirds, the tail accounts for almost 1/3 of their length. Cocks have a wingspan of 32-34" and weigh 2 1/2-3 1/2 lbs. Adult hens are 20-25" long with a wingspan of 24-29" and an average weight of 2-21/4 lbs.

Identification in Flight:
Brightly colored male appears much darker than the female. Other features of the cock are the white collar around its neck and long dark tail. The male will sometimes cackle in flight, but this is not a sure identification factor. Following a pheasant in the sun or in low light can confuse the identification of the sexes. When in doubt, don't shoot! Hunting in South Dakota is for male pheasants only.

- Distribution of food and cover is important. Twenty acres of cover scattered throughout a crop field is more effective than 20 square acres.
- CRP has been a boon to pheasant populations. In South Dakota, 675,000 acres have been taken out of agricultural production and planted to permanent cover.
- Pheasants Forever, Inc. is an organization that was formed to protect land and enhance pheasant and other wildlife populations throughout North America through public awareness and education, habitat restoration, development and maintenance, and improvements in land and water management policies. I highly recommend that all upland bird hunters join Pheasants Forever. Membership is $20 a year and includes $5 for the magazine, *Pheasants Forever, The Journal of Upland Game Conservation*, published 5 times a year. Contact your local chapter or write: Pheasants Forever, Inc., 3522 La Bore Road, St. Paul, MN 55110.

Color

Many South Dakota upland bird hunters consider the adult male pheasant the most handsome of all gamebirds. It is certainly a magnificent, brilliantly plumed bird. Well established in North America, the wild pheasant was introduced in South Dakota in the late 1800s following the plowshare and agricultural development in the state.

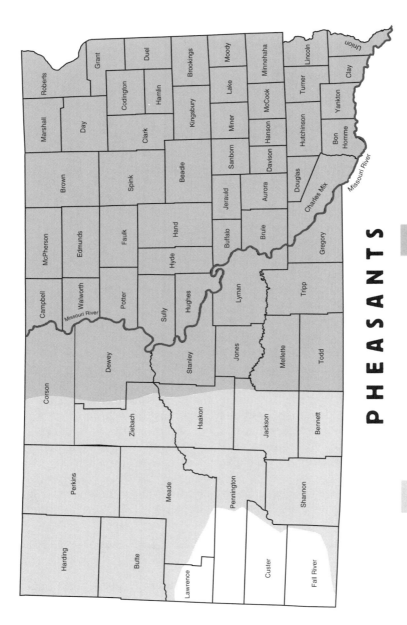

PHEASANTS

Prime Area

Very Productive

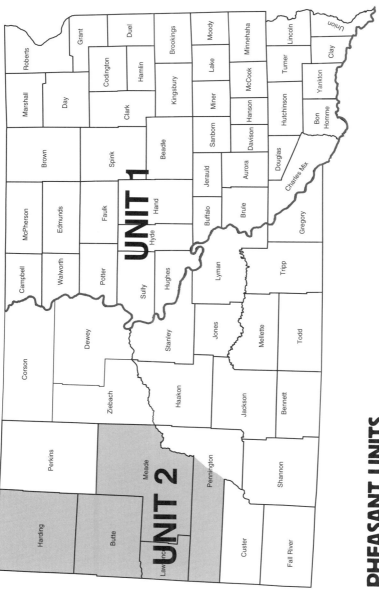

PHEASANT UNITS

The cock has ear tufts and bright-red cheek patches around its eyes forming wattles around much of the head. The beak is bluish-white and chicken-like. The rest of the head and neck is iridescent green separated from the body by a white collar. The body is colorful with many rich metallic, bronze, brown, red, black, and gray markings. The long, pointed tail is light brown with dark bars. The legs lack feathers but have spurs.

The hen is smaller and has several shades of mottled light browns, with dark markings throughout her body. She does not have a white ring around her neck. The female has a pointed, light brown, barred tail that is shorter than her partner's. The hen's legs are bare and lack spurs.

Cock pheasant feeding in a CRP field.

Sound and Flight Pattern

Cocks will often utter a coarse cackle when flying (cuct-et, cuct-et, cuct-cuct). Hens are mostly silent but can make a high pitched queep-queep.

Although pheasants would rather run than fly, they are strong flyers for short periods. They take off explosively in any direction except the one you are expecting. The rounded wings are short compared to their body size. The wings are cupped and built for sudden power strokes. Within seconds, pheasants can hit speeds of up to 35 miles per hour. The pheasant locks its wings and can glide up to a quarter-mile, flap its wings, and start the glide again. Many cock birds will fly and glide nearly a mile before landing with their running gear down. The distance of the flight depends on the proximity of cover the bird is looking for as an escape route.

Similar Gamebirds

Early in the season, young pheasants of both sexes can be confused with young sharp-tailed and prairie chickens. Young pheasants have brown bellies with bare legs and long tails. Sharptails have shorter tails, white bellies with feathered legs, and a plump shape. All three species have different flight patterns, wingbeats, and vocal sounds. With a little practice, it is easy to identify these characteristics.

Flock or Covey Habits

By fall, young birds have reached adult size and the broods have broken up for pre-winter conditioning. Pheasants are in mixed-sex pairs, singles, or small flocks in late fall. In years of high pheasant populations, large flocks of 40 or more birds will remain in protective cover close to food sources.

Winter is a critical time for pheasants in South Dakota. Great losses can occur during severe winters. It's important for pheasants to have heavy protective cover and adequate winter food to minimize losses and achieve a breeding population.

Reproduction and Life Span

Pheasants nest on the ground in a wide variety of cover types—open grassland, CRP fields, ditch banks, fence rows, hay meadows, alfalfa fields, or any brushy area with heavy cover. Nests in undisturbed cover have the best chance for success, while nests in sparse habitat have little chance of survival. Pheasants lay 8-12 eggs with an incubation period of 23 days. If the nest is destroyed, the hen is quite persistent and will renest. Pheasants raise only one brood each year, but during the early fall you may see birds of different sizes because of renesting.

Hatching activity peaks in mid-June, coinciding with the mowing season for alfalfa and hay in many South Dakota counties.

Clutches of eggs differ in number. The average is 8-12, but usually only 30% or less of young pheasants survive to the following spring. A two-year old pheasant is comparatively old. Studies have indicated that less than 4% of the pheasant population is over three years old.

Pheasant population numbers are affected by diversity of cover crops, weather, seasonal changes, and long-term land practices. The quantity and quality of the habitat is the determining factor in the population numbers for any species. The CRP has contributed greatly to higher nesting success.

Kash Lovec turns on a running rooster

Feeding Habits and Patterns

Pheasants normally roost on the ground in cover such as CRP fields or grassy draws. In cold weather, they roost in cattails and other dense cover. Pheasants leave their roosting place at daybreak and begin feeding after sunrise. During overcast days or bad morning weather, they may change their feeding habits considerably. If there is a change in weather or a front approaching, the pheasant will feed longer to take advantage of the light.

At daybreak, pheasants gather along edges of roads, rock outcroppings, or in grain fields to feed and collect grit. Daybreak and sunset are excellent times to drive gravel roads and spot birds for the next day's hunt. Once full of food and grit, the pheasant seeks denser cover along waterways and draws, preferably with a canopy of cover such as willows, cattails, rose bushes, or other high vegetation to rest. In the middle of the day, birds may move to dusting areas for short periods, and on cool days, occasionally

Arnie Gutenkauf hunting CRP.

lie out in the open to sun themselves. Later in the day, the birds begin moving to feeding grounds and grit spots before returning to their roosting places.

Young pheasant chicks eat insects to get protein needed for growth. Soon they learn to eat a wide variety of foods. Young and adult South Dakota pheasants dine mostly on cereal grains. Wheat, barley, oats, corn, beans, peas, sorghum, weed seeds, grasses, wild oats, thistle, sunflower seeds, fruits, dandelions, sweet clover, insects, snails, and many other plants and animals are consumed by pheasants. Pheasants obtain water in many forms, including insects, fruits, green vegetation, rain, dew, and snow. Creeks, ponds, and ditches are useful but not necessary. Wetlands are used by pheasants mostly for protection.

Preferred Habitat and Cover

Ideal pheasant habitat has a balance between non-cultivated land and cultivated land. Large blocks of dryland farming provide a food source for pheasants but lack cover for protection. Large areas of shrub grasslands and plains grassland have cover but no food.

Diverse cover types and food crops perform a variety of functions in pheasants' lives. Trees, shrubs, woody plants, and thorny bushes mostly found around waterways provide the pheasant with shade and protection from wind, sun, and predators. Undisturbed vegetation provides nesting and brood cover. Wetlands, cattail marshes, weedy patches, and brushy draws are used for loafing, dusting, and roosting. Edges of fields, fence rows, ditches, narrow draws running into grain fields, and roadsides provide travel lanes for food or escape.

While training dogs one August, I observed through my binoculars, a red fox with pups by her den beside a creek bottom. The willows were high and the cover heavy. Around the den was a large mound of open grassland about 30 yards square. There was a group of young pheasants chasing grasshoppers, paying little attention to the vixen and the pups rolling around in the dirt. After a time, the female fox got up, stretched her front feet forward and yawned, sending the pheasants back into the cover. I approached the site with my dogs, putting the fox family down the hole and the pheasants on the run for heavy cover. The dogs pointed several birds, but most of the pheasants funneled down along the creek. I returned to the den and examined the bones and fox scat scattered around the site. I did find a number of pheasant bones, but to my surprise the scat was mostly rodent bones, grasshopper wings, fruits, and other vegetation I could not identify. The habitat provided the young birds with an escape route, thus keeping them safe from the fox. That fall the pheasant hunting on this stretch of creek bottom was outstanding. The combination of different vegetation cover in an area is the key to good pheasant populations and pheasant hunting.

Jerry Grinstein rooting out a pheasant.

Locating Hunting Areas

In South Dakota, the hunter will find the right combination of cover types plus croplands together:
1. along major river bottom lands and their tributaries;
2. around irrigation projects;
3. in grain croplands (especially corn fields), dryland areas interrupted by brushy draws, and steep grassy slopes, marshes, reservoirs, and other terrain unsuitable for tillage;
4. in CRP tracts (many CRP fields are bordered by grain cropland);
5. near large water impoundments with cover and adjacent croplands.

Looking for Sign

Pheasant droppings are similar to those of chickens. The birds scratch the ground to uncover food and make well-defined dusting bowls. Favorite loafing places will have feathers.

Hunting Methods

There are possibly as many ways to hunt pheasants as there are pheasant hunters. Here are some things that work for me. Learn the birds' daily routine (feeding habits, roosting areas). Early in the morning when the birds are feeding, hunt

Lyn Grinstein thanks Winston for a fine retrieve.

A couple of happy pheasant hunters

along the edges of grainfields, old homesteads adjacent to crops, draws running into croplands, high-cut stubble fields close to vegetation areas, cover along fence rows with feed, and reservoirs and stock ponds located near food sources. These are the places where birds have food and escape routes.

It may take only an hour or so for the pheasant to get enough grain and grit. After they loaf, the pheasants will move into CRP tracts, high cover, and weedy hangouts. Later in the season, due to hunting pressure or cold weather, pheasants will hide in heavier cover like cattails. Hunt the CRP fields, creek bottoms, large draws, and woody thickets in the middle of the day. Late in the afternoon, as birds move back to feeding areas, hunt the same cover as you did in the morning.

Hunting large fields of CRP or croplands without dogs can be futile, but hunting the same area with a good dog can be outstanding. Two or more hunters can walk the fields from opposite ends, cutting the edges of the field. This prevents pheasants from running out. Another approach is to move along in a zig-zag pattern, stopping often to give the pheasants a chance to flush. Pheasants often circle around and are pushed into the trailing person. The important thing about this maneuver is that each hunter remains aware of the others' locations.

When hunting creek bottoms and long draws, blocking by two or more hunters with or without dogs can be effective. Meandering creeks, oxbows, and turns can provide a place to cut off birds. Isolated patches of cover should be approached from different ends.

One of my favorite ways to hunt pheasants is to follow a creek bottom with my dogs, running the birds ahead and forcing them into the small side draws that either run out or lead to stubble fields. Later, I hunt the small draws slowly. Some of the pheasants will hold for the dogs.

Hunting with Dogs

A dog that hunts close and likes to retrieve birds is the best kind of pheasant dog. Fast-moving pointing dogs occasionally pin down pheasants, but many good pointers have a lot of trouble with them. While the dog is on point, the pheasant runs out. Pointers that work close or trail are worthwhile pheasant dogs.

Flushing and retrieving dogs are the best all-around pheasant dogs. A dog working back-and-forth in front of the hunter within 25 yards will be successful. It takes a smart pheasant to escape a flushing dog.

After shooting a pheasant, the first responsibility is to find the bird. Any well-trained bird dog, whatever the breed, will save many downed and crippled birds.

Table Preparations

Pheasant breasts are white meat and the legs are medium-dark. I draw my birds as soon as possible and hang them in a cool place for at least a week. This seems to reduce stringiness and add flavor. Pick or skin the bird just prior to cooking.

Shot and Choke Suggestions

Early in the season and in close cover: No. 7½-6 shot, 1⅛-1¼ oz. of shot.
Chokes: improved and modified.
Mid- and late season: No. 7½, 6, or 5 shot, 1¼ oz. of shot.
Chokes: improved, modified, and full.
Over dogs and all around: No. 6 shot.

TERRY

Pete always got up early. Not because pheasant hunting is better in the morning, it just seems old folks do that. Ink Blot would only raise one eyelid to make sure the old man wouldn't leave without him. If you add seven years to a dog's life for every one year in a man's, they'd be about the same age. Old! Both had gray whiskers.

Pete went to the kitchen, put the teakettle of water on the stove, and three tablespoons of coffee crystals in the thermos. Blot got up and blocked the front door so Pete wouldn't forget him. The old man made two sandwiches, one bologna and mayonnaise, the other peanut butter and jelly, wrapped the two in waxed paper, and put them in his lunch box along with two apples, four dog biscuits, and a Coke. He filled the thermos, grabbed the lunch box and placed them next to the dog at the front door.

The lab raised his head two inches and smelled the lunch box, his eyes following Pete around the room.

Pete dressed warm, putting on his tin cloth hunting coat. The worn pockets showed outlines of shot shells. He opened the front closet, took out a battered model 12 and a single shot twelve gauge, both ancient. The dog's big brown eyes were glued to the guns as he got to his feet.

The pickup coughed a couple of times and belched once before it started. Blot's nose against the windshield had already thawed a small peek hole through the frosted glass. The bright orange sun hadn't been up long enough to do its job.

Pete went over and picked up the kid. Terry was small for a seventh grader but eager. The slight youngster wore a Minnesota Twins baseball cap, coveralls and Nike running shoes. The straight blond hair emphasized the cornflower blue eyes. The kid jumped in on the passenger side of the pickup, but the lab didn't move over, and the door slammed against the bright red jump suit. Terry looked under the dog's head at the old man and he looked back. He shook his head and said, "Those ain't much for huntin' boots. Are you dressed warm enough?"

The kid said ,"Hi" first and then "Yes".

"Terry, we're still going to hunt your grandfather's farm. He told me there's plenty of pheasants on the place. I guess Bill already told you he couldn't go with us this morning."

"The grain elevator operation needs two loads of corn early so he and your grandmother had to go to town, Terry. Bill said he was looking forward to taking you on your first pheasant hunt . You know, Kid, this is the first opening day of pheasant season that Bill and I have missed hunting together in twenty years. Terry, we'll do all right without him."

"I brought a little lunch for us. I hope you like peanut butter and jelly."

"Let me tell you, Kid, I've missed a lot of birds in my time and I'll miss some more if I shoot long enough, so don't get upset if you don't shoot a bird today. I ain't shootin' much these days. I just like to get the dog out now and then. I won't take my gun along, so we can concentrate on getting you a big long tail rooster. Don't think about how pretty they are and don't close your eyes when you shoot. Both are bad news, Kid."

Pete parked in back of the big red barn, out of sight of the chicken coop so Blot wouldn't get so excited seeing all those chickens. The old man got out of the pickup with Blot helping him along. The kid jumped out the other side. The sun was higher now and the frost was starting to melt on the corn stalks. A rooster crowed in the distance.

The old man handed the kid the single shot gun and two shells and said, "Put one in the gun and one in your pocket, but keep the gun open until Blot gets excited. He'll get real nervous when he smells the birds and run back and forth in front of us. Don't worry, I'll be right in back of you. Shoot only at the pretty ones. If a hen gets up I'll yell."

The old man, the old dog, and the kid started between a row of bent over corn stalks and the long fence row. The old lab worked the heavy cover slowly, its tail swinging back and forth like the pendulum on a grandfather clock.

Pete could see rooster pheasants running ahead, but didn't say a word. He knew it wouldn't be long before the birds would stop and all hell would break loose.

"Figure it this way," the old man said to Terry. "Hold the muzzle high, be aware of the dog, and give the bird time to get some elevation. Then shoot!"

They walked until they hit the corner of the cornfield and the fence lines. Blot was sailing around with his nose to the ground making some serious game. He sounded like a pig digging up turnips.

"Close the gun and get ready," Pete said.

Terry moved four steps to the side, clearing some bushes, then moved forward. She was ready. Five roosters catapulted into the crisp cobalt blue sky. Blot didn't have far to go to retrieve that long tailed rooster.

Ben O. Williams, 1996

GREATER PRAIRIE CHICKEN

Tympaniuchus cupido pinnatus

QUICK FACTS

Local Name

Pinnated grouse, fool hen, prairie grouse, yellow legs, square tail, prairie hen, wild chicken

Size

Adult cocks are slightly heavier than the hens. The adults range in length from 16 to 19 inches with a wingspan of 27 to 29 and a weight between 2 to 2½ pounds.

Identification in Flight

Many hunters find it difficult to differentiate between prairie chickens and sharp-tailed grouse while the birds are in flight. Prairie chickens have a squared-off tail, darker coloration, different wing beats, and a less cupped wing in flight than the sharptail.

- The greater prairie chicken was a tall grass prairie species but extended its range westward as cereal crops replaced the native mixed prairie.
- Most of the original range of the prairie chicken was turned into agricultural land. Cultivated land does help the chicken; yet if the cropland is too widespread, replacing most of the prairie, the bird will disappear.
- In some states, there has been a trend to increase the amount of grasslands and decrease the amount of tilled land. If these new grasslands are properly managed there may be a brighter future for the prairie chicken.
- Prairie chickens were not native to the Dakotas, but later adapted to the mixed prairie states when the cover and food supply was in balance.
- The courtship performance of the prairie chicken cock is done on an open raised area, called a booming ground.
- Hunting prairie chickens is best done in early fall. Later, the birds flock in large groups and are hard to approach.

Color

A generally drab brown chicken-like bird, the adults have brownish heads with a slight crest, orange eyebrows, and blackish pinnated feathers. The key marking are dark brown and buff on the upper parts of the body and heavily barred feathers on the breast. The tail looks square but is short and rounded. The male has yellowish sacs on the sides of the throat. The female's sac is very small. Adults have yellow orange toes and their feet are feathered to the toes.

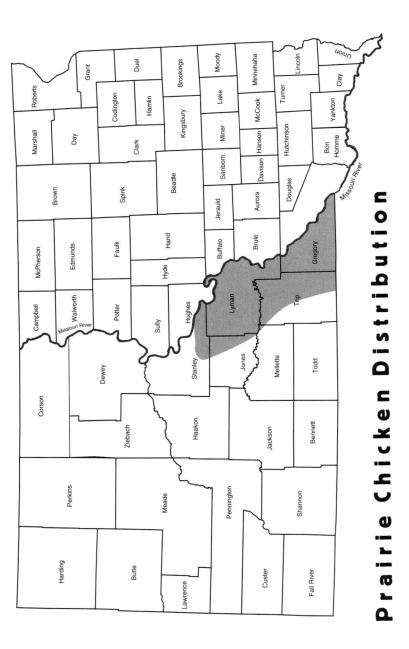

Prairie Chicken Distribution

Sound and Flight

The sound the prairie chicken makes is similar to the sharptail, but the "chuckles" are softer. The chicken's take-off is rapid, the wing beats are continuous for long periods of time (almost pigeon-like). Early in the season, birds will fly shorter distances. Later in the fall, the prairie chickens will band together in large flocks and will fly long distances and will be hard to approach.

A prairie chicken on his booming ground.

Similar Game Birds

Bag limits are set for prairie grouse in general which includes any combination of sharptails and prairie chickens. Flying birds are not easy to distinguish, but prairie chicken and sharptail in the hand are easy to identify. Grouse can be confused with immature pheasants and many times they inhabit the same fields. When in doubt, don't shoot.

Flock or Covey Habits

When the chicks hatch, the hen and brood stays together throughout the summer and fall. By late September, the birds are in full plumage and will start forming loose winter flocks with other brood groups. As cold weather arrives, food supplies dwindle and large groups will form. Their range will expand as they search for food and roosting habitat.

Reproduction and Life Span

The prairie chickens' courtship begins in March and will last as late as June, but most activity on the booming grounds is in early April.

Nesting begins in April or early May. Prairie chickens tend to use open cover like pastures, hayfields, grasslands, or CRP fields. Nests are dished out and often will have a canopy overhead. The nest can be fairly close to the booming grounds and more than one hen may occupy the same area. A prairie chicken's clutch of eggs is from 8 to 12 and incubation takes about 24 days. Unlike most other upland game birds, re-nesting is not as common if the first nest is destroyed. Some late broods will hatch as late as July. The hen has full responsibility for the rearing of the young. She leaves the nest a few hours after hatching, allowing the young chicks to follow. The chicks respond to her instructions closely. Mortality can be low during the early life of the chicks if weather conditions are good. The loss of young throughout the summer months may bring the brood size down to five or six birds by hunting season. The average annual mortality rate for juveniles is about 65%. Habitat and the land carrying capacity plays an important part in keeping numbers of young birds alive.

Mark Kayser hunting prairie chickens.

Feeding Habits and Patterns

Food requirements of young prairie chickens are similar to those of sharptails. Large quantities of insects are consumed early in life along with many greens. Prairie chickens will feed on wild fruits and small grains as they become abundant. Buds and twigs are eaten in the winter when cultivated crops are covered with snow. Prairie chickens roost in the open prairies or in CRP tracts. The bird leaves early in the morning to go to the feeding grounds, and will feed as close to the roosting area as possible, if food is available. Later in the year, the prairie chicken may have to travel great distances for food. Once they've fed, the birds return to the prairie grasslands and CRP field to collect grit, dust, and rest. The prairie chicken likes high ground in the grassland and will spend many hours below hilly crest lines to loaf, sun themselves, and look out across the prairies for danger. Like other game birds, the birds will return to the feeding grounds after sunset before going to roost.

Preferred Habitat and Cover

Grassland is the fundamental habitat required by prairie chickens. The prairie conditions, amount, and variety determine the carrying capacity for chickens. Other type of cover within the grassland (marshes, swales, brush land) may be useful but it is not essential to the bird. Shorter cover is used for booming grounds, loafing and feeding for the young. Denser grass is cover for nesting, roosting, and feeding. Also, rolling prairies are better suited for prairie chickens than flatlands because the hills, ridges, and depression have the different types of grasses and densities the chickens require. Large blocks of grasslands are essential for prairie chickens. If smaller parcels of croplands are interspersed with the grasslands or adjacent to it, the chicken habitat improves, but if the agricultural lands become dominant over a large area,it has a detrimental effect on the population.

Unfortunately, the large native prairies of the past are mostly gone, replaced by pastures, hayfields, and croplands. These would be acceptable for the prairie chicken if it wasn't for intensive management practices. Moderate grazing and less hay harvest can play an important element for today's prairie chicken habitat, but proper management is the key.

Locating Hunting Areas

Prairie chickens depend on large tracts of rolling prairie that have been well managed. Some blocks of CRP can be beneficial to these birds if it has the right habitat. Crop fields close to or adjacent to large grasslands are used by the birds during feeding.

1. Prairie chicken are early risers and start feeding before sunrise. It takes several hours for chickens to fill their crops. The birds repeat the feeding in mid afternoon before going to roost. Look for feeding areas close to grasslands early in the season.

Chuck Johnson works a draw.

2. Chickens will use food sources close to grassland prairie first. As food becomes scarce, the birds will expand their range.
3. When prairie chickens are using the grassland after feeding in the morning the birds prefer to be along the hillsides just off the ridge lines. Also look for areas in the grassland where birds are feeding on particular plants like prickly lettuce or seeds.
4. Use binoculars for bird movement. Many times the birds will move great distances and tracking them with glasses can be helpful.
5. Unlike sharptails, prairie chickens do not use brushy cover or woody areas unless conditions are extremely cold.
6. Early in the season, booming ground locations can help in finding prairie chicken hangouts for fall hunting.

It's hot, dirty work, but sombody has to do it.

Looking for Sign

Prairie chicken droppings are off white to green-brown and very similar to sharp-tailed grouse droppings. In roosting areas, the droppings will be in a small circular matted down space where the birds have spent the night. Many times the family groups or flocks will roost in the same location. Prairie chickens, like other game birds, like to dust and form dusting bowls on sandy soil or open places where the soil is silty. Many of the dusting sites are used over and over. Dusting bowls will have many feathers and a close examination can determine how recently the birds were present.

Hunting Methods

Prairie chicken populations do fluctuate from year to year. Weather conditions during the nesting season and good management of the prairie and other factors play an important part in large and small numbers. Early in the hunting season, the

A prairie chicken and sharptail grouse brace.

prairie chickens are still in family groups or small flocks. At this time they do not move great distances. In fact, many of the chickens will spend all of their time in the prairie if greens and other food and cover are available.

Chickens like to hang out on grass hillsides and below the edges of hills during windy weather. On warm sunny days, birds use the crest of rolling hills with less dense cover to loaf and rest. The best bet for hunting is to concentrate on the big blocks of well managed mixed prairie or the CRP tracts that have a mixture of grasses and vegetation that chickens use. Also hunt the particular area of the grassland that the birds will use at certain times of day—hillsides in open areas during mid-day, fields in the morning and early evening. Early in the morning or late afternoon, many birds move to crop fields adjacent to large blocks of grasslands. Late in the season chicken hunting changes to mostly pass shooting. The birds are in large flocks and then they are traveling from resting or roosting places to feeding areas. Large flocks of most game birds cannot be approached within shooting range.

Hunting Dogs

Pointing dogs are great for prairie chickens. This is one of the game birds that like big open rolling grasslands. Early in the season prairie chickens hold well but when flushed, can fly fairly long distances in the big country. With big, running, pointers you have a better chance of relocating the birds. Dogs that retrieve are useful in tracking downed birds in the high grass cover. Flushing and retrieving breeds can certainly be used for hunting chickens, but the hunter just has to cover more ground.

Late in the season, the chickens will not hold well for dogs and hunting becomes difficult.

Shot and choke suggestions

Early in the season 7½ -6 shot, 1 to 1¼ ounces of shot
Choke: improved and modified
Mid season and beyond 5-6 shot, 1¼ ounces of shot
Choke: modified and full

Table Preparations

Prairie chickens have dark meat and compare favorably with sharptails. Birds shot early in the season will be very tender and delicate. Old timers have said, "The sooner cooked after being killed the better." Treat prairie chicken the same as sharptail. Field dress as soon as possible. Hang or refrigerate birds for a few days before skinning.

PRAIRIE BOOMERS

It was nine fifteen when Ray pulled in the drive and parked his hunting rig between the garage and dog kennels. Arnie's shorthair, Rex, and English pointer, Skeeter, sounded off in unison, as he drove up and stopped. There was no response from Ray's Munsterlanders, except for the sound of tails wagging against the sides of the compartments in the dog trailer.

The trailer is a converted veterinarian mobile clinic unit built like a tank. It has all the comforts of home for the dogs plus a few extras for people. The trailer holds fifty gallons of water for use in the kitchen galley and outside spigots. There are six dog compartments and ample room for hunting and dog equipment. The trailer's clearance is high, giving it mobility and with his 4 X 4 pickup he can travel most gumbo roads in the vast, mixed grass prairies of South Dakota.

Ray stepped out of the cab of the pickup, checked his dogs, and headed for the house. It was a three hour drive to Arnie's and a cup of coffee would taste good.

Arnie met Ray at the side door, shook hands, and sat down at the table. "Coffee?" asked Arnie.

"Sure will. How do the grouse and chickens look?" inquired Ray.

"A lot of birds, but not where we found them last year. There's more vegetation, so the birds are not as concentrated this year," said Arnie as he finished pouring the coffee. Pot coffee always smells good, he thought, as he returned the pot to the stove. "Help yourself to more, Ray. I'm going to load my gear and dogs. Oh, by the way, here's the latest report about the fall pheasant forecast. Sounds good too."

Ray eased the trailer down the drive, backed into the street, and headed south out of town.

Cirrus clouds were building on the western horizon. The misty morning dew clung to the buffalo berry, chokecherry, and plums. Rolling waves of western wheat grass had disappeared creating soft, moist, saturated air that poured through the side vents, chilling their faces. Arnie closed the side port, looked over at Ray and suggested taking the old Manson Creek Cut Off Road to S.R. 230. "I don't believe it's too wet, and we may see a few chickens flying back to the side hills after feeding." said Arnie.

"Yeah, might see some pheasants along the creek, too," he said, signaling right.

Ray swung out a little for the tight corner and on to the gumbo rutted road where they slowed to a crawl.

It took most of an hour to get there. The clouds were moving fast across the pale blue sky, the swirling wheat grass loosely visible in the rear view mirror. Along the narrow trail the post marker S.R. 230 had disappeared under a mud bath. Ray hit the brake pedal gently. "We darned near missed the turnoff," he said.

The dogs shifted positions and the grass quit swirling in the rear view mirror as they made the turn down the long slope toward the twin hills. At the first big draw, Ray pulled the pickup over and stopped. They were alone. Good friends, four dogs, rolling waves of prairies grass dancing in the breeze and chickens, they hoped, loafing in the little blue-stem and grama grass covered slopes.

"It's that time of day. The birds should be here, Arnie," said Ray.

"What do you think of hunting a while and having a late afternoon lunch, Ray?"

"Sounds good to me."

Both unloaded the dogs from the the truck, put water down for them, and put on their hunting vests.

"Ray, are you going to run both dogs?" Arnie asked.

"I think so. How about you?"

"No, I think I will run Skeeter alone. He runs big and has a good chance of locating the birds early," pointing his finger at the expansive terrain below the ridge line. "What do you think about separating and you run one hill and I'll run the other? When we get back we can compare notes," said Arnie.

"Good idea, Arnie."

Arnie put the shorthair back in his compartment. Rex was a great old dog and didn't put up too much of a fuss, but you could tell by his eyes that he wasn't unhappy. "Your turn will come." Arnie said to his dog. Arnie turned to talk to Ray, but he was already a third of the way up the grassy slope below the shale outcropping.

Arnie called Skeeter over and put on the remote training collar and crossed the big coulee toward the rolling hills. There was a small stock dam a quarter of a mile up the coulee and Arnie's intention was to have Skeeter search the edges of the reservoir first and then work the side hill to the ridge covering the different elevations. Skeeter had his own agenda and headed in Ray's direction. Arnie turned toward Skeeter, reached for the button on the remote trainer, blew one loud blast on his whistle first, and the pointer made a tight U turn toward his master. Arnie watched, his hand on his hip, waiting for his English pointer .

He watched Ray for a moment, negotiating the slope far out in the tan hills. Arnie's eyes caught a glimpse of black specks flying over the ridge. He signaled, moving his arm upward, and Ray responded, but Arnie shook his head and decided to keep to his own game plan.

Arnie walked a half a mile across the uneven rolling country toward the ridge, watching Skeeter work above and below the pond. The pointer was thorough crisscrossing the heavier vegetation around the water. The dog had had enough of the coulee and struck out toward the ridge for the sparse, bleached big bluestem and needle grass prairie hills. Skeeter was running two hundred yards ahead, at the same elevation as his master. He turned suddenly—as if he'd run into a brick wall, twisted, locked up motionless, tail held high.

Arnie changed gears. When he walked in past the dog, one chicken got up. It was an easy straight away shot. Skeeter scooped up the prairie chicken and was heading back toward Arnie when the flock flushed at the far edge of full choke range. Arnie watched them feather the wind, pitching down over the ridge.

Arnie smoothed the feathers down, admired the beautiful barred rooster, and slid it into his vest. He reached down and patted Skeeter's head.

It took Arnie many slow steps to reach the ridge top. The ridge was bare and rocky. Beyond the wide meadow was a wilderness of metallic gold against the sun.

A little while later, the pointer straightened out like a statue, head high with every muscle quivering, as Arnie walked along side. Arnie killed another chicken, could have had two, but he watched the rest of the flock fly low against the putty blue skyline.

He thought possibly his third and last bird of the day would come after lunch with his older dog Rex. Arnie headed toward the pickup. While walking he heard two shots fired. Ray, he thought.

Ray's two dogs were working far out ahead, their tails swaying, encouraging their noses. Ray walked perhaps two hundred yards, picking his way diagonally up the steep slope, gaining elevation slowly. The pair of Munsterlander's tails slowed, stopped, and the dogs became rigid. Ray moved as quietly as possible, breathing harder with each step. Both dogs relocated over a swell, moving out of sight. Ray's steps quickened! Reaching the top of the rise the tails came into view, high and steady. They moved again, working the cover, and trying to locate the scent. The birds had been there, but possibly flushed when they saw the hunting rig below them. Ray checked the ground and found fresh droppings and a few feathers. His dogs continued working the area like twin vacuum cleaners. Ray looked back down the hill toward Arnie.

Arnie was waving his arm, pointing in the direction of the ridge line. Ray motioned for his partner to join him. Arnie waved him to go ahead. Ray assumed the chickens wouldn't go far this time of year, but the flock might be scattered. At the top of the wide ridge, the little blue stem grass gave way to western wheat-grass mixed with green needle grass. The grass was high and lush on the rolling gumbo clay hills of the fertile grasslands.

The dogs' high tails were all that was visible, moving across the sea of waving gold. Ray stopped and watched his pointers, knowing they would find the birds in this vast ocean of prairie

Two hundred yards ahead the tails disappeared over the gradual swell. He did not hurry, but his course was a straight line toward the last sighting of tails. The gentle breeze felt good on his face, his eyes focused on the horizon, looking for two dark brown specks. He reached the highest land form, seeing only the golden hue of grasses blended into the mackerel sky. No dogs! Ray's eye searched every foot of cover; he knew his dog were on point some place. But where?

Grassland prairies play tricks on you. The sea of grass is not level, always rolling, hiding unseen things in its folds. He followed his instinct walking into the wind. The land gave way to a gradual slope. Out of the left corner of his shooting glasses he picked up a dark spot. He turned his head and two spots came into view, motionless. Ray took a deep breath, opened the breech of his double and checked the shells. By the time he walked to the dogs the breeze had picked up. He adjusted his glasses first, then his hat. The shotgun stock went just below his armpit as he walked past the dogs. Ray turned and whispered quietly to Turk and his partner. The dogs held tight and the Parker spoke twice. "Fetch em up!" he said.

Ben O. Williams, 1996

Ray DeJong holding two prairie chickens retrieved by his Munsterlanders.

Pete McLain with a fine pair of prairie chickens.

SHARP-TAILED GROUSE

Pedioecetes phasianellus

QUICK FACTS

Local Names:
grouse, sharptail, speckle-belly, pintail, prairie chicken, chicken

Size:
both sexes average 16-20" in length and weigh 1¼–2¼ lbs. The wingspan is 26-29".

Identification in Flight:
Appears almost white—have a rounded look and a short, pointed tail.

- Weather conditions are determining factors in sharptail behavior and location.
- Sharptail habitat is primarily mixed prairie rangeland interspersed with shrub and brush-filled draws and coulees.
- Number of sharptail can vary greatly between moist upland prairies and semi-arid shrub grassland.
- Sharp-tailed grouse are native to South Dakota and are well established in the state. The Great Plains sharptail is abundant and lives in the central and eastern part of the state.

Color

The sharp-tailed grouse is a plump, short bird with a pointed tail. The sexes are similar in appearance, however males have yellow eye combs and pale purple air sacs on the throat. Sharp-tailed grouse are mottled black, brown, buff, and white. The feathers on the top of the head are brown and black with a black line behind the bill running through the eye. The throat and cheeks are off-white. The breast and flanks have V-shaped markings that are difficult to see from a distance. The two feathers in the center of the tail are longer. These tail feathers on the male are a neutral brown color; on the female, the feathers are cross-barred with black. Both male and female sharptails have feathered legs and small pectination, or fringe, on their toes that serves as snowshoes.

Sound and Flight Pattern

The sharp-tailed grouse's take-off is rapid. When airborne, the bird makes sharp turns with rapid wingbeats, glides for some distance, and repeats this pattern over and over. Sharptails cluck (cac-cac-cac-cac) loudly when flushed and in flight. Early

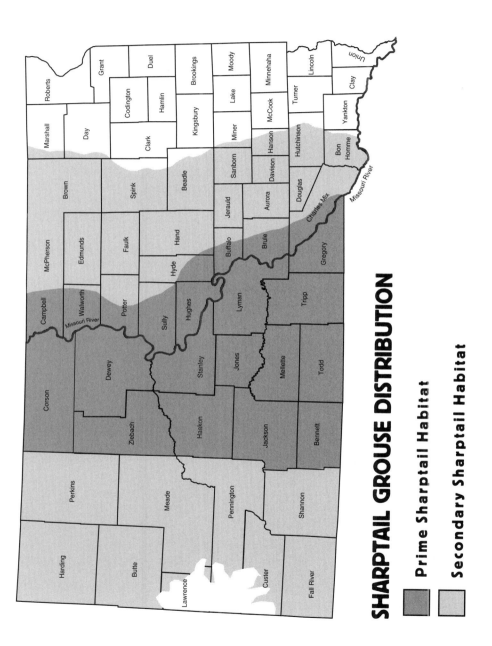

SHARPTAIL GROUSE DISTRIBUTION

Prime Sharptail Habitat

Secondary Sharptail Habitat

in the season young birds usually fly only short distances. Later in the fall sharptails fly greater distances when flushed. As the hunting season progresses, the birds may not hold for dogs unless they are in heavy cover or have not been hunted.

Similar Gamebirds

Early in the season young sharptails can be confused with immature pheasants and sage grouse. A flying sharptail could be mistaken for a female pheasant, but sharptails have a shorter tail with white edging and a different wingbeat.

Flock or Covey Habits

Once the chicks hatch, the female leads them away from the nest to open areas where they can feed. If the first nest is destroyed, the hen will try to renest, but only one brood is raised each season. Before the young are half grown, they are fully feathered with their juvenile plumage. In August, the post-juvenile molt takes place producing the winter plumage, and the young bird is practically an adult by September. The female and her brood stay together during the fall. The cocks do not associate with the young throughout the brooding season.

In early autumn, loose flocks begin to form. As winter approaches, sharptails assemble in large flocks in areas that have good habitat and food supply. Sharptails will move many miles in search of these conditions.

Sharp-tailed grouse on his dancing ground.

Reproduction and Life Span

Sharptails nest in the grassland prairies close to their dancing grounds. In April or May, the hen nests on the ground in a slight depression in cover of grass, weeds, or low shrubs. The hen lays an average of 10-12 eggs and incubation takes about 24 days. From June to September, the hen and her brood will be together. From September to March, the birds are in their winter flocks.

By the time hunting season begins in September, half of the brood may have already died of natural causes. The average yearly loss of eggs and mortality of young birds can be as high as 80%. Cover and weather conditions can cause fluctuations in sharptail populations.

Feeding Habits and Patterns

Sharptail grouse are primarily vegetarians. Young chicks and adults eat many insects during the summer months, but even then their diet is mostly vegetable matter. The summer food includes large amounts of grasses, succulent forbs, seeds, and fruits. In the fall a wide variety of foods are consumed. If the sharptail's range includes farmland, wheat, barley, oats, alfalfa, clover, and many other farm crops are eaten. The winter diet of the sharptail is very different. During this season the birds feed on buds, twigs, catkins from trees, berries, rose hips, shrubs, and other woody plants.

Sharptails roost in the open prairie and on CRP tracts. They leave before sunrise to go to the feeding areas. They may feed close to the roosting area, or they may fly great distances. Most of the time the birds fly to their feeding grounds. Many times sharptails will both roost and feed in different locations within the same CRP tract. Once full, the birds will collect grit and moisture. Sharptails, like other gamebirds, rest, dust, loaf, and preen themselves after feeding. The birds spend most of their day loafing in prairie grasslands and CRP fields. Later in the day the birds move out to their feeding grounds before going to their roosting spots.

Sharptails are not as predictable as other upland birds. Look for grouse on grassy ridges during years of lush vegetation. Grouse can be widely scattered and will travel extensively to find good food and habitat.

Preferred Habitat and Cover

The core of sharptail habitat is shrub grassland and brush. Cover types used by sharptails include native grass prairie, hayfields, pasture lands, and grain fields with hardwood forest edges. Sharptails like large expanses of grasslands interspersed with shrub and brush-filled draws and coulees.

Much of this habitat in South Dakota has been converted to dryland farming or has been grazed intensively. To a certain degree, sharptails have adapted to modern agriculture. However, if all of the large expanses of grasslands disappear, so will the sharptails.

John Stillman collects a sharptail from Winston.

Locating Hunting Areas

The best sharp-tailed grouse range has large expanses of well-managed grassland and rolling hills broken by wooded and brushy draws, interspersed with cultivated fields.

1. Look for heavy cover with woody, brushy draws. It makes little difference what kind of cover, as long as there is enough of it.
2. Sharptails feed on an abundance of vegetation types, but in the fall the birds concentrate in grain fields near their summer range and will use the fields as long as the food is available.
3. Weather and seasonal food sources play an important part in location of sharptails. For example, when it is raining, sharptails will not be in heavy cover.

Shoe and Remington pointing sharptails in sage.

4. Since sharptail ranges can be large, the birds usually fly to resting, loafing, and feeding areas. Traveling backcountry roads early in the morning and late in the day looking for bird movement can be effective.
5. Sharptails use trees, telephone wires, fence posts, old buildings, and other high objects to rest.
6. Use binoculars on flying or sitting birds to help locate sharptail hangouts.
7. Sharptails spend many hours resting around scattered patches of heavy cover, small tree clumps, woody reservoirs in isolated grasslands, and in croplands.
8. Knowing locations of established dancing grounds can help you find sharptails in the fall.

Looking for Sign

Sharptail droppings are white to green in color, much smaller than sage grouse droppings, but only a little smaller than those of the pheasant. In roosting areas, the droppings are together in saucer-sized concentrations in many locations. Dusting bowls and resting areas will have feathers.

Ken Taylor with Gunner.

Hunting Methods

Even when sharptail populations are excellent, finding the birds can be difficult because their flocking habits and the variety of foods they consume contribute to their wide range and multiple movements. Once you find them, you will usually have great hunting. If you do find a large population of sharptails, take note of the type of food and habitat available. You will likely find other populations in similar areas.

On warm, sunny days sharptails can be found in clumps of brush, small pockets of trees and shrubs, on north slopes, in draws, and close to creek bottoms. Hunt these areas midday—grouse like to feed on buffalo berries and chokecherries. Late in the afternoon sharptails move to grassy areas and grain fields to feed and later to roost. Sharptails will be on fairly dense grassy hillsides and on edges of ridges in windy weather. Grouse can be in grassy flats, open ridges, and lightly grazed grasslands in wet and cool weather. Searching certain types of grasses (e.g. little blue stem) can be productive.

Successful hunters cover large areas looking for diverse types of cover—edges of fields, high stubble, high grasses, brushy draws, shallow coulees with patches of chokecherry, snowberry, and buffalo berry bushes, or large CRP tracts—and hunt the particular kinds of cover at the right time of day.

Late in the season, if sharptails have had some hunting pressure, they can be jumpy and flush wildly.

Hunting Dogs

Flushing and retrieving dogs are useful on sharptails, especially in heavy cover and narrow, wooded draws. Close-working dogs work well in CRP fields (where cover can be heavy) for flushing and retrieving downed birds.

Pointing dogs are great for sharptails. When a flock is flushed early in the season it usually doesn't fly far and can be relocated. Late in the season, if birds are in open or sparse cover feeding in hay meadows or grain fields, they tend to be wary and flush out of shooting range. I use my pointing dogs on sharptails throughout the season with fairly good results. I use more than one dog to cover lots of country.

Late in the season I hunt only heavy cover and try to find birds that have not been hunted before. Sharptails are much more likely to hold for a pointing dog in these conditions.

I also watch where the sharptails go when they flush out of range. I sometimes pursue them with success.

Field Preparations

Sharptails have dark meat. Like other wild game, people have differing opinions about its taste. Sharptail should be field drawn and cooled down as soon as possible. Hang or refrigerate birds for a few days before skinning.

Shot and Choke Suggestions

Early in the season and in close cover—No. 7½–6 shot, 1 to 1¼ oz. of shot. Chokes: improved and modified.

OPENING DAY SHARPTAILS
Winner, South Dakota

September is a very hot month in the prairies. It is really far too hot to be bird hunting with dogs. The air is dry, the scent conditions are poor, and the high heat make hunting unpleasant and even dangerous for both dogs and men. Still, I am out in South Dakota, in the lovely small town of Winner, the pheasant capital of the state, hunting sharptails and prairie chicken. Winner has an annual Sharptail Grouse Classic hunt every year to promote their town and the great bird hunting in South Dakota. They invite outdoor writers from all over the country to participate in the hunt.

Ben Williams, my hunting partner and co-author, his wife, Bobbie, and my wife, Blanche, have been invited to the hunt. Winner is a small prairie town in the south central part of the state. It is in the heart of great pheasant country. This area is also known for its excellent population of both sharptails and prairie chickens. When we drove into town, we were greeted by a huge "Welcome Hunters" banner that was hung across the main street of town. It is a rare pleasure to find communities that welcome and respect hunters and the sport of hunting. The people of Winner were very friendly and made us feel at home. That night, we met at the golf course for a barbeque, where we met the other members of our group that we would be hunting with the next day. Our team would be hunting on the huge Rosebud Indian reservation southwest of town.

We met early for breakfast the next morning. After breakfast we drove to the reservation and split up into two groups. Two hunters joined Blanche and me and our dogs.

There was a light dew on the ground as we let Duke and Annie, my two wirehairs, out. We made several sweeps across the prairies and down through the coulees. The dogs covered the ground without success. Our team captain suggested that we move on to the large alfalfa fields. We broke up into two groups, each group covering a large alfalfa field. Thirty yards into the field Duke went on point.

Jim and Al moved in as the birds got up. They emptied their guns as the sharptail flew away untouched. Annie snapped on point at the corner of the field. Six birds got up. This time our group connected and we killed two birds. While the dogs retrieved our birds, we could hear shots from the other field. We saw several birds fall while a large number of sharptails flew out of the alfalfa field and sailed into the adjoining CRP field.

We followed up the birds, and my dogs made several more finds in the CRP. The birds were scattered and held well for a point. We picked up several more singles and rejoined the other group of hunters. It was time for a lunch break and rest for the dogs. The sun was now burning brightly, and the temperature was creeping into the 80s. After lunch we decided to hunt the large coulees. The birds should be in the coulees in the shade of the brush and trees. The dogs hit scent half way up the first coulee. A covey of sharptails flew out of the side, I dropped one and watched the others land at the end of the coulee. Blanche and I ran to the end as Duke and Annie penetrated the thick brush at the bottom. Blanche stayed on the side where she could get a shot, and I went into the tangle of brush. I could hear the birds fly as I got near the dogs. Fortunately, one bird went straight at Blanche. She dropped it with the first barrel.

The afternoon hunt continued with our group finding a covey in almost every coulee. By three o'clock we each had our limit of three sharptails and headed back to Winner for cocktails and the evening banquet.

Dinner and drinks with new and old friends is a nice way to end a great day. We had a fine hunt, good dog work, plenty of birds, wide open uncrowded spaces topped off by the warm hospitality of the people of Winner, South Dakota. It doesn't get any better.

Chuck Johnson

Arnie Gutenkauf accepts a sharptail from his German shorthair.

RUFFED GROUSE
Bonasa umbellus

QUICK FACTS

Local Names:
wood grouse, partridge, mountain chicken, birch partridge, mountain pheasant

Size:
Ruffed grouse are fairly large—15-19" long, with a wingspan of 23-25" and a weight of 1½-2 lbs. Adult males are usually larger and heavier than females.

Identification in flight:
Chicken-like in size and has a thunderous roar of wingbeats when flushing from the ground or a tree. In flight, the dark bars on the side are very prominent, as is the long, dark, fanned tail.

- Ruffed grouse are native to South Dakota.
- Adult ruffed grouse spend most of their lives in a small area.
- Plant succession is important in ruffed grouse ecology. Grouse cover is always changing.
- Perfect cover for ruffed grouse is predominantly mixed woodland.

Color
South Dakota has the gray phase ruffed grouse, which is common in the Northwest and at higher elevations. Both sexes have "ruff feathers" on each side of the neck. The head, back, and upper body are gray-brown, brown, black, and white with oval spots. Ruffed grouse have a long, fan-shaped tail with narrow bands of blackish-brown and one wide band at the end of the tail. The side and the breast of the grouse is light gray with large, dark bars and fading narrow lines through the breast. The legs are feathered to the toes.

Sound and Flight Pattern
The adult males will usually climb steeply, while the adult female will fly lower to the ground. Ruffed grouse can fly fast and will twist and turn, dodging brush and trees that are close together. Grouse will try to quickly get some obstruction between the hunter and themselves.

Flock or Covey Habits

After hatching, the ruffed grouse brood stays together until early fall. At this period in September, often after a storm, grouse may go through their fall shuffle of crazy flights to find a home range. There are many theories about the cause of this phenomenon, but none have been proven. Grouse do a lot of walking during this period, intermixed with short flights. There is some evidence of grouse regrouping in the winter, forming flocks of 3-8 birds.

Reproduction and Life Span

The nest of the female ruffed grouse is usually located against a stump, clump, or tree to protect her back. Her camouflaged colors blend into the material of the next. The hen may put leaves over her back to further conceal herself. She lays 8-12 eggs with an incubation period of about 22 days.

Young grouse are the size of marshmallows when hatched. The hen will leave the nest as soon as possible to get her brood into open areas where more insects are available. She can spot danger quickly and will call her chicks to scatter and use the "broken-wing" trick to distract an intruder. Within a few days the young birds are able to fly up to low branches to roost with much greater protection.

In winter, ruffed grouse habitat is often covered with snow. If the snow is wet, birds will roost on top of it or in trees. When temperatures are cold and the snow is deep and powdery, the grouse will sleep beneath the snow for protection and warmth. In winter, grouse movements are restricted to a few acres as long as food is available.

The young ruffed grouse has a high mortality rate, with habitat and weather conditions contributing to large losses. Population levels vary with the carrying capacity of the habitat. Ruffed grouse populations will increase steadily for many years, decline, then rise again. Ruffed grouse numbers vary greatly from year to year due to this cycle. Mortality of adult grouse from all causes can be more than 40%. The average life expectancy of a ruffed grouse is 2-4 years.

Feeding Habits and Patterns

Young birds eat many insects, which are vital to their growth. Late in the summer, the poults eat about the same amount of animal matter as the adults. Juvenile birds do not eat the variety of foods the adults consume.

The ruffed grouse diet varies greatly, the bulk being vegetable matter. Grouse and white-tailed deer are browsers and can be in competition with each other. In summer and early fall, the adults eat tender shoots, green leaves, insects, berries, and fruits. Later, the birds will add nuts, grain, and seeds to their diets. In winter, ruffed grouse will feed on many kinds of buds.

The feeding patterns of ruffed grouse are like most gallinaceous birds. Feeding starts at daybreak and continues until mid-morning, then the birds seek cooler covered spots to rest and dust. Late in the afternoon, the grouse will feed again until low light, and go to roost at dusk.

Preferred Habitat and Cover

Ruffed grouse live most of their lives within about two square miles, as long as there is an ample food supply.

The grouse inhabit brush, woodlands of dense cover, mixed evergreens, and hardwoods. The cover is often along small streams, creeks, springs, open grassland parks on steep hills, mountainsides of quaking aspen stands, and drainages coming out of mountains. Cover type used by ruffed grouse can vary greatly during feeding periods and seasons. Open grasslands have good supplies of insects and greens during the summer. Brushy and overgrown areas have seeds, fruits, and greens in the fall. Mixed woodlands of conifers and deciduous trees have fewer food supplies, but are used in the winter and spring feeding for fruits, nuts, and buds.

Locating Hunting Areas

Ruffed grouse are common in the Black Hills in Custer National Forest.
1. Intermountain grasslands and montane forests are the best hunting areas for ruffed grouse.
2. Much ruffed grouse hunting is on state and federal lands.
3. Many county and Forest Service roads follow drainages across the intermountain grasslands leading into the mountains. Most of the ruffed grouse are in this range where the hardwood trees, steep rolling hills, and waterways disappear into the evergreen forests.

Looking for Sign

Ruffed grouse droppings are about ¾-1¼" long and the diameter of a pencil. One grouse can produce many droppings, because much of what they consume has little nutritional value. Dusting spots can be along old roads and open places that are dry. A few feathers are left behind.

Hunting Methods

Ruffed grouse are always easier to find in the early morning or late afternoon. Midday, the birds are often in very dense cover or holing up in trees. Hunt along the forest edges of open parks, hayfields, pastures, berry patches, or brushy draws during feeding times. Hunt hardwood creek bottoms, moist areas that have springs, aspen groves, and bush hillsides in the afternoon. Look for grouse sign and if found, cover the area completely, walking slowly and looking up in trees for movement.

Hunting Dogs

Retrievers and flushing dogs help tremendously in heavy cover. The closer the dog works, the better. Winged ruffed grouse run after falling and can be very difficult to find due to their camouflage coloring. A good retriever in ruffed grouse country will rarely lose a bird because scenting conditions are usually better in moist habitat.

Pointing dogs do well on ruffed grouse, as most birds hold and leave a good scent. Big running dogs hold birds well, but my experience has been that grouse will sometimes fly into a tree before the hunter arrives.

When working dogs on ruffed grouse, bells and beepers are important.

Table Preparations

I believe young ruffed grouse are the most tender of all upland gamebirds. The breast and legs are white meat. In warm weather, field draw and wash out with cold water, hang, or place in a cooler with ice. I hang my birds for several days and either pick or skin them, depending upon how I am going to prepare them for the table.

Shot and Choke Suggestions

All season: No. 8-7½ shot, ⅞-1¼ oz. of shot.
Chokes: improved and modified.

GRAY PARTRIDGE

Perdix perdix

QUICK FACTS

Local Name:
   Hungarian partridge, Hun, Hunkie, European partridge

Size:
   South Dakota's only true covey bird. Both sexes are 12-13" in length, have a wingspan of 15-17", and weigh 13-16 oz.

Identification in Flight:
   Huns are strong flyers with rapid wingbeats. They make quick turns in flight. Early in the season, they usually fly short distances making right or left turns, frequently flying to a knoll or ridge and then dropping out of sight. Their bright, rusty tail is conspicuous in flight.

- The gray partridge, usually referred to as the Hungarian partridge, is not native to North America.
- If good habitat is maintained in a particular location, it will support a covey of Huns year after year. Climate, soil, and topography are important factors in gray partridge habitat.
- In South Dakota's big, open country, the grasslands and associated cover types have to be well managed to carry Hungarian partridge populations.
- Huns, like most covey birds, are limited to their occupied range but have some movement during their pairing break up.
- Old abandoned homesteads with shelter belts are excellent Hun hangouts.

Color

The sexes are similar in color. The adults have reddish-brown and gray backs, cinnamon heads, gray breasts, gray sides with wide vertical chestnut bars, and often a dark brown horseshoe on the lower breast. Both males and females can have a horseshoe, but it is more common on the male. During breeding season, males have a red ring around their eyes. The center two tail feathers have bars, and the outer tail feathers are bright, rusty red.

Sound and Flight Pattern

Coveys rise in a single noisy burst of whirring wings and loud, harsh shrieks that sound like a rusty gate being opened (keee-uck-kuta-kut-kut). Huns have rapid wingbeats alternating with glides.

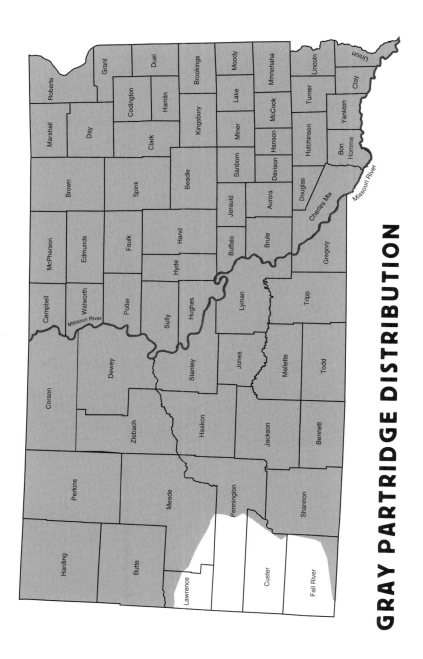

GRAY PARTRIDGE DISTRIBUTION

Similar Gamebirds

Hungarian partridge, along with bobwhite quail, are covey gamebirds. When a covey is scattered, a single Hun could be confused with a young sharp-tailed grouse or bobwhite.

Flock or Covey Habits

The entire covey generally takes off together and flies in a tight formation. If the covey is broken up, birds will call and assemble as soon as possible. Coveys are family groups and remain together until spring breakup. In late fall and winter, more than one covey may band together.

Hungarian partridge.

Reproduction and Life Span

The hen partridge makes a simple nest—a slight depression in the ground with a few leaves, grass, and feathers. It is usually in bushes (snowberry), long grass, or under other plant cover (lupine). During the egg laying process, which can take up to 3 weeks, she will carefully cover the eggs with grass or dead leaves. The average number of eggs is 15, but can be anywhere from 5 to 22. If the first nest is destroyed, the hen may renest at least once, but she will lay fewer eggs. The incubation period is 24 days and the peak hatching time in South Dakota is from mid-June to mid-July. Only the hen sits on the eggs, but the male remains in the area. When the chicks are hatched, the parents share the chore of raising the brood.

If disturbed, the young birds freeze and the parents attempt to draw the intruder away. As summer progresses, the brood becomes more mobile and moves about freely, extending their range. They roost in a circle, much like bobwhite quail.

The brood is the fall covey, but adults that have no young will sometimes join a covey. Vegetation, climate, and seasonal weather conditions are the important factors in population fluctuation from year to year. The annual mortality rate of Hungarian partridge can be over 70%.

Chuck Johnson's Duke pointing a covey of Huns.

Feeding Habits and Patterns

Huns are early risers and will start moving long before sunrise. They are primarily vegetarian. The main sources of food are cropland grains, seeds of herbs, and leafy greens, although young Huns eat many insects during their growth period. Adults will also eat insects when available. In some areas of South Dakota, waste grain may make up 60% or more of the birds' diet. In prairie grasslands or large CRP tracts where grain is not available, Huns will feed on a wide range of seeds, forbs, and grasses. Greens are probably taken as soon as they become available. Many greens in CRP tracts start early in spring and remain late in the fall due to protective cover overhead, thus giving wildlife an extended period to feed on green vegetation.

During the winter, Huns can work down through the snow in search of food. Huns living in open grassland remain on the prairie as long as food is available. When it is not, they move to heavier brush draws or open areas without snow. Windy winters can be beneficial to grassland partridge.

As fall approaches, Huns feed on mature weed seeds and cereal grains. The birds' main moisture comes from dew, rain droplets, snow, and greens. Standing water is used by partridge at times, but is not essential. Regardless, many times Huns are

Mark Kayser hunting with Clyde and Shoette.

found around an open water source because water complexes usually have useful Hun habitat associated with them.

If the weather is warm, Huns look for shady places to hang out. In cool or cold weather, they will move into denser cover.

Grit is definitely essential to Huns and is collected in many different places. In the fall and winter, when the birds' diet is mainly grain and/or seeds, grit is particularly needed.

In the late afternoon they move out again to their feeding areas. Resting and feeding areas can be close together or a considerable distance apart. When close, the birds may walk to and from these spots.

Preferred Habitat and Cover

Gently rolling topography—bare knolls, draws, and shallow depressions—seems to suit the gray partridge best. Soils that are sandy, loamy, loose, and highly fertile make good Hun habitat. Only the higher elevations and montane forests do not support Huns. Climate that is cool and moderately dry appears to be best for the Huns.

Important habitat needs are related to vegetation combinations. Two essential types of cover are needed by partridge: grassland and cropland combination and grassland herbaceous cover (native grasses, hay, alfalfa, and other weed seed vegetation). I have found that Hun coveys are not as plentiful in grassland/herb habitat combinations and their daily movements encompass a larger area than coveys occupying grassland/cropland combinations.

As long as the grasslands have plenty of brushy, woody draws with large amounts of weedy herbs and other cover types that are well-managed, Huns will occupy these areas.

Locating Hunting Areas

As mentioned above, hunting areas have to be linked to habitat combinations. South Dakota has thousands of square miles that fit this formula. To locate Hun country look for:

1. Grasslands and dryland crops interrupted by draws, grassy slopes, and rolling hills;
2. Irrigation projects with grain crops and other agricultural crops interspersed with cover types;
3. Grasslands with multiple vegetation types and cover that is not overgrazed. The more cover, the better;
4. CRP fields surrounded by cover and croplands;
5. Areas used by both sharptails and pheasants.
6. Hungarian partridge, early in the morning or evening, along established roadways collecting grit and flying to different areas. (If a covey is found in this manner, more than likely other coveys will be in the same area.) Always ask permission before hunting private land along roadways.

Chuck Johnson concentrates on a Hun.

Looking for Sign

Gray partridge droppings are pale green with a dark green end. Droppings will be in large circular deposits in roosting areas because the covey sleeps in a circle. Huns will usually roost in the same area for many nights. CRP fields are excellent places for Huns to roost. Dusting bowls and relaxing areas will have scattered droppings and feathers. Hun droppings do not last as long as other gamebird droppings—if found, you can be assured the birds are in the vicinity.

Hunting Methods

When Hungarian populations are excellent, the birds are not hard to find. They are very active early and late in the day while feeding and moving about. They glean food at a fast pace. Early in the season hunt likely feeding stations along the edges of crop and hay fields, and CRP fields that have green herbs available.

Young Huns' movements are relatively short—usually flights are less than a quarter-mile. As the birds mature and become stronger, their flights will increase.

I think of a covey's lifetime range as a circle. When the Huns are plentiful or the habitat is excellent, covey circles overlap. The circles become larger and do not overlap as much in sparse years. Once you learn where covey circles are, finding the birds becomes easier. I have hunted many of the same circles (where the habitat has not changed) for over 30 years. That is one of the ways I predict the population density for the upcoming season.

Once the covey is found and flushed, the birds will stay together as long as possible. Most of the time the same covey can be pursued over and over. When the covey is finally separated, like any other covey bird, the singles will sit tight and the birds will call each other, trying to assemble. Quite often they will run or fly back to their original flushing point.

After feeding, Huns will return to an open area to loaf and find grit. If the weather is warm, Huns will gather in shady cover such as juniper bushes or chokecherry

Charley Waterman working a grassy draw.

bushes.Huns may occupy a rock outcropping to sun themselves in cool weather. They will relax along creek bottoms, bushy draws, and cool, moist areas midday. Huns also like to use steep hillsides to rest or relax.

Hunting Dogs

If the Huns have an excellent hatch and the coveys are numerous in the fall, hunting without a dog can be good. If you do not have a dog, follow along the edges of fields, fence rows, patches of cover, or creek bottoms.

Retrievers and flushing dogs can be very effective when hunting Huns along weedy draws, CRP fields, brushy bottom lands, or any area with heavy cover that will help to hold the bird close to the hunter. In most cases, Huns will flush at a greater distance when they are hunted with flushing and retrieving dogs.

Close-working pointing dogs can be outstanding, especially if the hunter has slowed down a bit and would just like to hunt short distances. When the Huns are pointed and flushed, close-working dogs can do wonders finding singles and locating the covey again.

I have had my own Brittany blood lines for over 40 years. I use more than one dog at a time with beeper collars so I can hear the dogs in this rolling terrain and coulee country.

I prefer a partridge dog to hunt wide because there is more country than there are Huns. Many coveys live in big, rolling hill country. I walk the highest points along ridge lines or tops of sloping hills. When I'm in more level terrain, I still try to seek the highest ground. Using this method, I can scan miles of country and see the dogs working. Also, I can get to the dogs faster by going downhill, and see where the coveys go if they happen to leave before I arrive. If hunting Hun country with many draws leading down to a main water course, I hunt the draws from ridge to ridge instead of following them. It may make your blood pump a little faster, but you'll have a better chance of locating the covey. Hun hunting can be tough no matter what you do, but it is worth the effort.

Shot and Choke Suggestions

Early hunting season: No. 7½ shot, & 8¼ oz. of shot.
Chokes: improved and modified.
Late in the season: No. 7½ shot, 1¼ oz. of shot.
Chokes: improved, modified, or full.

Table Preparations

Gray partridge have medium-dark meat on their breast and legs. Draw the birds as soon as possible in warm weather. Hanging in a cool place or refrigerating for a few days seems to help the flavor and reduce stringiness. I skin the bird just before preparation for the table.

BOBWHITE
Colinus virginiaus

QUICK FACTS

Local Name
Common bobwhite, quail, partridge

Size
The bobwhite is a small plump bird with a short beak and tail. They measure from 9 to 11 inches in length and have a wingspan of 14 to 16 inches. Their average weight is about 6 ounces. Females are slightly smaller.

Identification in Flight
Coveys rise in a burst of noisy, whirling wing beats. Once the covey takes off the birds will scatter and fly in many directions making quick turns around objects. They will only fly a short distance however, and can be relocated.

- The bobwhite is one of the most widely distributed game birds in the U. S. and is the most hunted of all the quail species.
- Mortality rates among wild bobwhites are very high and are in direct proportion to food supply, cover and weather conditions throughout the season.
- Hunting bobwhite in the fall has very little or no effect on the number of quail that will survive over the winter. Excess birds should be harvested. Under best conditions only half of the fall population will survive.
- Bobwhite hunting was best when the country was occupied by small farms with diverse field crops and many edges for cover.
- Old homesteads overgrown with weeds and shelter belts with heavy cover are good hangouts.

Color
Bobwhites are brown with reddish sides with some blackish and white marking. The back, neck, and top of the head are mostly brown to reddish with mottling of blackish-brown. The under parts of the bird are a grayish-white with black tipped cross bars. The male has a white throat patch and a broad white stripe that starts at the upper bill above the eye and runs down the nape of the neck. The top of the head and the stripe through the eye is dark, accentuating the white stripe and patch. The female is almost identical to the male except for a yellow-buff eye stripe and throat patch. The head of the bobwhite is the easiest way to identify the species and sex. The eyes, bill, legs, and feet are black.

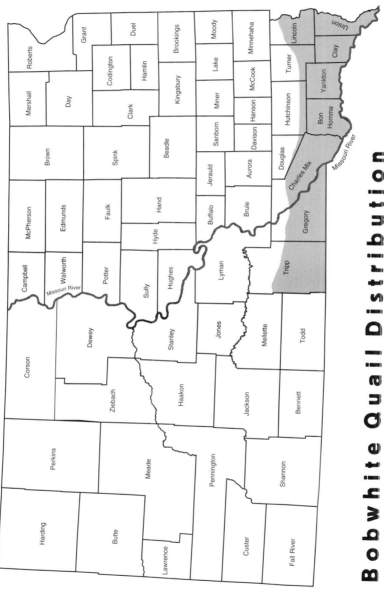

Bobwhite Quail Distribution

Sound and Flight Pattern

In spring and summer, male bobwhite have a very distinctive whistle, usually bob-bob-WHITE. When pairs are separated or fall coveys scattered, bobwhites become very vocal and call to one another. The assembly call, ka-loi-kee ka-loi-kee, is then used. Both males and females have many other conversational notes to keep in contact with each other.

Bobwhites have short cupped wings which enables them to have fast, thunderous take-offs. For a short distance the bobwhite can reach speed up to fifty miles an hour at which point it sets its wings and glides. Bobwhites will occasionally run on the ground, but usually sit tight.

A steady English pointer locked on a quail.

Similar Game Birds

Hungarian partridge, a covey bird like the bobwhite, is much larger and will stay in a tighter formation than the bobwhite when flying.

Flock or Covey Habits

Bobwhite sit very tight, but when they explode into the air they will scatter in all directions. Their flight after getting up is much shorter than most upland game birds and bobwhites waste no time in regrouping. Coveys are family groups and the birds will stay together until spring break-up. At night, the birds roost in a tight circle with their heads facing out. The range of the bobwhite is around one quarter of a mile.

Reproduction and Life Span

The nest is a shallow depression in the ground with grasses and leaves as a lining. The nest usually will have a canopy overhead, such as a plant or a clump of grass. The male and female share the rearing responsibilities and stay together as a family group until spring. The hen takes two to three weeks to lay her eggs before she begins to incubate them. The average clutch is twelve to fifteen eggs.

The male stays close by the nest to help if danger approaches by using himself as a decoy. If the nest is destroyed the bobwhite will renest, but normally will raise only one brood a year. As soon as the last egg is hatched, the parents will lead the young away from the nest in search of food. Within several weeks after hatching the young quail can fly short distances. When they are disturbed, the young birds will freeze and the adults will decoy the intruder away. Annual mortality of birds is very high. The turnover for bobwhites can be upwards to 85% and is directly related to weather and the availability of food and cover.

Feeding Habits and Patterns

The young quail feed exclusively on insects at first but will change to green vegetation as soon as it becomes available. As summer progresses, the covey moves more freely and will expand their area. By fall, the birds are full grown and feed mostly on greens, fruit, seeds, and cereal grains. Quail also eat many weed seeds such as rag weed, smart weed, and thistle seed. Bobwhites will continue to eat many kinds of insects as long as they are available. Grit is also consumed by bobwhite and is used in the gizzard to aid in digestion.

With the ripening of fruit and seeds in the fall bobwhites will seek out new areas in their home range. The birds use farm fields and fence rows with good cover for most of their autumn feeding activity. The birds begin feeding and drinking at dawn. Bobwhites will collect dew drops if available; otherwise they will go to surface water areas to drink. In summer and fall food is plentiful, the weather is good, and cover is adequate for escape routes. As winter approaches food and cover become more scarce and the habitat reaches its lowest point. Quail numbers drop to the carrying capacity of that particular area. Winter can be hard on bobwhites because they are locked into small areas and do not expand their range like other upland game birds

Preferred Habitat and Cover

Most of the original habitat for bobwhites is gone. Farm tracts are larger and cleaner resulting in less cover, weeds, fence rows, and woody places.

Bobwhite are a good example of birds that are associated with edges, where different types of cover and fields come together. Bobwhites need these edges to perform all their daily and seasonal activities. It is important that their cover and feed are in close proximity to one another. The greater the edge and the more cover types, the more cover it will support. Today, bobwhites are birds of the farm, but need the hedges, brushy field borders, and other places unsuitable for cultivation, such as marshes and draws. Quail habitat depends upon the diversified vegetation, crop-land, grassland, brushland, and woodland plots that are near water.

Locating Hunting Areas

Hunting areas have to be linked to the habitat combination. Southeastern South Dakota lies on the northernmost edge of the bobwhite's range. (See map)
1. Cropfields of corn and small grains mixed with weed fields are summer and fall hang outs for feeding, dusting, and loafing quail.
2. Grassland, hay, alfalfa, clover, and legume fields that haven't been overgrazed are used mainly in the summer for roosting and some feeding.
3. Brushy areas, hedges, thickets, untilled low places, scattered shrubs, and wild fences rows are used in fall and winter for feeding, roosting, loafing, and escape routes.
4. Woodlands, hardwood draws, riparian bottoms, woody patches, tree lots, and shelter belts are used in the fall and winter for roosting, feeding, and escape.

Looking for Sign

Quail droppings are very small, but since quail roost in such a tight circle forma-tion roosting ares are easily found. A covey will use the same locations for a long period of time as long as the cover does not change. Dusting and relaxing areas will have scattered feathers and droppings.

Hunting Methods

A quail's lifetime range is fairly small, only twenty to two hundred acres, com-pared to other game birds. Coveys will overlap each other's territory. Once you learn where a covey is present, finding the birds should not be difficult. Most times they use different kinds of cover at different times of day. Generally you are most likely to find quail in their food patches early in the morning and after-noons. Birds feed about thirty to forty minutes a day depending on the quantity

Bernie retrieves a bobwhite.

and kind of food available. The weather can play an important part in the feeding habits of the quail; storms moving in can force birds to feed almost any time of day

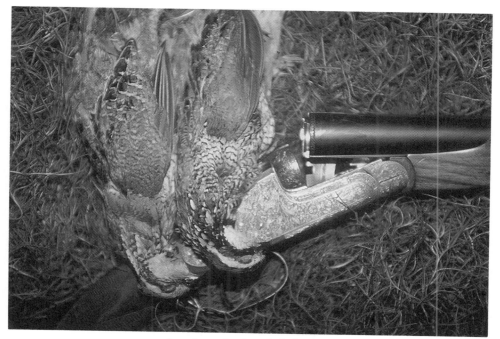

A male and a female bobwhite.

and for longer periods. Snow conditions will shorten their feeding periods and the birds will move into heavy brushy cover as soon as possible. Once a covey is found and flushed, the quail will scatter and will not fly a long distance. Singles rarely run far from where they alight. If birds are marked or the covey's general location is observed the hunter should move into the area of the birds and work all the cover slowly and methodically. Single quail set very tight. Flushed coveys explode in all directions with great speed. Picking out a single bird in a covey can be hard. If you concentrate on single birds and never try to flock shoot, you will be much more successful.

Hunting Dogs

Retrievers and flushing dogs can be helpful in hunting bobwhite especially in heavy cover, creek bottoms and weedy patches. Downed birds can be difficult to find without dogs because their size is small and the color blends into the habitat. Probably the most effective way to hunt bobwhite is with a good pointing dog. Bobwhite hold more readily with a pointing dog than any other western game bird, giving the hunter ample time to approach the covey. Once the birds are flushed and scattered, pointing dogs can be deadly on singles. In fact, with a good pointer it's possible to find most of the singles. A hunter with a pointer should be cautious about shooting too many quail out of a single covey.

Running pointing dogs in denser cover can be difficult. I use beeper collars which are very effective in locating running and pointing dogs.

Field Preparations

Bobwhite are a true delicacy. The meat is light in color and very tender. Draw the birds a soon as possible. Hanging them in a cool place or putting them in the refrigerator for a two or three days helps the flavor. Skin them just before preparation for eating.

Simple Recipes

Bobwhite can be cooked on the grill (see dove recipe)—or, skin the quail; cut down the back bone; cover with flour, salt, and pepper by shaking them in a zip lock bag. Brown them in margarine or butter in a fry pan. Add one 10 1/2 oz. can of mushroom soup or cream of asparagus soup and 3/4 can of water. Cover and simmer until tender.

Shot and Choke Suggestions

Although bobwhites are small and explode into the air, most shooting is at close range.

No. 7½ and 8 shot ⅞-1⅛ ounces of shot

Chokes: improved and improved / modified

Bob Tinker with his setters hunting the grasslands.

MOURNING DOVE
Zenaida macroura

QUICK FACTS

Local Name

Wild pigeon, turtle dove, wild dove

Size

Adults range in size from 11 to 13 inches in length and have a wingspan of 17 to 19 inches. Their average weight is about 6 ounces, with the females slightly smaller in size and with a shorter tail.

Identification in Flight

The mourning dove is a fast flier. It swerves and rocks in its flight until it reaches top speed and then usually flies arrow straight.

- These birds are native, but the state also receives many migrating doves.
- Since doves are migratory birds, they are regulated by federal & state laws.
- The mourning dove is the only dove or pigeon with a pointed tail.
- The dove is one of the fastest flying upland game birds in North America.
- Due to migration patterns, the best hunting for doves is early season.

Color

The male mourning dove has a beautiful soft slate-brown color blending with many subtle changing hues from the beak to the tip of the tail. The dove's head is a bluish gray with a bare patch around the eye and a black spot on each side. The throat and neck are an iridescent buff color. The feathers from the upper back to the center of the tail are olive brown with white outer tail feathers. The underpart of the body and wings are a lighter gray blue. Most noticeable are the round black spots on the upper side of the wings and a few dark markings on the outer tail feathers. The beak is black, while the legs and feet are a pale red. Females are similar in color, but the colors are more muted.

Sound and Flight Pattern

Both sexes make a mournful low-pitched cooo-cooo-coo-coooah sound, hence the name mourning dove. The cooing is more frequent in the morning and in the evening. When flying, their wings make a whistling sound. Fast, erratic motion, plus their small size make the bird a real challenge for the wingshooter. Flight speed is 30 to 40 miles per hour but mourning doves have been clocked up to 50 miles per hour.

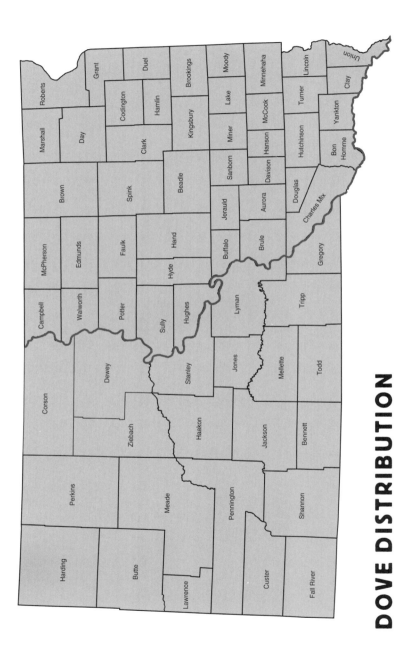

DOVE DISTRIBUTION

Similar Game Birds

The rock dove (domestic pigeon) has a square tail, mixed colors and is much larger in size, but both have similar flight patterns.

Flock or Covey Habits

Mourning doves reside in the state in the spring and summer and exhibit strong flocking instinct as fall approaches. Their migration south starts in September and large groups will feed, water, and roost together. The first sign of cold weather will push the local birds south, but other birds from the north move in right behind them. When the conditions are right the flocking of local doves and the migrating birds can make extremely good hunting.

Gerry Grinstein anticipates a rise on CRP.

Reproduction and Life Span

Mourning doves usually mate for life. Nesting is done in many types of bushes and trees, but evergreens seem to be preferred. Most nesting occurs in June and July. The nest is made by the female from sticks and twigs with rootlets as a liner. The nests are haphazard with flimsy construction. Storms and high winds can cause many nests to be destroyed. Doves are persistent however, and will build again. They usually have two broods and under good conditions in the right latitudes will have more. The female normally lays two eggs, which the male shares in incubating. The eggs hatch in about fourteen or fifteen days and it takes about the same amount of time for the young to begin to fly. Although the pairs leave the nest, they are still fed by the parents. As soon as the young are on their own the adults start the brooding process again. The young birds join other young to form small flocks until migration time.

During their first year about seventy percent of juveniles die while the mortality rate for adults is about fifty-five percent. Some birds do live as long as five to ten years, but this is uncommon.

Feeding Habits and Patterns

Doves will feed sporadically throughout the day when moving into a new location or during a weather change, but their typical daily activity consists of feeding early in the morning, flying to a watering place afterwards, and then going to a resting or loafing place mid-morning. Doves feed again in late afternoon, sometimes in a different feeding place than the one used in the morning. Mourning doves feed more abundantly in the afternoon than any other time of the day. After feeding, they return to their watering places before going to roost. Mourning doves require fresh

Ben Williams with his dogs, Clyde and Shoette.

water from ponds, gravel pits, streams, puddles, or any place good surface water is abundant, after each feeding period. Doves prefer to fly to a perch such as a dead tree or other raised object before they fly down to water. Because they have the ability to drink their fill in an extremely short period of time, they only need to drink a few minutes every day. Doves prefer a fairly hard surface to drink from and will land several feet away from the water's edge and walk to the site.

Eliza Frazier shooting a double.

Mourning doves are primarily ground feeders and will crouch close to the ground when eating, making them difficult to see. Almost 100% of the dove's diet is seeds of all kinds including weed seed, cereal grain crops, waste grains, and a variety of grass seeds. The size of the seed has a lot to do with their choice. Few seeds are too small, but some can be too large. After one feeding, many different kinds of seeds can be found in the crop and filling a crop may take several hours. Legume seeds are an important food supply and are mixed in many pastures and range lands. Farming practices today are conducive to creating habitat for large numbers of mourning doves, resulting in a long season and liberal bag limits.

Grit is an essential part of the doves' diet, and is used for pulverizing hard foods. Grit is stored in the gizzard and can last for days before more is needed. The types of grit particles (sand ,etc.) are wide spread. Even though doves will sometimes congregate while collecting grit, the number will not be enough for a hunting strategy.

Migration

The fall migration of doves takes place in September and October and many of the birds hunted in South Dakota are migrants from North Dakota and Canada. Dove families join together and form flocks of twenty to thirty birds. The cold weather plays an important part in the start of the fall migration. Migrating birds will start mixing with local birds. This makes the start of fall migration difficult to determine. If the weather is warmer in South Dakota and colder in the north, the mixing of migrants with local birds can make hunting doves ideal.

Migrating birds will feed in the same fields morning and evening as long as the food supply lasts. If the weather changes it will push the birds farther south to a new feeding location.

Doves have a strong flocking instinct and, as fall progresses, large migrating groups will be feeding and watering in the same locations as the local birds. Keep an eye out for increased numbers of birds around; it will pay off in good wing shooting.

Preferred Habitat and Cover

Mourning doves live in many kinds of habitat and are well adapted to most areas of the United States. The dove has the largest range of any upland game bird. It is at home all over South Dakota, but prefers mixed habitat and cover to dense forest or clear open plains. Doves prefer riparian habitat, woody draws, thickets, old homesteads, windbreaks, and other woody places adjacent to grain fields. Nesting cover can be trees surrounded by open land, woodland edges with agricultural land, a single tree in a fence row standing alone surrounded by crops or pasture, or a farmyard with ornamental or fruit trees. The common denominator in all nesting situations is that the home base is a tree for a nest site surrounded by open cover, with surface water relatively close by. Non-nesting mourning doves roost in heavy thickets, brush lined streams, or groves of heavy timber around old farmyards.

Good feeding areas must be within several miles of the roosting sites. Feeding locations in the fall, before and during migration, are mainly fields of agricultural crops such as sorghum, sunflower, soy beans, wheat, corn, oats, or millet. Hay fields, pastures, and grassy range areas also provide food for all seasons of the year. The three main habitat requirements for doves are feeding areas, roosting sites, and open water sources. These are widely distributed throughout South Dakota.

At the first sign of cold weather, which affects the feeding and watering areas through frost or snow, the birds will be on their way south.

Locating Hunting Areas

Locating good hunting areas depends on your ability to identify mourning doves flying from place to place and to learn the kind of habitat they are using at that time. Locating hunting areas before the hunting season is generally a good idea. Look for gravel pits, stock ponds, reservoirs, and other open water with dead trees or a high bank above the water. Doves prefer a gravely or sandy shore over a muddy area. Look for lone dead trees, fence lines, or power lines along crop fields where the birds will perch before feeding. Watch for moving birds, particularly in the morning and evening. Doves have particular flight lanes and will use them over and over again. The migratory bird will often use the same flight lanes as local birds. Feeding fields can be difficult to locate unless you watch the birds going into a field and once in the field, doves can be hard to see. Even though doves continually change their feeding and roosting spots, your best bet is to look for good dove locations—a parcel of land that has all the habitat requirements—food, roosts, and water.

Looking for Sign

Dove droppings are small, but can be found around watering and roosting sites along with feathers. If birds are using a site, the location of droppings can help determine where to sit or set up a blind.

Hunting Methods

Once you have found where the birds are watering, feeding, or roosting and the time of day the doves are using these areas, shooting can be fast and furious. Dove hunting under these conditions is much like duck hunting from a blind except you don't need to set up a constructed blind for doves. Any natural concealment, camouflage, and being motionless work well. Field shooting concealment can be along a feed row, in irrigation ditches, behind hay bales, or in a depression in the ground. If the crop cover is high enough, sitting or lying works well.

Roosting sites have enough natural cover to hide in and most shooting is done in dim light just before sunset.

Pass shooting can be effective if you can locate a flying lane the birds are using. Wingshooting in this matter will surely test your shooting skills as the birds will be flying high and fast. Jump shooting for doves in crop fields can be good at times especially if the stubble is high, although jumped birds can be difficult targets.

Dove decoys are very useful around watering places that have dead trees, a fence line along a crop field or around old homesteads where doves hang out. Doves decoy very readily. The cost is minimal and decoys are small enough to carry easily. It's worthwhile to have a few for all your dove hunting situations.

Hunting Dogs

Downed doves in any kind of cover can be hard to find. A dog that can retrieve can be helpful in finding lost birds. When hunting from a stationary position, the dog should be concealed.

Shot and Choke Suggestions

Doves are fast-moving targets and are small (5 to 6 oz.) with erratic flight patterns and can be an extremely difficult shot. 7 1/2 or 8 shot 7/8 to 1 1/8 oz. of shot. Choke: improved and modified.

Field Preparations

Skin out the breast and discard the rest and put in a cool place or an ice chest. Birds can be kept for a few days before preparing or freezing. Dove meat is darker than chicken and has no gamey taste.

Simple Recipes

Dove is a real delicacy, but can dry out if cooked too long. Split the breast in half through the breast bone; baste with butter, lemon juice and a bit of garlic; and cook on a grill. Sprinkle with salt and pepper.

MERRIAM'S TURKEY
Meleagris gallopavo merriami

QUICK FACTS

Local names:
> tom, gobbler, wild turkey, American turkey

Size:
> This is the largest North American upland gamebird. The male is 3½-4' long, has a wingspan of 4-5', and weighs 15-20 lbs. The adult hen is 2½-3' long and has a wingspan of 3-4', and weighs 7-10 lbs.

Identification in Flight:
> Turkeys prefer running to flying. They have powerful legs, and can reach speeds of 20 miles per hour on the ground. They are strong flyers and can clear a treetop easily and glide for long distances. Turkeys are easily distinguished in flight because of their large size.

- The Merriam's turkey is not native to South Dakota.
- South Dakota has a spring gobbler season and an either-sex fall season. (Hunters must have a conservation license, an upland bird license, and a turkey tag for each season.)

Color

The male's body plumage is brilliant metallic bronze with a rainbow of reflections. The wings are dark with white bars and the back and breast feathers are tipped with black. The head is mainly red with fleshy snood above the bill. The males have a long tassel (beard) that hangs from the breast and can be 10-12" long on an older male. The medium-long tail is bronze with darker bars, white tail coverts, and cream tail tips. Males have spurs.

The female is lighter and less brightly colored. The breast feathers have buff tips. The hen's head is darker than the male's and blackish blue. Females lack spurs and rarely have beards.

Sound

Turkeys learn early in life to communicate and have many different calls and sounds. Males, females, and young poults all have variations of tones, pitches, and rhythms. The early morning call by the hen is a soft tree yelp. The gobbling of the male is mainly used during the mating season, but occasionally a tom will gobble during the fall and winter.

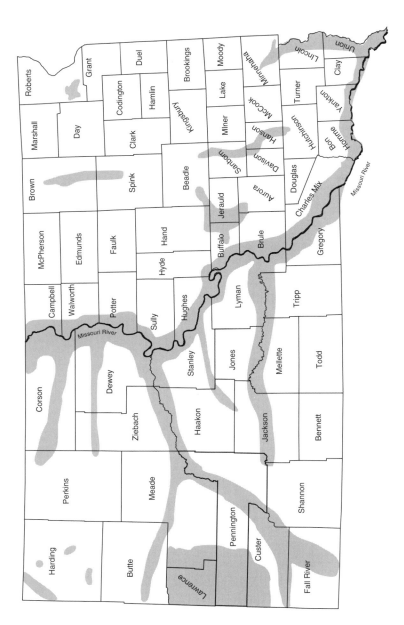

Turkey Distribution

Other calls that turkeys use are the yelp, the lost call, the cluck, the kee-kee, the cackle, the pit-pit, the purr, and the alarm putt. Seven of these calls are used by hunters, but this is only a small part of the turkey vocabulary.

Flock or Covey Habits

After hatching, the hen and brood stay together and are sometimes joined by other broods to form larger flocks. By fall, the juvenile gobblers have outgrown the hens and disrupt the social order of the flock. Some of the young males separate from the brood and band together. In winter, there can be many different kinds of flocks— brood hens with offspring, hens without broods, young gobblers separated from the brood, and adult males. In South Dakota, Merriam's turkeys often form large droves and move to lower riparian habitat or seek out food around ranching operations.

Reproduction and Life Span

Breeding season starts in April and lasts into May. The hen makes or finds a depression in the ground for her nest that is well concealed under branches, logs, or other thick cover. The nest is lined with leaves or grass and when she is not present, the hen will cover the eggs with leaves. The number of eggs the female lays can be as few as 8 or as many as 20, but is usually 10-12. The incubation period is about 28 days.

Merriam's Turkey in the Black Hills.

As soon as the eggs are hatched, the hen leads the poults away from the nest in search of food and protection. Poults learn to fly in about two weeks. The period before they fly is a dangerous time in their lives. The mortality rate of young birds depends on the weather, habitat, and other factors. The turkey's life expectancy is 6-10 years, although birds older than eight years are rare.

Feeding Habits and Patterns

Wild turkeys may have the most varied diet of any bird. It is easier to list what they don't eat than what they do. It has been said if turkeys can catch it or swallow it, they'll eat it. The most important plant foods eaten by turkeys are mast, fruits, and seeds. These foods are not produced in abundance each year. There are many other factors that affect birds' feeding habits, such as snow, ice, drought, fire, and flooding conditions along rivers. Turkeys may remain in trees for several days without feeding during heavy snow or rain. In winter, turkey droves will feed around cattle, ranch buildings, hay stacks, and grain bins.

Turkeys fly down to feed at daybreak. In spring, hens will fly down first and call. The gobbler may stay on the roost and call for up to an hour before flying down. By mid-morning, feeding has tapered off and the birds begin moving about. Around noon the turkey usually spends time resting, dusting, and preening. Turkeys spend a lot of time dusting in sandy areas, under trees with soft soil, and even in anthills. In the summer and fall, when the weather is hot, the birds will be in cool, shady locations. In the early afternoon, the flock increases its movements and feeding picks up for 2-3 hours before roosting.

Preferred Habitat and Cover

Habitat used by Merriam's turkeys in South Dakota is of two types—riparian hardwood along streams adjacent to farmlands and ponderosa pine forests. Much of the ponderosa pine forest is rugged terrain with brushy hardwood draws, steep slopes, and long ridges with open meadows and mixed prairie vegetation.

Locating Hunting Areas

A great deal of the pine forest turkey habitat is on public land and most of the riparian forest is private.

1. After driving to a likely hunting spot, walk to a ridge, sit, listen, and glass the area for turkeys or turkey habitat.
2. Walking logging roads and trails is helpful in locating sign and bird habitat.
3. Many county roads follow riparian drainages. When good habitat is located, get permission from the landowner before hunting.

Looking for Sign

Droppings can reveal sex. Gobblers make large-diameter droppings that are "J" shaped. Hen droppings are corkscrewed or piled.

Turkeys shed each feather on their body once a year, so looking for feathers is usually productive.

Footprints along trails, roads, and moist areas are easiest to spot. An adult male's tracks are much larger than a hen's. Piles of leaves that have been scratched or disturbed can indicate feeding places. Dusting areas will have many feathers and droppings. Waterholes have numerous tracks, feathers, and droppings. Finding turkey sign can be more helpful than any other method for locating the birds in an area.

Hunting Methods

1. Learn to use a turkey call.
2. Wear camouflage or clothing that blends with the foliage.
3. For spring hunting, be in the woods before dawn.
4. If you hear a gobble (it can be audible a half-mile away), move to within 200 yards and set up.
5. When calling to a tom on the roost, a cluck works best.

6. If no turkeys are heard or found in the morning, walk a ridge slowly, listening, glassing, and looking for turkey sign.

7. In the fall, walk logging roads and ridges and view wide areas with binoculars.

Shot and Choke Suggestions

Rifles are legal for taking turkeys in South Dakota: the .222, .223 or .22 mag are very effective.

I prefer to use a 12-gauge shotgun with a full choke with loads of 4, 2, and B.B. Many books do not recommend these loads, but I have found that they work well in the open forests of South Dakota.

Table Preparations

Wild turkey is outstanding table fare. Draw the turkey as soon as possible. I like to hang my birds for a few days and pick them just before freezing or eating.

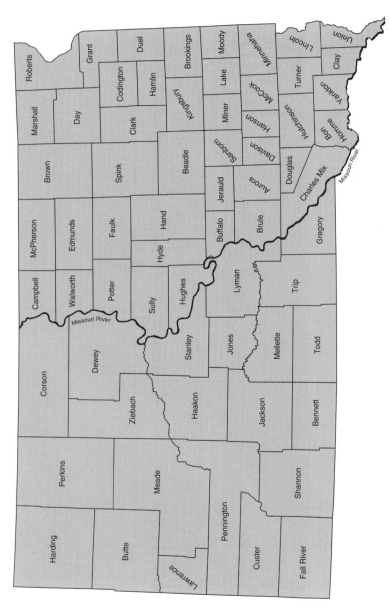

Duck and Goose Distribution

DIVING DUCKS

Deep Water Feeding Ducks

Divers frequent large lakes, coastal bays, inlets, and deep rivers. As their name suggests they feed by diving. These ducks can dive to great depths using their large feet for propulsion and holding their wings tight against their bodies. They can pull up large amounts of aquatic plants before coming back to the surface to feed. Widgeons, a puddle duck, will frequently gather where diving ducks are feeding and steal the succulent plants away from the divers and share them with other widgeons.

Diving ducks have rapid wing beats and fly in different formations than puddle ducks. The diving ducks' feet are set near the rear of their bodies, making landing and walking on land difficult. Divers have a low profile and swim with their tails close to the water. When landing, divers slide into the water. On take off they paddle with their feet across the surface before becoming airborne.

Unlike puddle ducks, the diver's speculum (wing patches) lack iridescence and are very dull in color, but are still good field marks to observe.

Most divers eat more aquatic insects than puddle ducks, making them second choice as table fare. Redheads, canvasbacks, and ring-necked ducks are the exception. They feed on wild celery and wild rice, making them excellent for the table.

The diving ducks most sought after by waterfowlers are the redhead, canvasback, ring-necked duck, lesser scaup, and the common goldeneye.

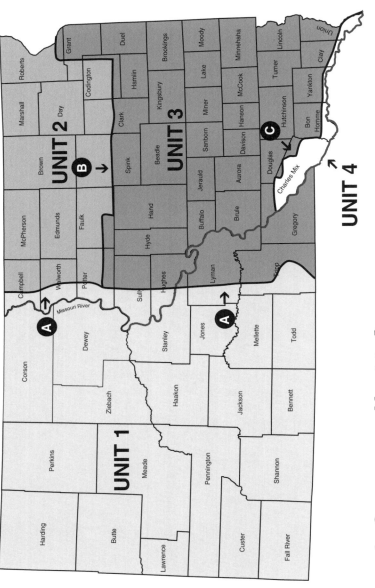

Duck Season Unit Areas

Unit 1: Oct.7 - Dec.5; Dec. 9-31
Unit 2: Sept.30-Nov.28
Unit 3: Oct.7-Dec.5
Unit 4: Oct.14-Dec.12

Data from 1995 South Dakota Hunting Handbook. Always consult current state hunting regs.

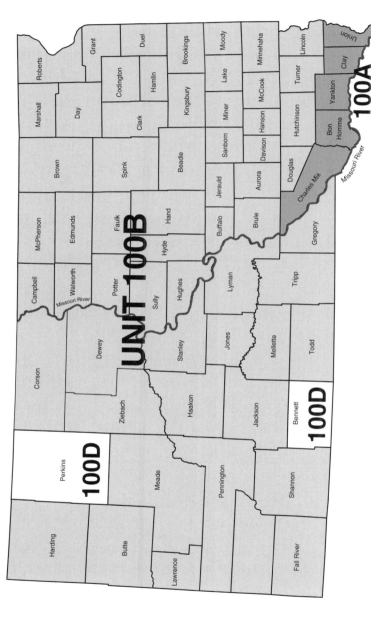

Nonresident Waterfowl Hunting Units

Licensed nonresident waterfowl hunters may only hunt waterfowl within the area designated on thier license

Data from 1995 South Dakota Hunting Handbook. Always consult current state hunting regs.

CANVASBACK
Aythya valisineria

QUICK FACTS

Local Name

Can, gray duck, bullneck, whiteback, canny, canvas

Size

The canvasback is a large duck 18-21 inches long with a wingspan of 28-36 inches, weighing up to three pounds.

Identification in Flight

Cans are strong flyers and their wing beats are rapid. They migrate in irregular V's. In flight, the canvasback is easily recognized by its large body, long wings, and pointed tail. The white body and the long, dark head, neck, and tail are highly visible when flying.

Speculum

male: pearl gray
female: pearl gray

• Canvasbacks begin to move into the prairie states in September to late October, but depart by early November. The canvasback's name derives from the fine gray and white on its back which looks like a piece of canvas. The most noticeable aspect of this duck is its dull red head with its long, black, sloping bill. The numbers of canvasback have declined over many years due to loss of critical habitat.

Color

The male's head is dull red and the forehead slopes into the large black bill. The eyes are red, the breast and rump are black, and the sides of the body are gray and white with heavy waving lines. The belly is white, wings dark black, and speculum pearl gray. The female is mottled gray-brown. The head, neck, and rump are brown with a white belly. Eyes and bill are black while the feet are gray, similar to the male's.

Speed and Sound

The canvasback is the fastest flying duck in North America, reaching speeds up to 70 miles an hour. Their wing beats are rapid and noisy. The male is generally silent except during breeding season. The female utters a low quack.

Food and Habits

The canvasback is a deep diving duck and will reach depths of 20 feet in search of food. They will bring the greens to the surface, cut off the green, and eat the roots. At times the baldpate, a puddle duck, will feed on the waste greens left by the canvasback. Eighty percent of the canvasback's diet is vegetable matter, most of it gathered in deep water in bays, sloughs, or ponds. Its favorite plant foods are wild celery (eelgrass), pondweed, water lily, wild rice, grass, and arrowhead. The other 20 percent of the duck's diet is aquatic animal matter. Canvasbacks will feed on dead salmon when available. Canvasbacks are excellent swimmers and divers. The canvasback needs a long, running start using its feet and beating wings to launch itself from the water. Canvasbacks are sociable and will mix with other ducks to feed and rest. At times, the canvasback will decoy fairly easily, but large decoy spreads are needed.

Migration

Canvasbacks travel in the fall in large flocks. They form long lines and loose, wedge-shaped formations at high altitudes. When the north country starts to freeze up, canvasbacks are forced to start their migration. As long as food and open water is available they will linger throughout the migration route. Canvasbacks look for large bodies of water to rest and feed. When large flocks are on the water, the birds are very wary and can be difficult to approach.

Table Fare

During the market hunting days, the canvasback was considered the most desirable eating duck available and brought the highest prices. A canvasback is still a very desirable table bird.

Photo: Blanche Johnson

Chuck Johnson prepares a decoy spread.

COMMON GOLDENEYE

Bucephala clagula

QUICK FACTS

Local Name

Whistler, bullhead, goldeneye, American goldeneye, copperhead

Size

The goldeneye is a medium-sized duck, 17-20 inches long with a wingspan of 25-32 inches, weighing 1¾ - 2½ pounds

Identification in Flight

The goldeneye travels in small flocks. Their flight is strong and swift with a distinct whistling sound. The male common goldeneye has more white on its body, wings, and tail than any other diving duck. The female has a brown head with white wing-patches and belly. The silhouettes of both males and females, in flight, have large heads, round bodies, and short thick necks.

Speculum

male: white

female: white

- In flight, the common goldeneye and the Barrow's goldeneye look much alike. The common goldeneye has an iridescent green head with a white cheek-patch. The Barrow's goldeneye has a purple head with crescent shaped cheek-patch.
- Common goldeneye are found east of the Rocky Mountains and the Barrow's goldeneye are found west of the Rockies.
- The goldeneye's wings make a vibrant whistling sound in flight. The name whistler fits the birds well.
- Three quarter of the goldeneye's diet is animal matter and is less desirable as table fare than most ducks.

Color

The male goldeneye's head is iridescent green with a round white spot on the cheeks. The back of the body, upper sides, and belly are a contrast of black and white. The wings are black with white coverts and speculum. The eyes are gold. The bill short and black and the feet are orange yellow.

The female has a brown head, and mottled gray back, chest, and sides. She has a white ring around her throat and a white belly. Her wings are brown with a white speculum. The bill, feet, and eyes are similar to the male.

Speed and Sound

The common goldeneye's flight speed is about 50 miles per hour. These birds are strong flyers with rapid wing beats that make a loud whistling sound.

Drakes make a low piercing sound (spee-spee). The hen has a soft quack. In the fall, the goldeneye is fairly quiet.

Food and Habits

The common goldeneye's main diet is mostly animal matter. They dive for long periods of time turning over small rocks in search of aquatic animal life such as insects, larvae, crustaceans, and small fish. The other 20 percent of the diet is made up of plant foods. Most of their feeding takes place on lakes and large river systems.

When in danger goldeneyes will often dive. On take off, they take a long time skimming across the water until getting airborne. Once in the air they will circle several times to gain altitude

Migration

The fall migration starts in late September and continues until early December. When migrating, goldeneye travel in small, loose flocks of 6 to 12 birds, often at high altitudes. The common goldeneye winters in most of the 48 contiguous states and will gather in large flocks or rafts on big bodies of water.

Table Fare

The goldeneye is edible, but is not considered an outstanding table bird.

LESSER SCAUP

Aythya affinis

QUICK FACTS

Local Name
Bluebill, broadbill, little bluebill, blackhead, butterball

Size
The lesser scaup is a medium-sized duck, 15-18 inches long with a wingspan of 26-33 inches, weighing 1¾ to 2 pounds.

Identification in Flight
Lesser scaup travel in tight flocks erratically twisting and turning as a single unit. The best identification in flight is the short white strip showing in both sides of the wing, rapid wing beats, dark head and tail with a white belly.

Speculum
male: white
female: white

• The lesser scaup is easily confused with the greater scaup. The lesser scaup has a white stripe visible on both sides of the wing running down only half of the wing length. The greater scaup has a white stripe on both sides of the wing but it goes almost the full length. The lesser scaup has a short, broad, light blue bill hence, the names broadbill and bluebill. The lesser scaup is more abundant, has a larger breeding range, and frequents the prairie states in greater numbers than the greater scaup. During fall migration, lesser scaup fly long distances and concentrate on large bodies of fresh water to rest and feed whenever possible.

Color
The male lesser scaup's head is dark purple. The chest and rump are black. The back is wavy gray white, the sides light gray, and the belly white. The wings are dark brown with off white splashes. The white speculum is visible on both sides. It has yellow eyes, a bright, light blue bill, and gray feet.

The female is dull, mottled brown with a white belly. The hen has a distinctive white patch at the base of her bill. The bill, feet, wings, and speculum are similar to the male.

Speed and Sound

The bluebill is very lively and fast in flight. Due to its twisting and turning, the duck appears much faster than it is. It can attain speeds around fifty miles per hour. When large groups fly close together over the water, the whistling sound of their wings can be loud. The lesser scaup is a wonderful sporting duck for waterfowlers. The lesser scaup is not very vocal. Females and males make a purr, purr sound.

Food and Habits

The lesser scaup is more an inland duck than the greater scaup and prefers to feed in lakes, ponds and marshes. During the late fall and winter, lesser scaup will use bays and larger bodies of fresh and brackish water to feed.

About sixty percent of the lesser scaup's food is vegetable matter. Some of its favorite plants are wild celery, pondweed, wild rice, bulrush, widgeon grass, and smartweed. The other forty percent is aquatic animal matter such as crayfish, mollusks, snails, small fish, and aquatic insects.

Lesser scaup take a long run on the water before launching into the air, but once air borne they are swift. Their legs are placed to the rear of their bodies, making walking awkward, but it does help in diving and feeding at great depths. Landing on water is easy for the scaup. Like most diving ducks it skids on the water surface before coming to a stop.

Migration

The lesser scaup's fall migration is slightly after ring-necked ducks and redheads and is usually delayed as long as there is open water and available food. If weather conditions remain moderate, the lesser scaup leisurely migrates south and will not arrive at its wintering grounds until late December. Lesser scaup fly long distances between stops, concentrating on large bodies of open water to feed and rest.

Table Fare

Lesser scaup, when feeding on large amounts of vegetable matter, can be delicious.

REDHEAD

Aythya americana

QUICK FACTS

Local Name
Red-headed, raft duck, American pochard, fiddler, broad bill

Size
The redhead is a medium-sized duck, 20-22 inches long, with a wingspan of 29-35 inches, weighing 2-2½ pounds.

Identification in Flight
The redhead is a speedy flyer with rapid wingbeats. These ducks travel in large flocks, using a wedge-shaped formation. During the fall migration they do not fly at great heights. When flying at close range, their red head and black chest and rump are highly visible. Redheads always look like they're in a hurry.

Speculum
    male: dull pearl gray, off white edges
    female: dull pearl gray, off white edges

- When migrating, redheads seek out large open water and stay in huge flocks called rafts. Redheads are curious ducks, not very wary, and can be approached or called rather easily. Redheads range through all the flyways and are often found with canvasbacks. During early morning and evening, rafts of redheads will move closer to shore to feed in shallow water.
- When flying at close range and on the water their head shape distinguishes them from the canvasback. Redheads have round heads; canvasbacks have sloping foreheads.

Color
The male has a round, rusty head and yellow eyes. His chest and rump are black and his belly is white. The back and sides of his body are gray with grayish-brown wings. The bill is gray with a white band at the tip. The feet are gray.

The female is mottled gray-brown with a white belly. She has dusty white markings around her eyes and at the base of the bill. The bill, feet, and wings are similar to the male's.

Speed and Sound

The redhead is a fast flyer and can reach speeds up to sixty miles an hour. This duck has rapid wing beats and is an erratic flyer. At times, a flock will make twisting turns in unison with one another.

Redheads are noisy. The male makes a loud cat-like meow and the female has a loud squawk.

Food and Habits

Redheads are deep water divers and feed mainly on the leaves, stems, and roots of aquatic plants. Ninety percent of their food is vegetable matter; the rest is small amounts of aquatic animal life. Redheads choose the same types of food as canvasbacks, but they utilize more of the plant's parts, eating the leaves, stems, bulbs, and roots.

When landing on water, redheads lose elevation rapidly and their wings and feathers make a ruffling sound. When they near the water, they set their wings and slide into a landing. At take off, redheads make a long run using their feet to become airborne. Redheads are gregarious and are often found mixed with canvasbacks, widgeons, and other species of ducks.

Migration

The redhead's fall migration starts in late September and continues until the first part of November. Redheads migrate after canvasbacks and, although they usually do not travel with other species of ducks, early in the season they will often associate with the scaups. Late in the season redheads migrate in large flocks traveling in long, low lines or irregular shaped V's.

Table Fare

Most of the duck's food is vegetable matter and many people rate it better than canvasback. It is considered a fine table bird.

DUCKS GALORE !

"The big northerns are here! Get on the plane and get out here for some great shooting!" was the call.

I had been in South Dakota earlier this year for a combination pheasant and duck hunt. While the hunting was great, our friends and hunting partners kept talking about the fabulous duck hunting later in the season. When the big northern mallards start coming down from Canada the hunting is unbelievable. The call came on Thanksgiving day and by the next day I was on a plane to Sioux City, Iowa. Jim, my hunting partner who lives in Sioux City, picked me up and we drove the two hours to our club on the Missouri river in eastern South Dakota.

Early the next morning Jim, his wife Cindy, and I were heading out to our blind. It was still dark and cold as Jim's big johnboat cut through the waves toward the small island where our blind was located. We beached the boat behind the blind, set up our decoys, made coffee, and waited for the first flight of ducks.

At daybreak, a flock of thirty big mallards came in over the trees and lit in the decoys. "Damn it!" I exclaimed as I hit my head on the top of the blind. In my hurry to stand up and shoot I forgot to fold back the lid of the blind as I stood. Jim's big ten-gauge L.C. Smith boomed twice and two ducks fell. Cindy got two ducks with her first shot and I managed to get one going away. Since the water was ice cold we decided to pick the ducks up by boat. Ten minutes later we had collected all the ducks and returned to the blind. Before we had time to pour coffee another flock of mallards came into the decoys. We took them as they were setting their wings. Four more ducks on the water. After retrieving the ducks we poured coffee and settled in. We had a propane heater and a small cook stove. While Cindy and I watched for ducks, Jim made breakfast. Ham and eggs with cold bread. "Chuck, take a look at the size of those ducks. See how big and bright colored they are and how the tail feathers curl."

"They are beautiful". There was a lull after breakfast. The ducks were off the river in the cut corn fields feeding. We could hear shooting from the cornfield blind where two other club members were hunting. "Patience," I told myself, "the ducks will be back by mid morning."

Around 10 a.m. we heard the sound of wings. Hovering over the tree tops was the largest flock of ducks that I have ever seen. There were at least two hundred ducks with wings cupped flying into our setup. The only sound was the wind and the wings of the ducks. We watched in awe as the ducks lit on the water. No one moved. We were in a trance. Suddenly, the ducks spooked, rose up and flew.

"Why didn't you shoot?" I asked Jim.

"I was mesmerized." he answered. "I never saw anything like that before. What a sight. Besides, we already have a number of ducks and there will be more flocks before the days over."

We had shot our limit by noon and returned to the old house that we used as a clubhouse and lodge. Jim and Cindy curled up in the living room and watched a Nebraska football game while I went out into the fields to try for a pheasant. Later that day Jim and Cindy drove back to Sioux City—they had to work the next day.

The following morning I had the blind to myself. The ducks started coming in as soon as I got in the blind. I let the first small group of ducks land, hoping that they would provide live decoys for more ducks. Sure enough another bunch of ten ducks came in on top of the first ducks. I stood up and shot—one duck down—click, click. Something was wrong. My Remington 1100's extractor was broken. I had to take each shell out by hand, so I was limited to one shot on each group of ducks. I really concentrated on each group, carefully picking out one duck and making sure of my shot. At least being limited to one shot sharpens your focus.

There were hundreds of ducks flying that morning. I could see several flocks in the sky at all times. Every five to ten minutes another flock of ducks would come in over the trees, cup their wings, and set in my decoys. With careful shooting, I had my limit of five ducks by 11 a.m. It was time to get back to the lodge, pack, and head for Sioux City and catch my five p.m. flight home.

Chuck Johnson, 1996

RING-NECKED DUCK

Aythya collaris

QUICK FACTS

Local Name

Ring bill, black head, ring-neck, broadbill, blackjack, butterball

Size

The ring-necked duck is a medium-sized duck, 15-17 inches long, with a wingspan 22-26 inches, weighing 1½ to 2 pounds.

Identification in Flight

The ring-necked duck is a strong flyer with rapid wing beats. They form small flocks and fly in loose formation at low elevations. Their coloring is much like scaups, with a dark head, neck, back, and rump, and white belly.

Speculum

male: pearl gray faint white edge

female: pearl gray faint white edge

- On the water, males appear to be very black with gray sides.
- The ring-necked duck is often confused with the lesser scaup when seen in flight because its shape and color are similar. The ring-necked duck's name is confusing; it does have a rust colored band around its neck, but because of the dark purple head and neck it is hard to see. A better name for the ring-necked duck would be the ring-bill because it has a highly visible white band on its bill.
- During their fall migration, ring-bills are found in all North American flyways. The long feathers on the duck's crown make the head look puffy or distorted.
- Ring-necks are good divers in deep water, but prefer fresh water in the interior, instead of coastal waterways

---

Color

The male ring-neck has an iridescent purple-black head, neck, and crown. The crown and neck have a narrow chestnut band. The bill is dark grayish-blue, black tipped, and has two white rings around it, one at the base and the other next to the black tip. The eyes are yellow. The back, chest, and rump are black. The sides are off-white. The wings are greenish-black brown with pearl gray speculums. The feet are gray blue.

The female's body is blackish-brown with a white belly. The sides, head, and neck are brown. The hen has a whitish eye-ring and face patch. Her eyes are brown. The bill has a light, small ring, but it's not as pronounced as the male's. The feet and wings are similar to the male's.

Speed and Sound

The ring-necked duck is a strong flyer with flight speeds up to forty-five miles per hour. It will make twists and turns in flight.

The male is usually silent, but will make a weak whistling sound. The female utters an occasional purr.

Food and Habits

About eighty percent of the ring-neck's diet is vegetable matter. They are good divers and will seek out food at depths up to forty feet. Aquatic plants that ring-necks like to feed on are pondweed, water lily, sedges, and duckweed. Ring-necks eat various parts of the plant, such as leaves, stems, seeds, and bulbous roots.

Ring-necks prefer freshwater interior marshes and sloughs to large open lakes, streams, and coastal waters. Since they use small bodies of water, they are more alert and nervous than other diving ducks.

Ring-necks must run along the surface before they take off, but rise readily from the water, making a whistling sound with their wings. When landing, ring-necks usually come directly in without circling making a sliding splash.

Migration

Fall migration starts in mid October, a little ahead of lesser scaups. Ring-necks migrate in small flocks of less than a dozen birds and fly in open formations. They decoy readily and will pitch in at great speeds without circling to get to their favorite places. Ring-necks have certain hot spots and will return year after year, refusing to use places that look similar to us.

Table Fare

The ring-neck is an excellent table bird, but does not rate as high as canvasbacks or redheads. Though small, it is fat and tender and certainly better than many other diving ducks.

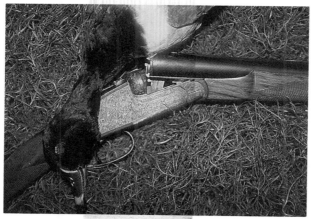

Ring-necked duck.

RUDDY DUCK

Oxyura jamaicensis

QUICK FACTS

Local Name
    Ruddy, butterball, spiketail

Size
    The ruddy duck is small, 14-16 inches long, with a wingspan of 21-24 inches weighing 1 to 1½ pounds.

Identification in Flight
    The ruddy duck's flight is often uneven, noisy, and tail heavy. They fly low over the water and prefer to follow the course of the waterway. In flight, ruddy ducks look small, stubby-necked, and drab.

Speculum
    male: brown
    female: brown

- The ruddy duck is a North American species and is scattered throughout all four flyways. The male ruddy duck is the only North American duck that carries his fan tail erect when on the water. The ruddy duck is a prairie grass bird and nests in sloughs associated with bulrushes, cattails, and tall reeds.
- The ruddy duck is a unique bird and has little in common with other groups of ducks, though it acts more like a diver than a puddle duck.
- The ruddy duck has great difficulty walking on land because of the placement of its legs.

Color

The ruddy duck's crowned head is black to below the eye with a white face patch. The bill and feet are blue-gray. The body is barred brown with a lighter brown belly. The wings are brownish with off-white markings. The tail is brown.

The female is a lighter barred brown and the face patch is buff with a dark stripe. The bill, feet, and wings are similar to the male's.

Speed and Sound

The ruddy has small rounded wings and is noisy and rapid in flight. Ruddy ducks fly low over the water in a jerky pattern. The speed of the ruddy duck is about forty miles per hour. In the fall, the male is not very vocal and the female will make a weak cluck.

Food and Habits

Ruddy ducks eat about seventy-five percent vegetable matter, such as the leaves, stems, seeds, and roots of pondweed, bulrush, widgeon grass, wild celery, and other green aquatic plants. Twenty-five percent of the ruddy duck's diet is animal matter, composed mostly of ten percent aquatic insects and fifteen percent crustaceans.

In fall and winter, ruddy ducks like large, freshwater sources or shallow brackish bays. Ruddy ducks do not dive, but sink slowly using their tails as rudders and their powerful feet to swim for foods.

Getting off the water appears to take great effort. They use their feet to scamper along the surface of the water. They would rather swim or dive than fly. Ruddy ducks land by sliding into the water with a splash.

Migration

Ruddy ducks migrate in September—earlier than most diving ducks. Like the redhead, they are already present in the northern plains states and will start their migration in September, but most will move to their winter range in November if weather conditions are favorable. Ruddy ducks usually migrate at night and fly in fair-sized to large flocks.

Table Fare

The ruddy duck is small and feeds mostly on vegetable matter, making a delicious table bird.

PUDDLE DUCKS

Surface Feeding Ducks

Puddle ducks are also called dabblers because of their feeding habits. These species are commonly found feeding in the water or in cereal crop fields. These birds frequent fresh water rivers, potholes and marshes and always rest on or near water.

Characteristic of puddle ducks are the centrally located legs making walking and running easy on land. They tip up to feed in water using their small feet for balance and rarely dive except when endangered. The feet are smaller and the speculum is iridescent in color in comparison with the larger feet and drab speculum of the diving duck. The puddle ducks ride high in the water and hold their tail erect when swimming. These birds can land almost vertically using small ponds and closed areas with overhanging trees to their advantage. Their take off is influenced by the placement of the feet to the body as they spring off the water. The puddle duck always leaps straight up in the air.

The puddle ducks most sought after by waterfowlers are the American widgeon, northern pintail, gadwall, mallard, blue-winged teal, green-winged teal, cinnamon teal, northern shoveler, and wood duck.

Mallard drake.

AMERICAN WIDGEON
Anas americana

QUICK FACTS

Local names
Baldpate, white belly, gray duck

Size
The widgeon is a medium-sized puddle duck, 18-23 inches long, with a wing span of 30-35 inches, weighing one and a half to two pounds.

Identification in Flight
Widgeons fly in compact flocks and can be identified at a distance by their constant twisting and turning flight. They are more erratic than most other ducks. The male has white shoulder patches and a white crown. The best identification in flight of both sexes is the white belly outlined by brown sides and chest.

Speculum
male: bright green shading to black
female: dull greenish-black

• Widgeons are called poachers—many times this duck will take greens away from coots and deep water diving ducks when they break the water surface. Widgeons have a very low profile when sitting on the water. The American widgeon prefers to nest on high ground in dry locations and often sets up housekeeping a considerable distance from water. Good habitat, drought, disease, parasites, accidents, and prairie fires are controlling factors for widgeon populations. Predators contribute only a small degree of losses to widgeon populations.

Color
The male has a gray head with a bright white crown which makes it look bald. Behind the male's eye is a wide metallic green stripe. The back, breast, and sides are reddish-tan marked with wavy black lines. The belly and under parts of the wing are off white. The bill is a grayish blue. The female does not have the white crown or the green stripe—her head is dusky brown. The female's color is more drab, as is the case with most female ducks. Her white belly is easier to see than the male's. Her bill and feet are darker blue-gray.

Speed and Sound

Widgeons are strong swift flyers hitting speeds of 50-55 miles per hour. Wing beats have a high whistling sound. The male utters a high pitched whistle (whew, whew, whew) when flying or feeding. The female makes a low pitched quack.

Food and Habits

Green vegetable matter makes up 95 percent of the widgeon's diet. Most of their feed is from water related sources (pond weeds, grasses, wild celery, etc.). Widgeons will feed on some natural or cultivated green crops. Widgeons frequently gather where diving ducks are feeding on deep aquatic plants. When the diver comes to the surface the widgeon will steal the morsel and share it with other widgeons. They usually feed on small impoundments and shallow bodies of water.

Migration

In the fall, widgeons usually migrate in small flocks around the first part of September in a leisurely fashion later than teal and before mallards.

Table Fare

The widgeon is smaller than a mallard and rates very high as excellent cuisine.

Male widgeon taking off from the water.

BLUE-WINGED TEAL

Anas discors

QUICK FACTS

Local Names
Blue-wing, white-faced, August teal

Size
The blue-wing is a small duck, 14-16 inches long with a wingspan of 24-31 inches, weighing about a pound.

Identification in Flight
Blue-winged teal travel in small, close flocks, low over ponds and marshes at great speeds, twisting, turning and dodging around trees. Both sexes have a blue wing patch. At close range the white crescent on the side of the male's face is distinguishable.

Speculum
male: green
female: green

- The speculum is green on the blue-winged teal. The sky blue lesser and middle wing coverts give this teal its name. In poor light, blue-wings are difficult to tell from other teal, but their flight is more erratic and twittering is easily heard.
- Blue-winged teal may be the most numerous breeding duck in the prairie states. Locally raised blue-winged teal have to be hunted early in the season in the prairie states because of their very early migration. These birds decoy readily, but their erratic flight can certainly test a hunter's skill.

Color
The male blue-winged teal has a white crescent on each side of the face and also has a white patch on each flank near the base of the tail. The body color is a dull mottled pink-brown. The female is mottled brown. The bright, light blue wing patch on both sexes is the best form of identification. However, the female blue-winged teal and the female cinnamon teal are almost identical.

Speed and Sound

The blue-winged teal's flight speed is 30 to 40 miles an hour, but it can reach speeds up to 50 miles per hour if need be. Teal depend on erratic flight movements more than their speed.

The males make a whistling peep and the hens make a faint quack.

Food and Habits

The blue-winged teal is a surface feeder, and feeds mainly in shallow water ponds, creeks, edges of reservoirs, marshes or irrigation ditches. Blue-wings do not tip up to feed, but reach out with their heads under water.

About 70 percent of the blue-wing's diet is vegetable material, with 30 percent being animal matter such as insects, larvae, snails, worms, and other aquatic life. These ducks will feed in grain fields when available.

Blue-wings like to circle an area repeatedly before landing and will fly almost in unison when in a small flock, swooping down for a sudden stop, and sliding on the water's surface. When taking off from the water, the blue-winged teal springs into the air and can achieve a great burst of speed quickly.

Migration

Blue-winged teal are generally the first ducks south in the fall. Birds fly in small, compact flocks. Males will leave for their winter ground well in advance of the hens and immature birds, as early as August. As a result, more female and juveniles are shot during the hunting season. Blue-winged teal travel great distances and will even migrate during the day if they need to get to their winter grounds

Table Fare

Blue-wings are an exceptionally delicious table bird as are all teal. Most are fat and tender.

CINNAMON TEAL
Anas cyanoptera

QUICK FACTS

Local Name
Red teal, river teal, red breasted teal

Size
The cinnamon teal is a small duck, 14-17 inches long, with a wingspan of 24-26 inches, weighing about 12 to 14 ounces.

Identification in Flight
The cinnamon teal's flight is similar to other teal, but they travel more in family and smaller groups. The red color of the male is easily recognized in flight. The male and female have a blue wing patch much like the blue-winged teal.

Speculum
male: bright green
female: bright green

• The cinnamon teal is a western duck and is rarely seen east of the Mississippi River. The bird's name comes from the beautiful, rich, dark, cinnamon color on its head and neck. The Central Flyway has a few cinnamon teal, but not in large numbers like their close relatives, the blue-winged teal. Cinnamon teal depart their breeding grounds in early fall for their wintering grounds.

Color
The drake's head, neck, and breast are vivid cinnamon-red. The back and rump are a mottled brown. The tail is brown. The wing coverts are bright, sky blue and white and the speculum is bright green. The legs are yellow-orange and the bill is black.

The female is mottled brown over her entire body and her wings are almost identical to the male. The female cinnamon teal's color is so much like the blue-wing teal hen that identification is difficult for most hunters.

Speed and Sound
The cinnamon teal is a small duck and appears to travel swiftly. It can fly at speeds up to 40 to 45 miles an hour.

The call of the cinnamon teal is very close to the bluewing's. The male makes a whistling peep and the female utters a low harsh quack.

Food and Habits

The cinnamon teal is a surface feeder and likes to work the edges of shallow ponds, lakes, sloughs, and marshes in search of food. It seems to like the small alkali bodies of water. They feed much like a shoveler duck feeding in the mud. The cinnamon teal's diet is about 80 percent vegetable matter. Their favorite foods are pondweeds, salt grass sedges, bulrush, and other plants associated with small bodies of water. The other 20 percent of the diet is made up of animal matter, mostly insects and mollusks.

Cinnamon teal seldom fly in large flocks and is not a sociable duck. They rarely mix with other species. This duck lands like other teal and when taking off they will jump quickly into the air. Cinnamon teal are somewhat tame and will decoy readily.

Migration

Migration starts early in September, but cinnamon teal usually spend more time on their way south than any other teal. Mostly, they travel at night and feed during the day. The cinnamon teal prefers to travel in family groups and small flocks.

Table Fare

Cinnamon teal are not shot in great numbers but, like their relatives the bluewings, they are good table birds.

GADWALL

Anas strepera

QUICK FACTS

Local Names
Gray duck, creek duck, red wing, speckle-belly

Size
The gadwall is a medium-sized puddle duck, 18-20 inches long, with a wingspan of 31-36 inches, weighing 1½ to 2 pounds.

Identification in Flight
Gadwalls fly swiftly in small flocks in a straight line—not twisting or turning. Wing beats are rapid. It has a white belly with a dark rump. You can see the speculum as it flies.

Speculum
male: black, but predominately white
female: black, but predominately white

- This is the only puddle duck with a white speculum. The greatest numbers of gadwalls are in the Central Flyway. It prefers to nest in prairies and is associated with alkali marshes. Gadwalls will often feed and mix with flocks of widgeon and pintails. The plowing of virgin prairie for cultivation has diminished nesting sites for the gadwall.

Color
The name, gray duck, is a fitting name for the gadwall, a slender gray-brown duck with a black rump. It has a pale brown head and neck with a white belly. Wing coverts are black and brown. The speculum is black with a large block of white. The bill is black with the lower edge orange. The feet are orangish-yellow

The female is mottled brown and can be confused with a hen mallard, but is smaller. Her wings and feet are identical to the male's.

Speed and Sound
Gadwalls are not fast flyers compared to other puddle ducks, but can reach speeds up to 45 miles per hour. They take off from water by springing forward into the air.

The male makes a small whistling call mostly during the breeding season. Males utter a single low pitched quack. The female has a call similar to the hen mallard, but softer with a series of quacks (kanak, kak-kak, kak).

Food and Habits

The gadwall feeds on more vegetable matter, 90 percent, than any other puddle duck. Most feeding takes place in small ponds, spring creeks, marshes and water areas that hold green vegetation. The duck feeds by tipping up and paddling its feet for balance while collecting vegetation from the bottom. Gadwall's favorite diet is green leafy plants.

Migration

In fall, gadwalls are often the first ducks to head back to their wintering grounds, but will stop many places and feed on the way. Many gadwalls will travel with other puddle ducks during migration.

Table Fare

The gadwall may not be as tasty as the mallard since it does not consume large amounts of cereal crops, but the green vegetation it does eat makes it a highly edible bird.

GREEN-WINGED TEAL

Anas crecca carolinensis

QUICK FACTS

Local Name

Teal, green-wing, common teal, red headed teal, winter teal

Size

The smallest of ducks, 12-16 inches long, with a wingspan from 20-25 inches, and weighs about twelve ounces.

Identification in Flight

Green-winged teal are very strong flyers, though their flight is erratic and swift. The green-wing has a white belly as opposed to the dark belly of the blue-wing. Green-wings travel in large flocks during fall migration.

Speculum

male: iridescent green and black

female: iridescent green and black

• In the fall green-winged teal leave as late as possible, being pushed out only by storms and cold weather. Green-winged teal have short necks and will appear shorter in flight than blue-wings. These birds decoy easily and will make several passes before landing. This teal's small size makes them appear as though they are travelling faster than they really are. Green-wings migrate south through all flyways.

Color

The male has beautiful plumage—the head and neck is a cinnamon brown with a wide iridescent stripe on the sides of the head starting from the eye and going to the neck. Shoulder, back and sides are grayish with very fine markings. The chest is tan with dark spots. The wings and primary feathers are brownish gray. The bill is dark bluish-gray and the feet are a light gray.

The female is mottled brown with a white belly. The bill is grayish-black with small black spots. The wings and feet are similar to the male.

Speed and Sound

The green-winged teal can fly at speeds of up to 50 miles per hour. Due to its small size, it gives the false impression of higher speeds. This duck's wing beats are rapid and make an audible whistling sound.

The male makes a short, high pitched whistle and a low pitched piping sound. The female has a faint three note quack.

Food and Habits

The green-winged teal feeds in sloughs, marshes, small streams, and ponds. It feeds by tipping up and kicking its feet to maintain its balance.. The green-wing teal will stir up the muddy bottom in search of aquatic plants in shallow places.

About 90 percent of this duck's food is vegetable matter. Since they are late migrators, they will feed on dead salmon along western rivers. Green-wings take advantage of all kinds of food and will also feed in grain fields.

Migration

Green-winged teal leave for their winter grounds late compared to other puddle ducks and will stay as long as there is open inland water. They usually migrate in large flocks and like to linger on their way south as long as they have open feeding grounds.

Table Fare

From a gourmet's standpoint, green-winged teal rates very high. Though small, this tender, juicy, bird is outstanding table fare.

MALLARD

Anas platyrhychos

QUICK FACTS

Local Names
Greenhead, curly-tail, stock duck, wild duck

Size
The mallard is a large duck, 24-28 inches long, with a wing span of 30-40 inches, weighing 2½ to 3 pounds. The hen is slightly smaller.

Identification in Flight
The flight of the mallard is not particularly rapid, but strong. The body appears large and dark in flight. The white tail and underwings contrast with the dark chest and green head on the male. The female is drab brown with white markings on the tail, and white and iridescent blue on the wings.

Speculum
male: iridescent blue, white on leading edge
female: iridescent blue, white on leading edge

- The mallard is the most common and best known duck in North America. These ducks are found in all flyways throughout the United States. Mallards are strong fliers and have been known to fly nonstop for hundreds of miles. These ducks fly in large flocks, usually in a V formation. When the lead bird tires another will take its place breaking the wind. Many mallards concentrate on refuges, lakes, impoundments, and potholes in the fall and will not leave until forced out by snow or freezing weather.

Color
Males have an iridescent green head. The body is dark brown with a gray-white belly, dark rump, and a white tail plus two curling blue feathers above the tail. He has a white ring around his neck. The bill is greenish-yellow and the feet are bright orange. Wings are grayish-brown with blue and white speculum.

The female is dull brown with a white tipped tail. The bill is darker than the male's, but the feet are the same color. She has a similar speculum.

Speed and Sound
Mallards are strong flyers and can reach speeds up to 65 miles per hour. The male utters a low sound (kwek). The female is noisier with her loud quacking which can be heard great distances (quack, quack-quack, quack, quack-quack).

Food and Habits

Vegetable matter makes up about 90 percent of the mallard's diet. Since the mallard is so widespread over North America the duck eats a wide variety of food. Mallards feed extensively on cereal crops. Flock after flock of mallards will leave the water early in the morning and late afternoon in search of grain crops, returning to the water after each feeding.

Migration

Migration starts in September, but peaks around the first part of October, depending on the weather condition farther north. Mallards are literally pushed out by freezing conditions. As long as there is open water and harvest fields to feed in, they will stay.

Table Fare

Most people will agree the mallard is a real treat and rates as one of the best waterfowl for the table.

Mallard drake.

PINTAIL

Anas acuta

QUICK FACTS

Local names
Sprig, sprigtail, spiketail

Size
The male pintail averages 27 inches in length and has a wing span of 34 inches. The body length is longer than the mallard due to the long tail. The sprig weighs about two pounds. It is a slender duck with narrow pointed wings. The female is slightly smaller than the male.

Identification in Flight
The pintail is a fast, agile flier with graceful lines. The long pointed tail and neck lend themselves to speed. The duck can make short turns and banks at incredible speeds. Pintails migrate at high altitudes, in loose formation, and large flocks.

Speculum
male: glossy green, edged with buff and white
female: dull brown, edged with white

- With its swift flight, it has been called the greyhound of the air. Pintails are one of the first ducks to migrate south in the fall, yet one of the first to migrate in the spring. There is evidence some pintails migrate in one flyway in the fall and find another to return in the spring. Pintails have a high profile when sitting on the water.

Color
Pintails are elegant in appearance. The males have dark brown heads with slender, long, white necks and bellies leading down to brown rumps. The back and sides are mottled gray and the top wing surface is gray brown with a black border edged in white. The tail is brown-gray with two long center feathers extending beyond the rest. The male is one of the easiest duck to identify flying or sitting on the water. The hen pintail is a mottled brown similar to a female mallard. The feet and legs of both sexes are slate gray.

Speed and Sound

Pintails are the fastest on the wing of all waterfowl, with speeds up to 65 miles per hour. Down wind it has been clocked up to 90 miles per hour. The male has a short flute-like whistle most often heard in the mating season. The female makes a soft, hoarse quack unlike that of the mallard.

Food and Habits

Most feeding is done in shallow water systems on vegetable matter such as bulrushes, sedges, pondweeds, grasses, wild celery, etc. Pintails may also feed on animal life which many times is mixed in the greens. When shallow water freezes, pintails will feed in croplands while migrating. The pintail is a gregarious duck and will mix with other species of duck while feeding or migrating. Pintails take off by beating their wings against the water surface, lifting them straight up at high speeds.

Migrating

Pintails of the central flyway from Saskatchewan, Alberta, and North Dakota start their fall migration in early September, regardless of the weather. Pintails do not tolerate cold temperatures and many times migrate directly to their wintering grounds, stopping over for only short periods of time to feed and rest.

Table Fare

Pintail feed primarily on greens and its meat is considered a true delicacy.

SHOVELER

Anas clypeata

QUICK FACTS

Local Name
Broad bill, spoon bill, butter duck, mud duck, shovel bill

Size
The shoveler is a medium-sized duck, 18-20 inches long with a wingspan of 27-33 inches, weighing 1¼ to 1½ pounds.

Identification in Flight
The shoveler flies in small flocks comparatively low to the ground and its flight is direct when migrating. When not migrating the shoveler flies much like teal, twisting and turning. In flight, the spoon-shaped head is carried low and the bill seems large compared to the body. At close range, the cinnamon colored belly and white chest are visible.

Speculum
male: bright green
female: bright green

- No other duck possesses a bill like the shoveler and the name spoon bill fits the duck well. This distinctive feature is the easiest way to recognize the shoveler. Shovelers sit low on the water with their bills pointed downward. These birds are widely distributed throughout North America, but the greatest numbers occur in the Pacific and Central flyways. Shovelers are similar to blue-winged and cinnamon teal in color and habit.

Color
The head of the shoveler male is iridescent green, much like the mallard drake. The belly is cinnamon colored with a white chest and tail. The wings are light blue, the wing bar and speculum is iridescent green, almost identical to the blue-winged teal. The bill is black and the feet are orange.

The female is mottled brown with an off-white tail. Wings are brown with pale blue and white bars. The hen's bill is green with orange overtones and the feet are orange.

Speed and Sound

The shoveler duck is a fast flyer and can reach 60 miles per hour. The spoonbill prefers to fly in a straight course, but if alarmed their flight becomes more erratic, similar to teal.

Shoveler males make a very weak sound (woh-woh) and the female has a soft quack. The shoveler is not a very vocal duck when compared to other puddle ducks.

Food and Habits

Spoonbills are surface feeders and are found feeding in shallow water, lake ponds, marshes, and sloughs. The shoveler feeds by skimming food from the surface or following other species of ducks, cleaning up food that other ducks leave behind. They will also tip up to feed, but will never dive below the surface when feeding. Sixty-five percent of this duck's diet is vegetable matter and 35 percent is aquatic animal matter. Some of the spoonbill's favorite foods are pondweed, salt grass, water lily, sedge, mollusks, insects, and small fish. Shovelers are sociable and mix with other species of duck with similar feeding habits. They land on water almost vertically, with a splash, and take off with a rather loud beating of wings. Shovelers jump off the water.

Migration

In the fall, migrating spoonbills will often travel with blue-winged teal and widgeons. Shovelers commonly travel in small flocks. The first sign of frost helps to push the duck south to their sunny winter homes. Good populations of shovelers collect during early fall in the northern prairie states.

Table Fare

When the spoonbill is feeding on mostly vegetable matter, it can be fairly good to eat, but does not compare with most puddle ducks.

WOOD DUCK
Aix sponsa

QUICK FACTS

Local Name
Wood widgeon, woody, acorn duck, squealer, summer duck

Size
The wood duck is a medium-sized duck, 15-18 inches long, with a wingspan of 28-30 inches, and weighs about 1½ pounds.

Identification in Flight
Wood duck flocks are usually small. Their flight is swift and direct. If disturbed the woody will flair, twisting and turning. This bird carries its large head high. The white and black bars in front of the wing, dark chest and wings, and long tail are good identifying features.

Speculum
male: iridescent purple-blue-green
female: iridescent purple-blue-green

• The wood duck is one of the most beautiful of all North American waterfowl. Wood ducks nest in trees and man made nesting boxes, never nesting on the ground. Common hangouts for wood ducks are open woodlands around ponds, lakes, swamps, and riparian waterways. Woodies will often sit in trees. This species, historically an eastern bird, has made a great comeback in the west and are now present in all American flyways. The supplying of nesting boxes for wood ducks has greatly helped nesting relocation.

Color
The distinctive markings of the drake are very difficult to describe. Its beautiful coloration is unsurpassed by any other puddle duck. The male wood duck has a large white stripe on its iridescent green head, the eye is red with a white ring, and the bill is multicolored. The feet are dull golden. The chest has white flecking with a cinnamon background. The bird's flanks are a vermiculated golden tan, the belly white. The wing coverts and speculum are iridescent green, purple and blue.

The hen woody is also a beautiful duck. The female is brown with a white belly, iridescent bronze and white flecking on the sides and chest. Her head has a crest and a white ring around the eye. The bill is dark with traces of orange and the feet are a dull golden color.

Speed and Sound

The woody's flight speed is 45 to 50 miles per hour. They are not considered fast flying, but they can twist and turn through trees better than any other duck. The male and female make loud calls in flight (hou-w-eet). The female has a sharp alarm call (cr-r-ek cr-r-ek) and the male's call is a high pitched jeeeeeee.

Food and Habits

The wood duck's diet consists of 90 percent vegetable matter balanced with insects. Seeds, berries, and nuts are an important part of the woody's diet, so these birds will do more walking and feeding on the ground than most other ducks. Wood ducks also feed in shallow water for pondweed, duckweed, water lily, and other aquatic plants. Wood ducks seldom congregate with other species of ducks. They frequent wooded streams and ponds and can fly through timber dropping down, and landing with ease. Wood ducks take off almost vertically from water. The wood duck is a perching duck and sometimes spends time sitting and resting in trees

Migration

Wood ducks start their fall migration early and most will have returned to their wintering grounds by the end of October. Woodies migrate in small flocks and fly high when traveling. If food is available and the weather is warm, wood ducks will stay in one place for short periods of time before moving on.

Table Fare

The wood duck is one of the most delicious of the puddle ducks.

Wood duck drake.

CANADA GOOSE
Branta canadensis

QUICK FACTS

Local Name
Wild goose, Canada, honker, big gray goose

Size
To most waterfowl hunters the words "wild goose" mean only "Canada goose" with its clear honking call. Although hunters can readily identify the species, Branta canadensis, most are not concerned with all the races of the species and simply lump them into categories of small, medium, and large. Even game biologists don't always agree with one another on the number of different races within the species.

The different races of Canada geese range in size from 22 to 48 inches long, wingspans can range from 44 to 75 inches and weight can vary from 3 to 20 pounds.

Identification in Flight
All races and sexes have a black head; long, black neck; and a distinctive white chin strap from ear to ear. The body and wings are dark and can be distinguished at great distances. Only the size of the bird in flight is difficult to determine. The honker's wingbeats are fairly slow compared with other waterfowl. Canada geese are very vocal; they will make clear honking calls to one another while flying. Flocks usually fly in V formation or in a long line. The Canada goose appears slow in flight, yet it is capable of speeds up to sixty miles per hour.

- This goose is extremely intelligent and learns to avoid danger early in life. When feeding on land or water, two or three birds will always act as sentinels to guard the rest of the flock. Canada geese are very wary of unfamiliar objects and movements. These large geese are prized as fine game birds over most of the continent.Field shooting with decoys for Canada geese is a great challenge and is probably the most exciting method of hunting this wonderful game bird.

Color
The sexes and races of Canada geese are similar in color. The head and neck are black with a white chin strap which sets it apart from all other geese. The back and sides are dark brown with bars. The chest and belly vary from brownish to gray with the larger races usually lighter gray. The upper wings are brown and the primary feathers are almost black. The underwing is grayish. The tail is black and the tail

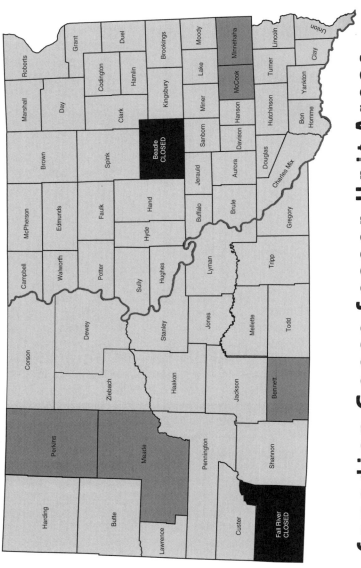

Canadian Goose Season Unit Areas

Unit 1; Sept. 30 - Dec. 24

Closed except by application

Closed

Data from 1995 South Dakota Hunting Handbook. Always consult current state hunting regs.

Majestic Canadian in flight.

feathers are almost black. The underwing is grayish. The tail is black and the tail coverts are white. The large eyes are brown. The feet and bill are black.

Speed and Sound

The Canada goose appears to fly slowly because of it long neck, large body, and rather sluggish wingbeats, yet the goose can reach speeds up to sixty miles per hour. Canada geese are very vocal and keep up a constant conversation with one another with their deep-throated, ah-honk ka rowl ah-honk.

Food and Habits

The Canada goose feeds largely on vegetable matter and spends more time on land than in the water. They are a grazing bird and eat a tremendous variety of grasses and cereal crops, particularly during their fall migrations. A large number of Canada geese concentrating on a single field are capable of doing great damage to cultivated fields before harvest takes place or on newly planted fields.

Canada geese are not usually early risers; they leave for morning feeding after sun-up, but they will stay on their feeding ground for long periods of time. When going to feed, the birds tend to travel in small flocks, possibly family groups. After their morning feeding is over, the geese will return to water to drink and rest on sand and gravel bars. Canada geese return to feed again late afternoon.

When on water the Canada geese will feed on green aquatic plants using their long necks or tipping up like puddle ducks. Animal matter is not an important part of their diet, even though they will chase and eat insects.

On clear days, Canada geese will fly quite high and will glide downward great distances to the place they have chosen to land. When landing in a field the birds will usually fly downwind, look over the landing spot, and then circle into the wind and land.

Migration

Canada geese migrate in V formation or in single lines with the lead bird breaking the wind for the other birds behind. When he tires he drops back and another goose takes his place in front.

Canada geese fly high during migration and in a direct route from one staging area to the other. Canadas may fly at night as well as during the day, but when the flock gets tired they stop to feed and rest.

In September, the small groups start gathering in large numbers on big bodies of water. Migration is in full swing in the month of October. Flock after flock will take off and follow the old timers toward their feeding, resting, and wintering grounds.

Table Fare

Canada goose has very dark meat and can become extremely dry if it is not cooked properly. Canadas are vegetarians and are a superb table bird.

LESSER SNOW GOOSE

Anser caerulescens

QUICK FACTS

Local Name

Snow goose, blue goose, wavie, white goose, common snow goose, arctic goose

Size

The lesser snow goose is a medium-sized goose, 26-31 inches long, with a wingspread of 53-60 inches, weighing about 4 to 6½ pounds.

Identification in Flight

The lesser snow goose has two color phases, white and blue. In flight, snow geese in their white phase appear to be snow white except for their black wing tips. During the blue phase they have a white head and neck with a slate gray body. The lesser snow's wing beats are much faster and flocks are much larger than the Canada goose.

- The blue goose is no longer considered a separate species from the lesser snow goose, but only a color phase. Both the blue and the white phases migrate together, but the blue are more common east of the Great Plains.
- The lesser snow goose migrates in large flocks, breaking up into long diagonal lines and irregular, loose, wide Vs. The snow geese migrate from one staging area to another.

Color

Both sexes of adult lesser snow geese during the white phase have snow white heads and bodies with black wing tips. The bills and feet are pink. Both sexes of the adult blue phase have white heads and necks with slate gray bodies and wings with dark primaries. The bill and feet are pink. The immature whites are dusky white and the immature blues are brownish gray with a white chin patch. The legs, feet, and bill are grayish-brown during both immature phases.

Speed and Sound

The lesser snow goose is a strong flier and has a flight speed of fifty miles per hour. The snows are the most vocal of all the waterfowl and when in large flocks can be heard over a mile away. When a large flock takes off the birds create a loud chattering sound. Their call is a high-pitched musical yelp—ou, ou, ou, ou.

Food and Habits
The snow geese feed almost entirely on vegetable matter. When migrating the birds will spend most of their time feeding in cereal crops like wheat and barley. Snows also feed on many different kinds of grasses. Like other geese this bird is a grazer and feeds on many kinds of vegetation.

When staging in a particular location snows will congregate by the thousands in grain fields and can cause great damage to unharvested crops. Snows arrive on the feeding grounds before daylight and return mid-morning to their resting places. About 2:00 PM they return and feed until dark.

When feeding in large numbers the snow goose has a reputation for being very wary. Snow geese always have some birds on guard looking for danger.

Migration
The snows depart from the arctic breeding ground in September and travel to their staging areas to rest and feed. The birds leave each staging area as the winter conditions force them on to the next staging area farther south. One day the fields are full of thousands of snow geese, but with a change of weather the birds are gone.

Table Fare
The lesser snow goose feeds mainly on cereal grains and greens. The meat is dark and fatty, not quite as good as the Canada goose.

Snow geese feeding in a wheatfield.

ROSS' GOOSE

Anser rossii

QUICK FACTS

Local Name

Little wavie, warty-nosed wavie

Size

The Ross' goose is a small goose, 21 to 25 inches long, with a wingspan of 47 to 54 inches, weighing 2½ to 4 pounds.

Identification in Flight

The Ross' goose is only slightly larger than a mallard duck. In flight, the field markings are the same as the snow goose. Ross' geese are much less vocal, travel in smaller flocks, and do not fly at high altitudes.

- The Ross' goose is the smallest of the North American geese. The Ross' goose has a short bill and wart-like tissue at the base. The bulk of the Ross' geese winter in central California. During migration they stage in Alberta, Saskatchewan, Montana, Oregon, and California. Ross' geese will mix with snow geese when staging and feeding.

Color

Both sexes of the adult are similar. The Ross' goose is a small white goose with black wing tips.

The tip of the bill is pink and the base has greenish wart-like tissue. The legs and feet are dark pink. Both sexes of the immature Ross' goose are similiar. The back of the juvenile's head, the neck, and back are light gray and the lower parts of the bird are white. The legs and feet are greenish-gray. The bill is greenish-pink.

Speed and Sound

The Ross' goose has a slower wingbeat and does not travel as fast as the snow goose. The air speed is about forty miles per hour. In flight, the Ross' goose is not as loud or as noisy as the snows. The call of the goose is a weak ke-gak, ke-gak, ke-gak

Food and Habits

On their migration routes through Alberta, Saskatchewan, and Montana, the Ross' geese feed on cereal grains such as wheat and barley. Farther south in Oregon and California they feed on barley and rice. In the fall, the staging areas are large bodies of water for protection while resting. The Ross' feed is similar to snows. They feed early in the morning and in the late afternoon.

The Ross' goose is a sociable bird and is commonly found mixed with other geese such as snow and white-fronted geese while feeding and resting.

Migration

The Ross' goose fall migration gets underway in late August when they depart from their Arctic breeding ground. The migration schedule in the provinces of Canada and in Montana seem about the same. Like the white-fronted geese, these geese seem in no great hurry to arrive at their wintering ground.

Table Fare

The Ross' goose is small compared to the snow goose, but I believe it is equal to the Canada goose in flavor.

Ross' goose.

WHITE-FRONTED GOOSE

Anser albifrons

QUICK FACTS

Local Name

Specks, specklebelly, tiger breast, marblebelly, laughing goose

Size

The white-fronted goose is a medium-sized goose, 27-30 inches long, with a wingspan of 54 to 60 inches, weighing 4½ to 7 pounds.

Identification in Flight

White-fronted geese travel in loose lines. The bird is mostly brown and is the only goose with a black and brown marbled belly. It has a white fronted face around the bill. They are very noisy and make a high-pitched laughing sound which can be heard for miles

- Most white-fronts fly from the breeding grounds to their staging area without stopping in between. The white-fronted goose's breeding ground is far north on the open, wet tundra. As early as late August, the birds start staging in areas of Saskatchewan. White-fronts are western birds and most of the fall migration takes place in the Pacific and Western flyways. The white-fronted goose is very wary and alert and will post lookouts while feeding.

Color

The adults of both sexes of the white-fronted goose have a dark brown head with white faces. The bodies are grayish brown with black barring on the breasts. The tail and the lower belly are white. The wing primaries are black and the secondaries black-brown. The bill is pinkish and the feet are yellow-orange. Immature birds have no white on their heads and have very little barring on the chest.

Speed and Sound

The specklebelly can fly at speeds between 45 and 50 miles per hour. Their wing beats are strong but slow. It is hard to judge their speed in flight due to their body size and wing motion.

I would rather listen to the wild laughing of the white-fronted goose than any other waterfowl. Once you hear the call—the rollicking, wild, laughing call—of the white-fronted goose you will never forget it. The notes are loud and melancholy, waah waah waah waah waah waah waah. When the white-fronted geese are feeding their sound is quite different but their conversation with each other is constant.

Food and Habits

Ninety-five percent of the white-fronted goose's feed is vegetable matter. Some of its favorite foods are cereal crops. When they are in staging areas they will spend most of their time feeding in the big grain fields. White-fronted geese are early morning feeders and are in the fields by sunrise. Unlike Canada geese, they do not linger while feeding and are back on open water within a couple of hours. White-fronted geese will use smaller lakes to feed on aquatic plants such as bulrush, cattail, wild millet, and sedges, but if disturbed they will seek out larger water areas.

When taking off they have to get airborne by running across the water for a considerable distance. Landing on land or water is not difficult for white-fronted geese.

Migration

White-fronts usually fly in large flocks, traveling in V formation or long broken lines, at considerable heights. Migration starts early in September. They travel from staging area to staging area and do not stop very often in between. White-fronts are some of the first waterfowl to reach their wintering grounds in the south.

Table Fare

White-fronts feed almost exclusively on cereal crops during hunting season and are considered the finest of all the geese for good table fare.

HUNTING WATERFOWL

Puddle ducks have two distinctly different stops and can be counted on to move both. Morning and evening hunting activities function around these movements. Puddle ducks feed around water and grain fields and always rest on water. There are three ways to hunt puddle ducks: jump shooting, pass shooting and staged shooting (over decoys).

Jump shooting means sneaking up or stalking ducks or geese. Make sure your approach is concealed until you arrive at a reasonable shooting distance. Another method of jump shooting is to drift a boat down a meandering stream. Successful jump shooting requires you to concentrate on several factors:

1. Water feeding areas
2. Field feeding areas
3. Feeding periods
4. Weather conditions

Jump shooting is very effective around small stock dams with high brims, small creeks, irrigation ditches, and streams with ox bows or high banks. Two examples of good hot spots would be a high banked, shallow meandering spring creek full of watercress or a back water marsh surrounded by cattails and willows.

Camouflage clothing is helpful, but any drab colored clothing matching the sur-roundings will do. Ducks have good eyes and movement in camouflage clothing appears no differently to a duck than movement in solid clothing. Ducks consider any movement as danger and are even more alert in windy conditions.

While jump shooting, a duck call can be quite helpful. The call can elicit a response revealing the bird's location on the water, but don't over do it. Early in the hunting season, when the first early migrants are mixed with the local species, most feeding takes place in the water on aquatic plants and hunting can be excellent through out the day.

Mid and late season jump shooting takes place after the birds have returned to their resting places. If the weather is clear, puddle ducks feed early in the morning and return to water mid morning. The best time to jump shoot field feeding ducks is when the birds have returned to water. Jump shoot hunting is best from 10:00 A. M. to 3:00 P. M. on clear days with large numbers of birds. Many species of ducks migrate in large flocks, but these huge concentrations will break up into small groups when feeding or resting.

Pass shooting is just that: shooting waterfowl somewhere along the route between their feeding and resting area. On clear days the birds fly fast and very high making shooting difficult. Ducks that have not been hunted will use the same route day after day but migrating birds establish their own patterns and their routes are not as predictable. Feeding areas change from time to time and weather will cause route deviations. Some of the most successful pass shooting occurs when, due to deteriorating weather, the waterfowl feed late in the morning. They will be flying low and can provide fast and furious shooting for a short period of time. Pass shooting requires many hours of observing the birds' movements with binoculars to determine the exact route they are using.

Another method I like to use is what I call back shooting. In back shooting you set up close to the water while the birds are out feeding in the grain fields and you pass shoot when the ducks come back to rest. Deteriorating weather conditions are not as critical during back shooting because the birds drop quickly to the water.

Decoy shooting is luring waterfowl into a spread of decoys. Adding another dimension to the art of waterfowling. The decoy can be made by one's own hand or purchased from a company. The number of decoys used depends upon the place hunted. Large spreads are usually not necessary unless hunting on big bodies of water.

Shooting over decoys is actually the other two methods of duck hunting combined. When the birds come in to a spread of decoys, they will either circle trying to set down or pass by. This is jump shooting and pass shooting at its best .

I believe that shooting over a block of decoys on land or water represents the most exciting and productive form of waterfowl hunting, be it puddle ducks, diving ducks or geese. All species respond to decoys if properly rigged. Decoy shooting does have its disadvantages over the other two methods; for example, the cost of the decoys, boats, motors, and other items used. More preparation time is needed to rig decoys, set up or build a blind, and maintaining the equipment you have accumulated. Is it worth it? You bet! The hours spent setting over a spread of decoys with your dog anticipating, watching and listening to every sound or movement is well worth the experience that one never forgets. A good part of the joy of waterfowl hunting is the discovery and use of all the special equipment.

In my mind I can still see the ten Canada geese coming into my rigs just before sunset–wings locked, the only birds of the day. I don't remember if it was a long drive home, or how cold it was picking up the decoys. I do remember talking to the geese with my call, crouching low in the pit blind, my knuckles white on the forearm of the shotgun, my heart beating, looking down at my dog, eyes as big as saucers and turning to my partner and saying, "Now." I've shot my limit other days, but I don't think numbers are as important as the feeling of any particular moment when it "all comes together."

IDENTIFICATION OF WATERFOWL

The identification of ducks and geese is extremely important to any waterfowler. Knowing the species on the wing is satisfying, rewarding, and essential to the wing-shooter for many reasons. The ability to identify each species comes with field experience and through the use of guidebooks, identification manuals and the pamphlets produced by state and federal agencies. It is critical for the hunter to identify the duck or goose before shooting.

Knowing that a flock of American widgeons is coming into a block of decoys and not canvasbacks,(which have hunting restrictions), can certainly make shooting and bag limits more rewarding. The desirability of bringing down a highly delicious, grain fed mallard over a common merganser will speak for itself.

What should one observe to help in learning waterfowl? Color, size, shape, motion, action, sound, and numbers of birds all play an important role in the identification of a species. Knowledge of the kind of habitat in use at different times of day, where the birds feed, travel routes and weather changes are beneficial to good wingshooting.

This part of the *Wingshooter's Guide to South Dakota* is intended to encourage you to recognize ducks and geese at a distance for better hunting success. The species of waterfowl discussed in this chapter are the birds most sought after by hunters.

Photo: Blanche Johnson

Day's end–Cindy, Brandy, Chuck and Blanche.

LOCATING HUNTING AREAS

To insure good shooting for waterfowl throughout the season you have to familiarize yourself with all possibilities in any given area. The task of finding good hunting places is best met by preseason scouting, to include obtaining permission to hunt private land and finding areas that fall under state, tribal, or federal waterfowl shooting regulations. If you live near the hunt, scouting can be easy. But if you are planning a distant waterfowl hunting vacation, preparation should start well in advance of the time you fire the first shot. The Wingshooter's Guide will certainly help save you valuable time towards achieving these goals.

Rivers

If a river flows through country with adjacent grain fields, hay meadows, and brushy cover it will hold ducks and geese. Rivers can be difficult to read. The only way to study a river is by floating or walking along its banks, all the while looking for good, out of the way holding spots for waterfowl. Wide sand bars and shallow back waters nearly always hold ducks. Larger rivers with side channels, brushy islands with exposed gravel bars can also provide some excellent waterfowl hideouts. Side channels with muddy flats, marshy dead end sloughs and out of the way back waters can also be productive. Any stream that meanders through agricultural land, is hidden from view or is in a remote area will hold a few waterfowl.

Lakes

Lakes hold large numbers of waterfowl if conditions are favorable for rest and feeding. As long as the habitat and conditions are good, ducks and geese will use the same body of water year after year. Many lakes are federally or state owned and are wildlife refuges maintained for waterfowl and waterfowl hunting. Large lakes attract mostly diving ducks but may have puddle ducks, especially if the areas are marshy and weedy. Lakes are much easier to evaluate than rivers because they can be viewed in their entirety.

Potholes and Sloughs

Potholes and sloughs can provide very good shooting early in the season for local and migrating ducks. Teal, mallards, widgeons, and gadwalls all prefer to use small bodies of water before freeze up. Look for sloughs or potholes in out of the way places. Many of these small watering holes are on private property and it goes without saying getting permission is essential. Reading local maps and observing the topography can be helpful in finding marshy areas. Sloughs and potholes follow low land formations and are usually found in chains. Take note of the habitat the water system has around it. For example, are bulrush and cattails around the perimeter? Are there grain fields close by? Are birds trading from one pot hole to another?

Fields

Locating good fields that ducks and geese are using is comparatively easy. Look for stubble fields that have low places with potholes and reservoirs in proximity. The best fields are large and open. Birds are very wary of irrigation ditches, fence rows, and other objects that obstruct their view.

GOOSE HUNTING METHODS

Canada Geese

The best ways to locate Canada geese are by scouting the big grain fields adjacent to major rivers for feeding geese or spotting geese flying to feeding areas. When the birds are found wait until they return to water. Get permission to hunt, dig a pit or set up a blind, set out decoys and return that evening or next morning (depending on the time of day you spotted the birds). Decoys can be set up on gravel bars or reservoirs when birds are out feeding. This is best done in the morning because birds usually return to their resting areas after sunset. Binoculars and spotting scopes are extremely helpful when looking for geese. Jump shooting can be productive on small rivers, ponds and reservoirs. Pass and back shooting can also be very good.

Snows, Ross' and White-Fronted Geese

Snow geese, Ross' geese and white-fronted geese are often seen in flocks together, sometimes numbering in the thousands, as they migrate to staging areas. Predicting the arrival of big flocks of geese moving in the fall can, due to agricultural practices and weather conditions, be difficult. It is essential to get information on local goose movement. You can start by contacting the wildlife management area or wildlife refuge you plan to hunt.

Hunting big flocks is best done using field shooting techniques, much like hunting Canada geese. Staging of snows can start as early as October or as late as November. Snows can range many miles to wheat and barley fields so the birds are best followed in a vehicle, using binoculars to locate their feeding area. Many different flocks will use the same place to feed on a given day, so watching or following the birds is not difficult. Snows are not as predictable as Canada geese and may not return to the same field. Using large spreads of decoys is the most successful method of hunting white-fronted geese. Use floating decoys on bodies of water or other wetland areas where the geese are resting. Back shooting (birds coming back to their resting area from feeding)or pass shooting can be productive. Boats and decoys are useful on large bodies of water, but are not always necessary. Many hunters successfully use shoreline or shallow water areas to hunt geese.

WATERFOWL ESSENTIALS: BLINDS, BOATS, CALLS, GUNS AND DOGS

Blinds

A blind is any type of concealment by which the person, dog, and equipment can be hidden from view while hunting.

Ducks and geese are very wary of places that do not look natural. For example, upon locating a pond or marsh rimmed with high willows or other tall brush, puddle ducks will circle and investigate the perimeter before landing. The important thing to keep in mind is that the blind should have overhead concealment as well as cover on all four sides. There are basic essential features that make a good blind, whether temporary or permanent. It should have enough room for one or two people to move about comfortably and safely, it should look natural so as not to scare quarry and offer some kind of protection from wind or bad weather. Be very choosy about the materials used for making a temporary blind. The blind must blend into the surroundings. It's important to be thoroughly hidden as well as motionless. The general rule of camouflage is to break up the shapes that look out of place with the natural cover. If a duck or goose flares, something is wrong; a boat, gun, dog, decoy or another piece of equipment is not thoroughly concealed.

Photo: Blanche Johnson

There are two different types of blinds, one for shooting around water and one for field shooting. Water shooting blinds can be temporary, built from deadwood, natural grasses, rocks or other material found close to the decoy set up. Temporary blinds can also be built with camouflage netting covered with grass, reeds, cattails, or whatever is available to blend into the background. Permanent blinds are usually built before the hunting season, some are used year after year, some are removed after the hunting season.

Permanently constructed blinds are stake blinds, pit blinds, piano box blinds, and sink boxes. Portable or movable blinds are made to float or set up quickly on land. Many kinds of boats can be covered with natural material or with camouflage netting and used as portable blinds.

Field blinds create greater problems than water blinds because there is little natural cover left after harvest. The most effective field shooting blind is one I call the pit board blind, (illustrated, page 130). The pit board blind is excavated to a depth of 36 inches. Pit boards are placed around the top of the blind and dirt from the pit is then placed around the boards. This blind is time consuming to construct and disassemble, but one of the best to use in field shooting.

I use portable field blinds and, with a little extra effort, find them very effective. My portable hay bale field blind (illustrated, page 129) consists of 4 foot high woven wire sheep fence covered on the inside with burlap bags and woven on the outside with wheat stalks, corn stalks, or grasses that blend with the surroundings. The good thing about the fence blind is that you can roll it up tight to conserving space and transport it easily. You could use snow fencing painted with flat light yellow paint and eliminate the burlap, but it takes more storage space.

Boats

Any kind of boat you can imagine can be used as a duck boat, but most effective are small, low profile craft, such as punts, prams, johnboats, canoes, gunning sculls, and some inflatables. The gunning scull,when moved by human power, is still the most efficient and deadly water craft available. Boats are expensive so choose a boat that can double for other recreation activities.

Because there are so many diverse water systems, there are no perfect duck boats. Different waters present different kinds of problems. Depth, flow, and overall area all determine the most effective craft to use.

I believe the best all around boat is the aluminum johnboat (illustrated, page 129). This utilitarian craft gets high marks because of its flat bottom construction, sled bow, size (12 to 15 feet), light weight, low profile, and seaworthiness. The johnboat can take a small motor, transports easily, and the cost is reasonable.

The other little boat I like is the coffin box (illustrated, page 128). The coffin box can be used for field shooting or as a water craft. When used in the water it has to be water proofed and it should be towed by a larger craft. In the field, coffin boxes covered with the material simulating the surrounds are also a deadly way to kill ducks and geese. The small size is a distinct disadvantage. You have to lie down for long periods of time and, when sitting up to shoot, turning can be difficult.

Decoys

Hunters have been using some form of decoys for centuries. The Native Americans used a wide variety of decoys woven from grass and various other natural materials.

Most waterfowl are attracted to their own kind and ducks and geese will land with other waterfowl species if conditions look favorable. Mallard decoys, for example, can be used for many species of waterfowl hunting. Each area of the country has it own particular species and when building or buying decoys keep in mind the ducks you plan to hunt. The mallard is America's most populous duck and the most commonly used decoy. The Canada goose decoy leads the field for goose hunting.

I highly recommend making your own decoys. It is time consuming but fun and gratifying. A teal or gadwall that swings into a block of your own decoys is very rewarding, not only for shooting but for the satisfactions of luring the birds in with your own handywork. However, most waterfowl hunters buy their decoys, and dollar for dollar, it's cheaper than building them. With today's new manufacturing technologies there are very good decoys available at reasonable prices.

Calls

To be successful at waterfowl calling, one must first be able to identify the calls and know the language of that species. Calling ducks into decoys is a very fine art and takes years of practice. Calling geese is much easier because geese talk a lot and the voices have less variety. The best way to learn calling is to listen to the wild bird in the field. You can also purchase an audio tape of the calls of ducks and geese.

I use duck calls; sometimes they work and sometimes they don't. It is my belief that some ducks are much more receptive to a call than others. Calling to geese (I call it talking) is more important than calling other waterfowl. Geese talk continuously to one another and they expect the birds on the ground (your decoys) to talk back. Because geese chatter constantly your mistakes are usually ignored. Everyone who hunts waterfowl should have several calls. Many are very beautiful objects in themselves, making calls just one more part of the sport to be enjoyed on several different levels.

Guns

What gun for you? The gun that feels good, fits and shoots well is the gun to use. Many old duck hunters will tell you that a 12 gauge pump, long barrel, full choke is the best gun ever made for waterfowl!

I use several guns for waterfowl shooting. For close in shooting I use a light weight, 20 gauge, 3″ shell, over and under improved and modified. I also use a 12 gauge, 2¾″ shell, side by side, improved and modified. In Canada, I use a 12 gauge 2¾″ shell, over and under, full and full.

Steel shot has changed the playing field in waterfowl shooting, whether you like it or not. The new nontoxic bismuth will also change waterfowl shooting in the future. I found shooting waterfowl with non-toxic bismuth to be extremely effective and to my liking.

A golden retriever and an English setter on duty.

Dogs

No matter what you hunt, upland game or waterfowl, dogs play an enjoyable and important part in the sport. The Labrador retriever is the most popular hunting dog in America, and has many wonderful traits. They are affable, and easy to train. There are many other good breeds of waterfowl dogs such as the Chesapeake Bay retriever, and golden retriever. Most water dogs are also especially good upland gamebird hunting companions.

Other breeds, such as Brittanys, can be used for waterfowl hunting but only the retriever breeds have the heavy coat and the strength to handle the hard job of retrieving in cold water. When killing a duck or goose over water, you have few choices: wading out for the bird yourself, rowing out in a boat, or sending out a retriever. Of the three, the last is the most fun and practical.

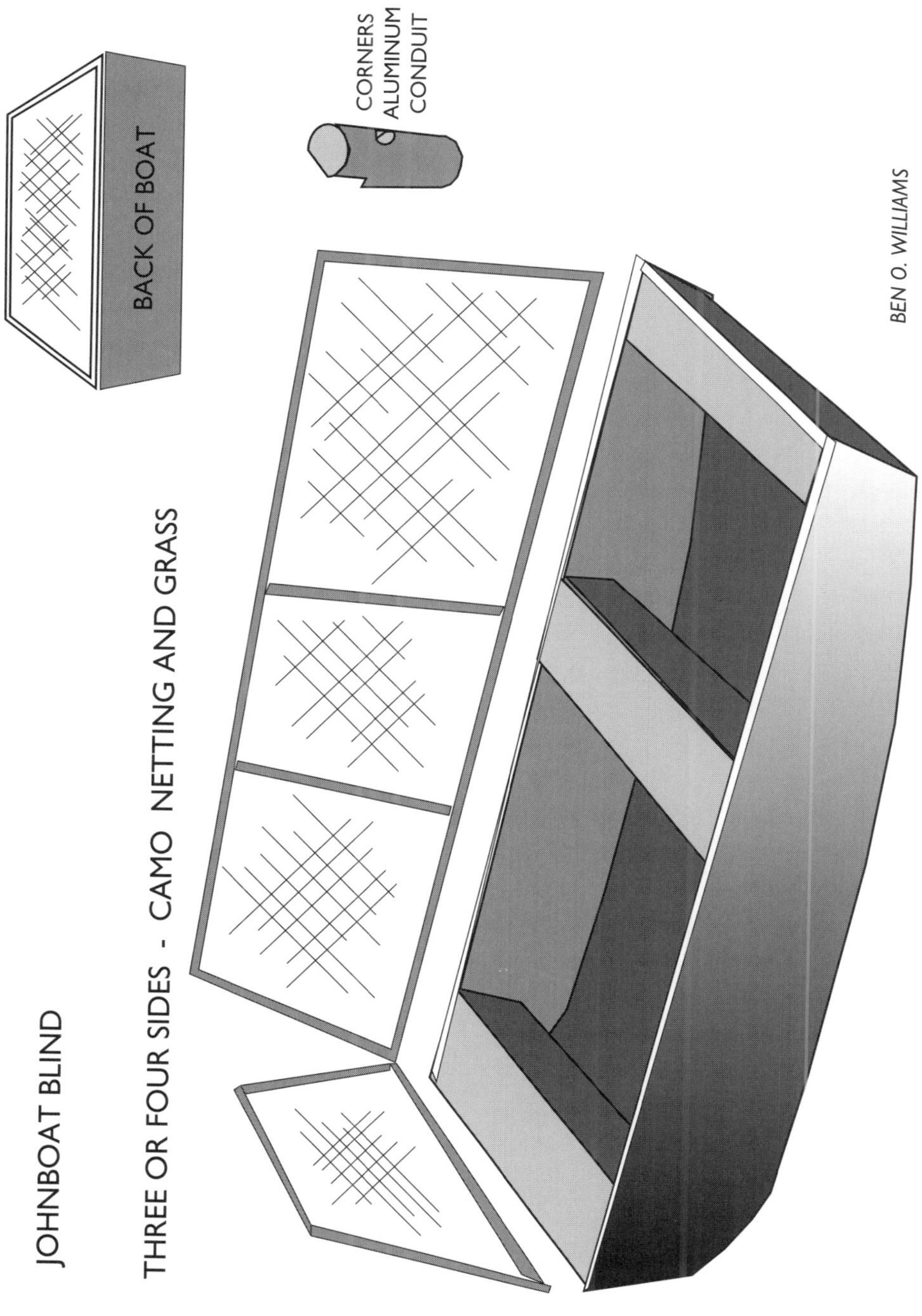

CORNERS ALUMINUM CONDUIT

BACK OF BOAT

BEN O. WILLIAMS

JOHNBOAT BLIND

THREE OR FOUR SIDES - CAMO NETTING AND GRASS

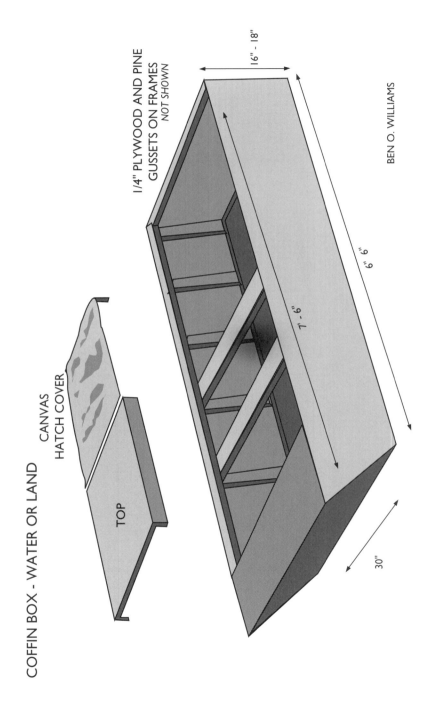

COFFIN BOX - WATER OR LAND

CANVAS HATCH COVER

TOP

1/4" PLYWOOD AND PINE GUSSETS ON FRAMES *NOT SHOWN*

16" - 18"

6' - 6"

7' - 6"

30"

BEN O. WILLIAMS

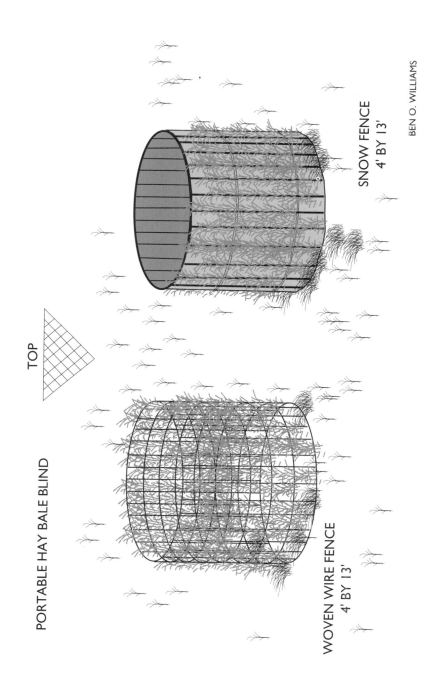

PORTABLE HAY BALE BLIND

TOP

SNOW FENCE
4' BY 13'

WOVEN WIRE FENCE
4' BY 13'

BEN O. WILLIAMS

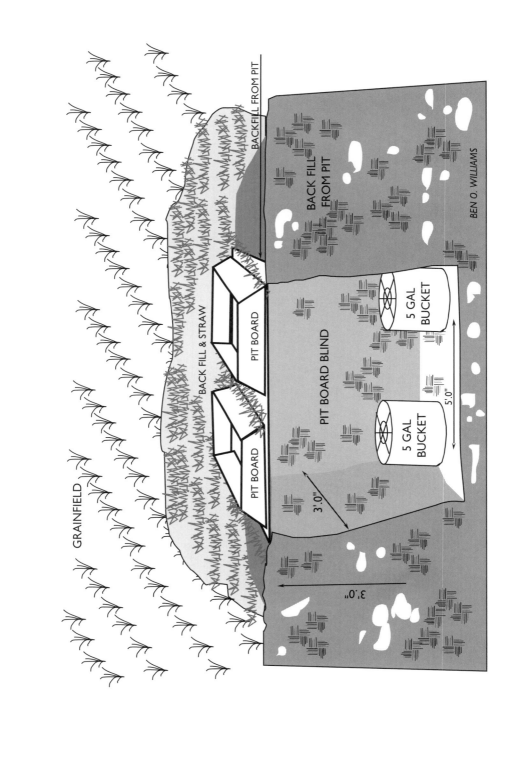

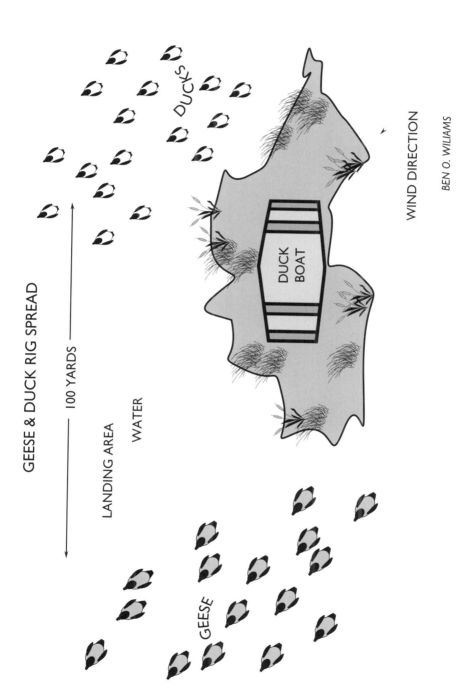

GEESE & DUCK RIG SPREAD

100 YARDS

LANDING AREA

WATER

DUCKS

GEESE

DUCK BOAT

WIND DIRECTION

BEN O. WILIAMS

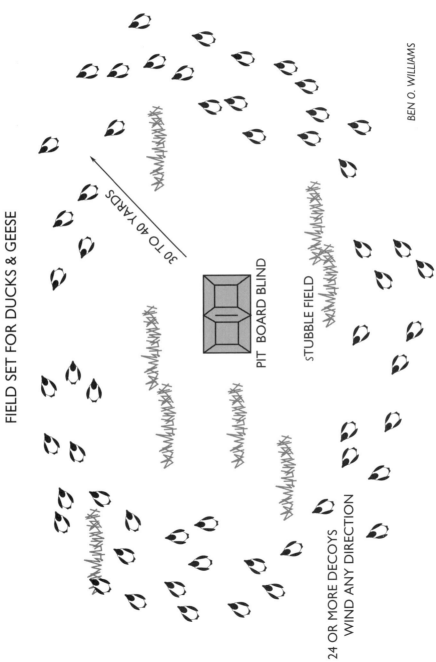

FIELD SET FOR DUCKS & GEESE

30 TO 40 YARDS

PIT BOARD BLIND

sTUBBLE FIELD

24 OR MORE DECOYS
WIND ANY DIRECTION

BEN O. WILLIAMS

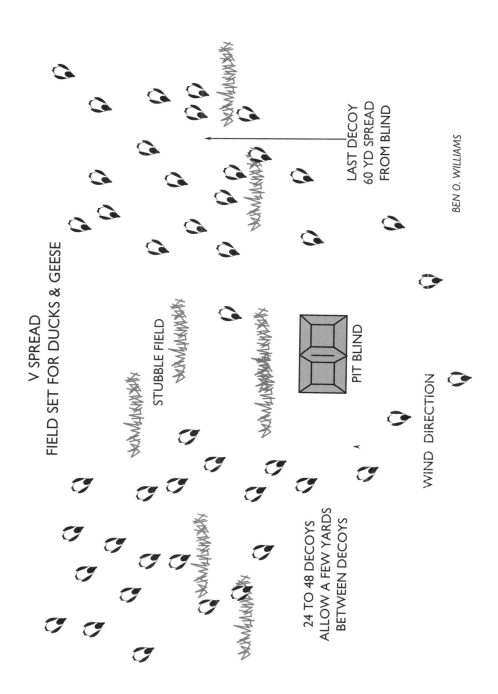

V SPREAD
FIELD SET FOR DUCKS & GEESE

STUBBLE FIELD

PIT BLIND

LAST DECOY
60 YD SPREAD
FROM BLIND

WIND DIRECTION

24 TO 48 DECOYS
ALLOW A FEW YARDS
BETWEEN DECOYS

BEN O. WILLIAMS

WATERFOWL COOKING

The flavor of any waterfowl is influenced by what the bird is feeding on. You have no control over what the duck you shot has been eating, but you do determine the species you shoot.

The first determining factor of the quality of a gourmet meal of duck or goose depends on the field preparation. Usually, when I shoot a duck, I pick the duck as soon as possible. By employing this method, I am able to avoid having to pick several birds all at once. When the weather is warm, I remove the entrails in the field. If it's cold, I do not draw the bird. I don't believe the time the bird is picked or drawn makes much difference in the taste of the game, as long as it is properly cooled. I hang waterfowl between four and seven days, depending on the size and weight of the bird.

If properly cooked, most ducks and geese are delicious and are the heart of some of the best meals I have enjoyed. The secret of waterfowl cooking is to use high heat for a short period of time, whether baking, broiling, or frying. Here are two recipes I use that are simple and delicious.

Place duck or goose on a broiler pan, preheat the oven to 450 degrees and bake. I cook teal and other small ducks 15 to 17 minutes, mallards or other large ducks 18 to 21 minutes. Experiment with the time for your particular taste. After taking the bird out of the oven, it will continue to cook for several more minutes. It looks very rare but will be thoroughly cooked. Remember; the longer the duck cooks the tougher it becomes.

When cooking in the field, camper, motel, or at home, frying ducks, geese and other game birds can also be delicious. Soak filleted breasts and legs in milk for 1 1/2 to 2 hours. Fry quickly over high heat in equal parts of butter and olive oil (inside should remain pink - don't overcook). Remove bird, lower heat, and add 1/2 cup bourbon and 1 cup sour cream, simmer briefly, salt and pepper to taste. Serve sauce over the bird.

Dinner delivered.

FEEDING PERIODS AND WEATHER CONDITIONS

When the weather is clear and sunny many puddle ducks and geese feed in cereal crop fields, usually once in the morning and again in the evening. As weather conditions deteriorate with low clouds, rain, or snow, movements of waterfowl will change considerably. The birds fly lower and feeding periods can change. These can be the most productive hunting days during the season as the birds seem to be uneasy and move often between their feeding and resting areas.

Windy conditions play an important part in determining where the ducks and geese rest. Birds prefer little wind and will seek out quiet water or will tuck up under a lee bank. Some hunters say birds are spookier during windy conditions, but I'm not so sure. I've hunted in high winds and found jump shooting to be superb.

FLYWAYS

Waterfowl is managed by the Department of the Interior's Fish and Wildlife Service and is an international resource crossing state and national lines. The department's management began in 1948 to allow different regulations relating to populations of waterfowl in that flyway.

The flyway systems are geographical regions with lines running north and south. There are four flyways in the United States: the Atlantic, the Mississippi, the Central and the Pacific. The flyways are helpful units that group states with common borders into administrative areas that work together to implement waterfowl management policy and to solve conservation problems. Many ducks and geese do follow a north–south geographic flyway, but not all waterfowl fit into a single flyway when migrating.

BLACK HILLS REGION

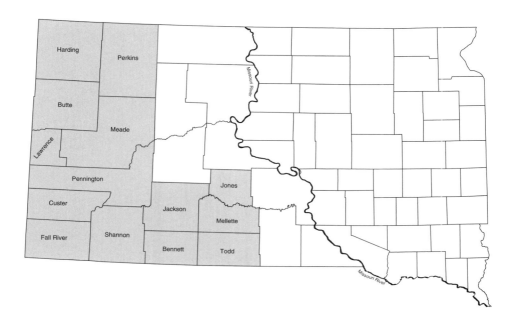

Western South Dakota boasts five national parks, forests and monuments. The area is characterized by the Black Hills in the west central section of this region and the Badlands in the southwestern corner. Predominant terrain consists of rolling hills and prairie land. Rapid City is the largest city found in this region and the second largest in South Dakota. This city of approximately 55,000 boasts a modern commercial airport, major retail facilities, and all other amenities you might expect from a growing metro area.

Wild turkeys and ruffed grouse are plentiful in the Black Hills and the Custer National Forest. The agricultural land and the prairies provide good hunting for sharptail grouse and Hungarian partridge, as well. The rivers and numerous small potholes provide excellent hunting for waterfowl.

Black Hills Mourning Dove Distribution

Black Hills Gray Partridge Distribution

Prime Area   Very Productive

Pheasant Distribution

Black Hills Region

Black Hills Sharptail Distribution

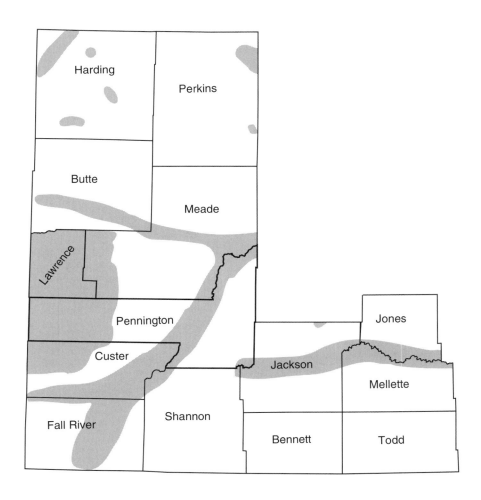

Turkey Distribution

Black Hills Region

PrairieChickenDistribution

BlackHillsRegion

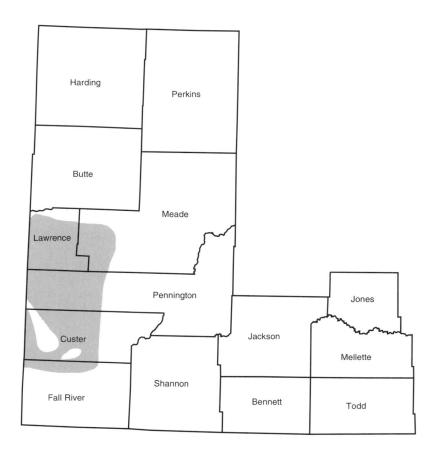

Ruffed Grouse Distribution

Black Hills Region

BELLE FOURCHE AND BUTTE COUNTY

Population–4,335	October Temperature–49.1
County Population–7,914	Annual recipitation–17.01
County Area–2,251 sq. mi.	Acres in CRP–3,136

Belle Fourche is the northern gateway to the Black Hills. North of town is prairie country. There is excellent ruffed grouse and turkey hunting in the Black Hills and prairie country north of town has fair upland bird hunting. The Belle Fourche Reservoir and nearby rivers provide good waterfowl hunting.

UPLAND BIRDS
Ruffed Grouse, Turkey, Hungarian Partridge, Pheasants

WATERFOWL
Ducks & Geese

ACCOMMODATIONS
King's Inn Best Western, 518 National. 605-892-2691. 30 units. Laundry. Dogs allowed in smoking rooms only. Dog exercise area nearby. $$

Reid Motel, 922 Harding. 605-892-2521. Kitchenettes. Dogs allowed-$5.00 fee per dog. Bird cleaning facilities. Cable TV. $$.

Super 8 Motel, 501 National. 605-892-3361. 43 units. Dogs allowed-no extra charge. Dog exercise area nearby. Cable TV. $$.

Ace Motel, 109 6th Ave. 605-892-2612. 14 units. Dogs allowed-$3.00 fee. Dog exercise area available. Cable TV. $$.

CAMPGROUNDS AND RV PARKS
Riverside Campground, 418 9th Ave. 605-892-6446. RV and tent sites, full hookups, showers, shaded areas. Open until October 31 (weather permitting).

RESTAURANTS
Korner Cafe, 623 Grant St. 605-892-6593. 6am to 3pm Mon-Fri.
Belle Inn Restaurant, South Hwy. 85 and 34. 605-892-4430. Open 24 hrs.
Bull Pen Bar & Grill, South Hwy 85. 605-892-2503 1pm to 2am daily

VETERINARIANS
Belle Fourche Veterinary Clinic, 430 Summit St. 605-892-2618. Dr. William Marlatt and Dr. James Myers.

SPORTING GOODS
Snoozy's Surplus, 501 State St. 605-892-6257.

AUTO RENTAL AND REPAIR
Can Am Automotive, 202 6th Ave. 605-892-4648
Wilbur Repair, Hwy. 212 W. 605-892-4556

AIR SERVICE
Belle Fourche Municipal Airport, North Hwy 85. 605-892-6345

MEDICAL
Belle Fourche Health Care Hospital, 2200 13th Ave. 605-892-3331

FOR MORE INFORMATION:
Belle Fourche Chamber of Commerce
415 Fifth Ave.
Belle Fourche, SD 57717.
605-892-2676, fax 892-4633

BUFFALO
AND HARDING COUNTY

Population–488	October Temperature–47
County Population–1,669	Annual Precipitation–14"
County Area–2,678 sq. mi.	Acres in CRP–30,776

Buffalo is a small farming and ranching community located in northwestern South Dakota. There are isolated tracts of the Custer National Forest located north and east of town. These forested areas provide excellent turkey hunting.

UPLAND BIRDS
Turkeys, Pheasants

WATERFOWL
Ducks & Geese

ACCOMMODATIONS
Tipperary Lodge Motel, Hwy 85. 605-375-3721. 605-375-3721. 20 units. Dogs allowed in downstairs rooms only-no extra charges for dogs. Dog exercise area nearby. Cable TV. $$

CAMPGROUNDS AND RV PARKS
Reva Gap Custer National Forest Campground, 20 mi. east of Buffalo on US 20. 406-657-6361. 4 sites. 10 day limit, open seasonally. Water available. Tents, travel trailers, & RVs accommodated. By reservation only.
Picnic Springs Custer National Forest Campground, 20 mi north & 6 mi. west of Buffalo. 406-657-6361. 7 sites. 10 day limit, open seasonally. Water available. Tents, travel trailers, & RVs accommodated. By reservation only.

RESTAURANTS
Oasis Restaurant, Highway 85, 605-375-9693. Breakfast, lunch, dinner.
Feedlot, Highway 85. 605-375-3403. 11AM–10PM. Lunch and dinner.
The Depot, Highway 85. 603-375-3766. Pizza.

VETERINARIANS
None, closest is in Belle Fourche.

SPORTING GOODS
Buffalo Hardware and Lumber, Main Street. 605-375-3322.

AUTO RENTAL AND REPAIR
Henderson Conoco, South Highway 85. 605-375-3255.

AIR SERVICE
None.

MEDICAL
Harding County Clinic 605-375-3744.

FOR MORE INFORMATION:
Harding County Chamber of Commerce
P.O. Box 273
Buffalo, SD 57720-0273

FAITH
AND MEADE COUNTY

Population–548	October Temperature–49.1
County Population–21,878	Annual Precipitation–16.56"
County Area–3,481 sq. mi.	Acres in CRP–28,278

Faith is a small, friendly, ranching community located in the heart of cowboy country.

UPLAND BIRDS
Pheasant, Hungarian Partridge

WATERFOWL
Ducks

ACCOMMODATIONS
Branding Iron Motel, Hwy 212 & 73. 605-967-2662. 16 units. No dogs allowed in rooms. Cable TV. $$

Prairie Vista Inn, Hwy 212 & 73. 605-967-2343 or 800-341-8000. 27 units. No dogs allowed in room. Cable TV $$.

Melissa's Bed and Breakfast, 1st St. & 1st Ave. 605 985-5238. 5 units(1 bed per room). Buffet breakfast (6:00am). No dogs allowed in rooms. No smoking. Cable TV $$.

CAMPGROUNDS AND RV PARKS
Faith City Park, 605-967-2261. Open year round, RV hookups.

Durkee Lake, 605-967-2261. Open year round, free.

RESTAURANTS
Granny's Cafe, Box 518. 605-967-2292. 5:30am–9:00pm.

Wrangler Cafe & Lounge, Box 99. 605-967-2999. 6:00am–10:00pm.

VETERINARIANS
Faith Veterinary Service, Box 488. 605-967-2212.

SPORTING GOODS
Afdahl's Hardware, Box 388. 605-967-2822.

AUTO RENTAL AND REPAIR
Auto Center, Box 37. 605-967-2490.

Tri-County Auto, Box 455. 605-967-2244.

AIR SERVICE
Faith Airport, Box 368. 605-967-2261. 4000' runway.

MEDICAL
Rapid City Regional Hospital, 353 Fairmont Blvd. Rapid City. 605-341-1000.

FOR MORE INFORMATION:
Faith Area Chamber of Commerce
Box 246
Faith, SD 57626
605-967-2001

HOT SPRINGS
AND FALL RIVER COUNTY

Population–4,325
County Population–7,353
County Area–4,742 sq. mi.

October Temperature–50.6
Annual Precipitation–15.83"
Acres in CRP–2,137

Located on the south eastern edge of the Black Hills, Hot Springs is a good spot to base a ruffed grouse or turkey hunt.

UPLAND BIRDS
Ruffed Grouse, Turkey

ACCOMMODATIONS

Dakota Inn, Jct. 79-385-18, 5 miles east of Hot Springs. 605-745-6655 or 745-6447. 20 units. Restaurant (dinner only), lounge. Dogs allowed-no extra charge. Dog exercise area nearby. Cable TV. $$.

Historic Log Cabin Motel, Hwy. 385 N. 605-745-5166. 17 units. Dogs allowed-no extra charge. Dog exercise area nearby. Hot tub & kitchenettes. Cable TV. Wide range of rates.

Super 8 Motel, 800 Mammoth St., Hwy. 18 By-Pass. 605-745-3888, 1-800-800-8000. 44 units. Restaurant (6:00AM-9:00PM), lounge. Dogs allowed with $25 deposit. Cable TV. $$

CAMPGROUNDS AND RV PARKS

KOA Campground, Hwy. 79, 5 miles east of Hot Springs. 605-745-6449. 73 sites, dump station, primitive cabins, full facilities. Open until October 15.

RESTAURANTS

Fall River Bakery, 407 N. River St. 605-745-6190. Coffee shop. 6AM-6PM, Mon.-Sat.

Heartland Restaurant and Lounge, Hwy. 385 S. 605-745-6693. Sandwiches, Steaks, Seafood. 8AM-2AM, Mon.-Sat. 8AM-midnight, Sun.

Maverick Restaurant, Jct. 385-79-18. 605-745-4215. Open 24 hours.

VETERINARIANS

Fall River Veterinary Clinic, Hwy. 385, Fall River Rd. 605-745-3786. Dr. Paul Wittenburg.

SPORTING GOODS

Coast to Coast Hardware, 207 S. Chicago. 605-745-5173

Pamida, truck bypass route. 605-745-4401

AUTO RENTAL AND REPAIR
Maverick Service, Jct. 385 and 79. 605-745-4215.
Southside Service, 445 S. Chicago. 605-745-5828.
Hills Edge Auto, Hwy 385 North. 605-745-3773.

AIR SERVICE
Hot Springs Airport, 7 miles southeast on Hwy. 18.
Cheyenne Aviation, Hot Springs Airport.   605-745-3555.

MEDICAL
Southern Hills General Hospital, 209 N. 16th St. 605-745-3159.

FOR MORE INFORMATION:
Hot Springs Area Chamber of Commerce
801 S. 6th
Hot Springs, SD 57747
605-745-4140 or 800-325-6991

KADOKA
AND JACKSON COUNTY

Population–736	October Temperature–50.5
County Population–2,811	Annual Precipitation–16.02"
County Area–1,872 sq. mi.	Acres in CRP–30,824

Kadoka is the eastern gateway to the Badlands, located on the northern border of the Pine Ridge Indian Reservation. There is good upland bird hunting on the farmland and prairie country around Kadoka.

UPLAND BIRDS
Sharptail Grouse, Pheasants, Hungarian Partridge

ACCOMMODATIONS

Best Western H&H El Centro Motel, 105 E. Hwy 16. 605-837-2287. 40 units. Dogs allowed-no extra charge. Restaurant on premises. Cable TV. $$

West Motel, exit 150 or 152 off I-90. 605-837-2427. 18 units. Dogs allowed-$3.00 charge per day. Cable TV. $.

Leewood Motel, I-90 Bus. Loop. 605-837-2238 or 800-982-1917. 5 units Dogs allowed-no extra charge. Dog exercise area nearby. Freezer space, bird cleaning area. Cable TV. $

Ponderosa Motel, & RV Park, exit 150 or 152 off I-90. 605-837-2362. 11 units. Open May 1 to Oct. 1. Laundromat, heated pool, cable TV. $$

CAMPGROUNDS AND RV PARKS

Ponderosa Motel & RV Park, exit 150 or 152 off I-90. 605-837-2362 or 800-675-7297. 20 RV hookups. Shaded sites, laundry, hot showers, heated pool, TV. Open May 1 to Oct. 1.

Kadoka Kampground, exit 150 off I-90. 605-837-2243. 25 sites. Open all year. Hot showers, heated pool, cable TV.

Dirk's Campground, exit 150 off I-90. 605-837-2292. 25 sites, 10 w/full hookups, 10 w/just water & elec. Laundry, hot showers. Dogs welcome.

RESTAURANTS

H & H El Centro, exit 150 or 152 off I-90. 605-837-2265 Open Memorial Day to Sept. 16. 6am - 10am/4pm - 9pm daily.

Happy Chef, Jct 73 & I-90. 605-837-2230. Open 6am - 10pm daily.

Sidekicks Restaurant, 605-837-2801. Open 6am - 9pm.

Pizza Shed, 2 Locust St. East. 605-837-2581 Open 4pm - 8pm

VETERINARIANS

Kadoka Veterinary Clinic, 303 Main St. South. 605-837-2431

Boyd L. Porch, DVM, 65 Ave. SW. 605-837-2697

SPORTING GOODS

Hogen's Hardware, 223 Main St. 605-837-2274

AUTO RENTAL AND REPAIR

Kadoka Standard Service, 605-837-2350

Scott's Auto Repair, 402 E. Hwy 16. 605-837-2866

AIR SERVICE

Kadoka Airport, 605-837-9198.

MEDICAL

Swisher Clinic, 104 1/2 Chestnut St. 605-837-2257. Open Mon.-Wed. only.

Kadoka City Ambulance, 837-2628

Hans P. Petersen Memorial Hospital-Philip, 2 miles north on Hwy 73. 505 W. Pine St. 605-859-2511

FOR MORE INFORMATION:

Kadoka City Finance Office

P.O. Box 58

Kadoka, SD 57543

605-837-2229

LEMMON
AND PERKINS COUNTY

Population–1,614
County Population–3,932
County Area–2,884 sq. mi.

October Temperature–47.8
Annual Precipitation–18.43"
Acres in CRP–62,667

Lemmon is the largest city in this Northwest part of South Dakota. This is an ideal city in which to base a combination North and South Dakota bird hunt. The Shadehill Recreation Area and the South Fork Grand River are located 15 miles south of town. The Grand and Cedar River National Grasslands, comprising 161,000 acres, is located west and south of town. This grassland area provides excellent bird hunting. Lemmon is located on the western boundary of the Standing Rock Indian Reservation. There is a large population of giant Canadian geese located in Perkins county. Hunting for ducks and geese is on a special drawing basis; see regulations section, page 1.

UPLAND BIRDS
Hungarian Partridge, Sharptail Grouse, Pheasants

WATERFOWL
Ducks & Geese

ACCOMMODATIONS

Budget Inn Motel, E. HWY 12. 374-3886. 26 units. Dogs allowed-no extra charge. Dog exercise area nearby. Kitchenettes and cable TV. $.

Lemmon Country Inn, 1 mi. east of Lemmon on US 12. 605-374-3711. 31 units. Restaurant next door. Dogs allowed-no extra charge. Cable TV. $$

Prairie Motel, 115 E. 10th St. 374-3304 or 800-341-8000. 13 units. Dogs allowed-$4.00 per dog. Dog exercise area nearby. Bird cleaning area, freezer space available Cable TV. $.

CAMPGROUNDS AND RV PARKS

Shadehill Recreation Area, 12 mi. east of Lemmon on Hwy 73. 1-800-710-2267. 32 sites, hot showers, RV dump station, hookups.

RESTAURANTS

The Steakhouse, east Hwy 12. 605-374-9511. Steaks, prime rib, seafood. Open 5pm

Meyer Family Inn, Hwy 12. 605-374-9534. Open 6am - 10pm days a week.

Busted T Cafe, 316 Main. 605-374-3680. Open 6am - 8 pm 7 days a week

VETERINARIANS
  Ron Ford, DVM. 605-374-5200

SPORTING GOODS
  Jerry's Hardware, 306 Main. 605-374-5466
  Rosenau's Hardware, 114 Temp St. West. 605-374-5955

AUTO RENTAL AND REPAIR
  K & R Auto Body, W. Hwy. 12. 605-374-5211.
  Wolff's Wheel Alignment, 301 1st Ave. E. 605-374-3377.

AIR SERVICE
  Lemmon Municipal Airport. Small craft, 4500' asphalt strip, no commercial service

MEDICAL
  Five Counties Hospital and Nursing Home, 405 6th Ave. W. 605-374-3871.

FOR MORE INFORMATION:
  Chamber of Commerce
  500 Main St.
  Lemmon, SD 57638
  605-374-5716

MARTIN
AND BENNETT COUNTY

Population–1,151	October Temperature–47.6
County Population–3,206	Annual Precipitation–47.6"
County Area–1,182 sq. mi.	Acres in CRP–8,262

Martin is a small town located just north of the Nebraska border in western South Dakota. It is bordered on the east by the Rosebud Indian Reservation and on the north by the Pine Ridge Reservation. The LaCreek National Wildlife Refuge is southeast of town. There is good upland bird hunting on both Indian reservations and the Lacreek National Wildlife Refuge. Between 4,000 and 10,000 ducks nest and visit the Lacreek N.W.R., providing terrific waterfowl sport. There is also a large population of giant Canada geese on the refuge. Bennett county has a limited number of waterfowl licenses available.

UPLAND BIRDS
Sharptail Grouse, Hungarian Partridge, Pheasants

WATERFOWL
Ducks and Geese

ACCOMMODATIONS
Kings Motel, east Hwy 18. 605-685-6543. 29 units. Dogs allowed-no extra charge for dogs. Dog exercise area nearby. Freezer space available. Cable TV. $

Western Heritage, east Hwy 18. 605-685-6543. 29 units. Dogs allowed-no extra charge for dogs. Dog exercise area nearby. Limited freezer space. Cable TV $$. **Crossroads Inn,** Jct Hwy 18 & 73. 605-685-1070. 34 units. No dogs allowed in rooms. Cable TV. $$

CAMPGROUNDS AND RV PARKS
Martin City Park, 3 hookups.

RESTAURANTS
Martin Auction Cafe, 605-685-1066. Open 6 a.m. to 1:30 p.m. Tuesday–Friday and Sunday; 6 a.m. to 8 p.m. Monday

Hot Stuff Pizzeria, 304 Main St. 605-685-6200

VETERINARIANS
Blackpipe Veterinary Clinic. 605-685-6336

SPORTING GOODS
Gambles. 605-685-6440
Ace Hardware. General Store, 201 Main. 605-685-6730
Coast to Coast. 605-685-6266

AUTO RENTAL AND REPAIR
Bair Ford-Mercury. 605-685-6646

MEDICAL
Bennett County Community Hospital. 605-685-6622
Martin Clinic. 605-685-6868

FOR MORE INFORMATION:
Martin Commercial Club
Box 610
Martin, SD 57551

MURDO
AND JONES COUNTY

Population–679
County Population–1,324
County Area–971 sq. mi.

October Temperature–49.3
Annual Precipitation–18.13"
Acres in CRP–33,118

Located midway across South Dakota on interstate I-90, Murdo has ample accomodations for hunters. You can find good hunting for upland birds here, without the hunting crowds that you will encounter in central South Dakota.

UPLAND BIRDS
Pheasants, Sharptail Grouse, Hungarian Partridge

ACCOMMODATIONS

Anderson Motel, 1/2 block north of I-90 business loop, 408 Lincoln. 605-669-2448. 5 units. Dogs allowed in rooms-no extra charges for dogs. Cable TV. $$

Best Western Graham's, I-90 exit 191 or 192. 605-669-2441. 45 units. Dogs allowed with prior manager approval- no extra charge for dogs. Full service restaurant and lounge on premises. Cable TV. Wide range of rates. $$ - $$$

Sioux Motel, 302 E. 5th. 605-669-2422. 24 units. Dogs allowed in rooms- $5.00 extra. Dog exercise area nearby. Bird cleaning area and freezer space. Cable TV. $$

CAMPGROUNDS AND RV PARKS

Camp McKen-Z, I-90 exits 191-192, two blocks east of 4-way stop. 605-669-2573. 50 pull-thru sites. Elec. hook-ups, laundry, showers, restrooms. Tenters welcome.

TeePee Campground, I-90 Business Loop, exits 191 or 192. 70 sites, 25 complete with sewer. 40 pull-thru sites with water & elec. hook-ups. Cabins, heated pool, showers, restrooms, laundry. TV. RV dump station.

RESTAURANTS

Triple H Restaurant, exit 192. 605-669-2465. Open 24 hrs.

Kentucky Fried Chicken, 600 E. 5th St. 605-669-3040

Sub-Station, 503 5th St. 605-669-3250 Open 6am-6pm.

Silver Valley Cafe, 211 Main St. 605-669-2959. Open 11am-11pm.

VETERINARIANS

Murdo Veterinary Clinic, 408 Cedar Ave. 605-669-2531. Dr. C.K. Kinsley

SPORTING GOODS

Lees department Store, 117 Main. 605-669-2291

AUTO RENTAL AND REPAIR

Cliff's Auto repair, 606 W. 5th St. 605-669-2811
Dean's Phillips 66 Service, 509 5th St. 605-669-2373
Murdo Ford-Mercury, 219 Main St., 605-669-2784
D&B Tire, 206 Washington. 605-669-2644

AIR SERVICE

No commercial service. 3400' paved.   Lighted if requested, no services.

MEDICAL

Jones County Clinic, 609 Garfield Ave. 605-669-2121
Ambulance, 305 Main St. 605-669-2841

FOR MORE INFORMATION:

Murdo Chamber of Commerce
Secretary Dorothy Anker
Box 242
Murdo, SD 57559

RAPID CITY
AND PENNINGTON COUNTY

Population–54,523
County Population–81,343
County Area–2,783 sq. mi.

October Temperature–48.7
Annual Precipitation–18.15"
Acres in CRP–26,615

Rapid City is South Dakota's second largest city. It is located on the eastern edge of the Black Hills, has a large commercial airport, and an abundance of retail stores, motels and resturants. The Black Hills has excellent ruffed grouse and turkey hunting. The prairies and farm lands east of Rapid City have fair to good pheasant hunting.

UPLAND BIRDS
Ruffed Grouse, Turkeys, Pheasants

ACCOMMODATIONS

Ramada Inn, I-90 exit 59 & LaCrosse St. 605-342-1300. 139 units. Dogs allowed-no extra charge. Cable TV. Perkins restaurant on premises, open 24 hrs. Lounge. $$

Budget Inn, Hwy 16 E. & Business Loop I-90, exit 59 or 60. 605-342-8594. 38 units. Dogs allowed-no extra charge. Cable TV. $$

Avanti Motel, 102 N. Maple. 605-348-1112. 40 units. Dogs allowed-no extra charge. Dog exercise area nearby. Cable TV. Restaurant/Lounge on premises. $$

Alex Johnson Motel, 523 6th St. 605-342-1210. 141 units. Dogs allowed-no extra charge. Cable TV. Restaurant/Lounge on premises. $$

Quality Inn, 2208 Mt. Rushmore Rd., I-90 exit 57. 605-342-3322 or 800-228-5151. 109 units. Dogs allowed-no extra charge. Cable TV. Wide range of rates, $-$$$.

Super 8, 2124 LaCrosse, I-90 exit 59. 605-348-8070. 119 units. Dogs allowed-$5.40 extra. Dog exercise area nearby. Cable TV. $$

EconoLodge of Rapid City, 625 E. Disk Drive, I-90 exit 59. 605-342-6400. 120 units. Dogs allowed-no extra charge, must be well attended. Dog exercise area nearby. Cable TV. Wide range of rates. $-$$$

CAMPGROUNDS AND RV PARKS

Rapid City KOA, I-90 exit 61, 2 1/2 mi. south from US 16 or SD 79 turn E. on St. Patrick to Hwy 44 Jct. 605-348-2111 or 800-852-2946. RV hook-up sites & cabins. Free pancake breakfast. Pool, spa, car rentals.

Elk Creek Resort & Campground, I-90 exit 46, 1 mi. east on Elk Creek Rd. 605-787-4884 or 800-846-2267. Tents, Full hook-up RV sites, 25 room motel. Restaurant on premises. Pool, spa, laundry, showers. Motel open all year/ Dogs allowed. Campground open April 15 - Oct. 15.

Happy Holiday Motel & Cabins, I-90 exit 57, 9 mi. south on US Hwy 16. 605-342-7365. 208 pull-thru spaces, full hook-ups, pool, spa, showers, laundry, groceries, firewood, rental cars. Open year - round.

Berry Patch Campground, 7001 S. Hwy 16, 4 mi. south of Rapid City. 605-341-8554. Pull-thrus with full hook-ups. Tent sites, camping cabins, hot tub, pool, laundry. Open April 1 - Oct. 31.

RESTAURANTS

Uptown Grill, 615 Main St. 605-343-1942. Open 11am - 1am daily

Bonanza Steakhouse, 1118 E North. 605-342-7484. Open 11am-9pm, Sun-Thurs, 11am-10pm, Fri.-Sat.

Firehouse Brewing Co., 610 Main St. 605-348-1915. Open 11am - 1am, dining till 9pm, Mon.-Thurs., 11pm, Fri.-Sat., Sundays 4pm-9pm.

The Millstone Family Restaurant, 1520 LaCrosse, 605-343-5824, & 2010 W. Main, 605-348-9022. Open 6am-11pm all week.

Mr. Steak, 2125 N. Haines. 605-342-1543. Open 11am-9pm,daily

Carini's Italian Food, 324 St. Joe. 605-348-3704. Open 11am-9pm, Mon.-Thurs., 11am-10pm, Fri.-Sat.

Gas Light Dining Saloon, Main St. Rockerville. 605-343-9276. Open 4:30-9pm Thurs.-Fri, 11am-9pm, Sat.-Sun.

Red Lobster, 120 Disk Drive. 605-348-9717. Open 11am-9pm all week.

Happy Chef, 2110 LaCrosse, 605-348-6898 & 2121 W. Main, 605-348-6667. Open 24 hours daily.

Conoco I-90 Travel Plaza, I-90 exit 61. 605-342-5450. Open 24 hrs.

VETERINARIANS

Canyon Lake Veterinary, 4230 Canyon Lake Dr. 605-348-6510 or 800-700-6510. 24 hr. service. James D. Mortimer, DVM

Animal Clinic, 1655 E.27 St., Valley Drive., 605-342-1368 or Mobile 381-1368. Dale R. Hendrickson, DVM

Dakota Hills Veterinary Clinic, 1571 E.Hwy 44. 605-342-7498. Dr. John Allen, Dr. Penny Dye.

SPORTING GOODS

Scheel's All Sports, Rushmore Mall. 605-342-9033

DakotaMart Outdoor Sports, 755 E. Disk Dr. 605-399-9590

Guns West, 601 Main St. 605-348-4867 or 800-246-3486

AUTO RENTAL AND REPAIR

Rent-A-Wreck, 1318 5th St. 605-348-3050 or 800-733-9735

Budget, Airport: 605-393-0488, Rushmore Plaza: 605-343-8499, or 800-676-0488

Avis, Airport, 605-393-0740

AIR SERVICE

Rapid City Regional Airport, 605-393-9924

Northwest Airlines, 1-800-225-2525

American Airlines, 1-800-433-7300
Skywest/Delta, 1-800-453-9417
United Express, 1-800-241-6522

MEDICAL

Rapid City Regional Hospital, 1011 11th St. 605-341-1000, Emergency-341-8222, All Emergencies-911

FOR MORE INFORMATION:

Rapid City Convention & Visitors Bureau
444 Mt. Rushmore Rd.
Rapid City, SD 57701-2754
605-343-1744

STURGIS
AND MEADE COUNTY

Population–5,330	October Temperature–48.6
County Population–21,878	Annual Precipitation–22.20"
County Area–3,481 sq. mi.	Acres in CRP–28,278

Sturgis is located on I-90 on the northeast side of the Black Hills The Black Hills provide great hunting for both ruffed grouse and turkey.

UPLAND BIRDS
Ruffed Grouse, Turkey

ACCOMMODATIONS
Days Inn, Hwy. 14A–Boulder Canyon Rd. Exit 30 off I-90. 347-3027. 53 units. Cable TV. No dogs allowed. Continental breakfast. $$

Spearfish Canyon Lodge, Spearfish Canyon, Hwy. 14A. 800-439-8544. 54 units. Satellite TV. No dogs allowed. Package deal, $70 includes room, dinner, drink from lounge, all for 2 people. Restaurant across the street, 8AM–8PM. $$

Super 8, Exit 30 off I-90. 347-4447. 59 units. Cable TV. Dogs allowed-$20 deposit per dog. Dog exercise area nearby. $$

Phil-Town Best Western, 2431 S. Junction. 347-3604. 56 units. 10% off for hunters, cable TV. Dogs allowed. Dog exercise area nearby. Bird cleaning area, freezer space. $$

CAMPGROUNDS AND RV PARKS
Bear Butte State Park Campground, 6 mi NE.. of Sturgis, off SD79. 15 sites, no hook-ups.

Boulder Park Campground, 5 1/2 mi. W. of Sturgis on Hwy 14A(Deadwood RD.). 605-347-3222. Elec., water, & sewer hookups. Showers, tables, daily or weekly rates. Open May 1 - Oct.1

Days End Campground, I-90 exit 30. 605-347-2331. 46 pull-thrus, 36 w/ water sewer, elec. & 10 w/ water & elec. Restrooms, showers, laundry, groceries, RV dump, firewood. Open all year. (Bath & laundry dependent on weather)

RESTAURANTS
G. Meister's Cafe, across the street from the Days Inn. 347-9241. Opens at 6AM. 10% discount for Days Inn guests.

Boulder Canyon Restaurant, Hwy. 14A. 605-347-3787. Open 6AM–10 or 11PM.

Country Kitchen, S. Junction. 605-347-3604. Open 6am–9pm.

VETERINARIANS

Dr. Ken Ireland, Dr. Carl Johnson,& Dr. Margie Jones, 713 Anna St. 605-347-3606.
Sturgis Veterinary Hospital, S. Junction. 605-347-4436.

SPORTING GOODS

Coast to Coast, 931 1st. 605-347-3681
Pamida, 2105 Lazelle & Park. 605-347-3641

AUTO RENTAL AND REPAIR

D & D Motors, 717 Anna. 605-347-2578.
Randy's Auto, 701 Lazelle St. 605-347-5197.
Farmer's Union Oil-Cenex, 1304 Main. 605-347-2351

AIR SERVICE

Sturgis Municipal Airport, 5 miles east on Hwy. 34. Small jets and twin engine aircraft. 605-347-3356

MEDICAL

Sturgis Community Health Care Center, 949 Harmon. 605-347-4741. If no answer 605-347-2536.
Ambulance Service, 1400 Main. 605-347-2574

FOR MORE INFORMATION:

Sturgis Area Chamber of Commerce
P.O. Box 504
Sturgis, SD 57785-0504.
605-347-2556

REGIONAL GUIDES AND OUTFITTERS

HIGH PLAINS GAME RANCH
HCR76, Box 192, Nisland, SD 57762
605-257-2365
Contact: Randy Vallery, 7am - 8pm
Land - 1280 acres
Game - preserve / pheasant, chukar, turkey
Personal Guides - available
Dogs - available / hunter's dogs welcome
Extras - clubhouse, lodging, meals, clays, group packages

HIDDEN VALLEY HUNTING CLUB
HC56, Box 51, Oral, SD 57533
605-424-2895
Contact: Bob Anderson, days
Land - 640 acres
Game - native / dove, ducks
        preserve / pheasant
Personal Guides - available
Dogs - available / hunter's dogs welcome
Extras - meals available, clays

DAKOTA HILLS SHOOTING PRESERVE
HC56, Box 90, Oral SD 57766
800-622-3603
Contact: Tom Lauing
Land - 6000 acres
Game - preserve & native pheasant, Hungarian partridge, chukar, turkey,
        sharptails, ducks
Personal Guides - available/ fully guided hunts only
Dogs - available / hunter's dogs welcome
Extras - clubhouse, lodging, meals, clays, airport transport, bird processing

GREAT LAKES REGION

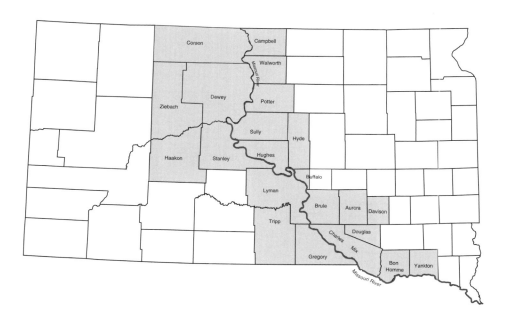

The Missouri River runs north to south through the center of the Great Lakes region. This region derives its name from the four major lakes formed by massive dams across the Missouri River, Lake Oahe, Lake Sharpe, Lake Francis Case, and Lake Lewis and Clark. The state capital, Pierre, is located central to the region on the Missouri River. This is prime farm land with ideal habitat for upland birds.

The Great Lakes area is famous pheasant country. Every community gears up for the opening of pheasant season and wholeheartedly welcomes hunters. Here you will also find a great deal of hunting pressure. If you are planning to hunt pheasant in this region, plan early. The Fort Pierre National Grassland, south of Pierre, has a large population of prairie chickens. In addition to prairie chickens you can hunt sharp-tails and pheasants on the grasslands. Hungarian partridge are found in all of the counties on both sides of the Missouri river. There are four Indian reservations in the region and all of the reservations have great hunting for upland birds and waterfowl.

The Missouri River and the many lakes provide outstanding hunting for both geese and ducks. You can hunt waterfowl in the morning and limit on pheasants in the afternoon. The Great Lakes region provides the bird hunter with great wingshooting for both upland birds and waterfowl.

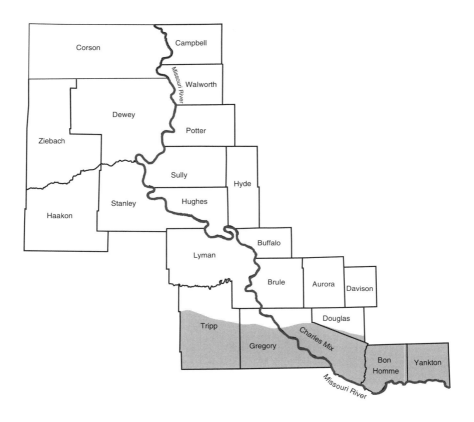

Bobwhite Quail Distribution

Great Lakes Region

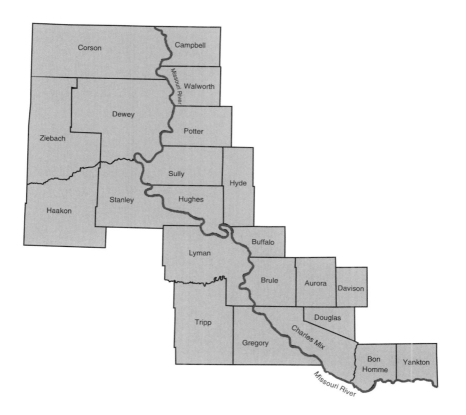

Gray Partridge Distribution

Great Lakes Region

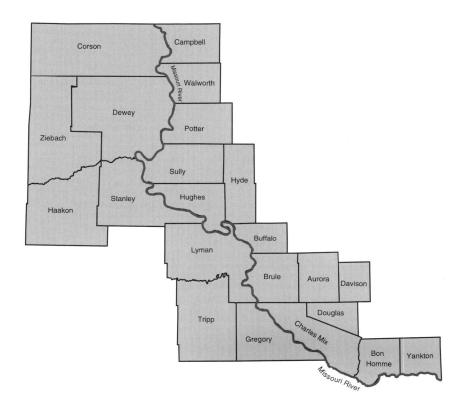

Mourning Dove Distribution

Great Lakes Region

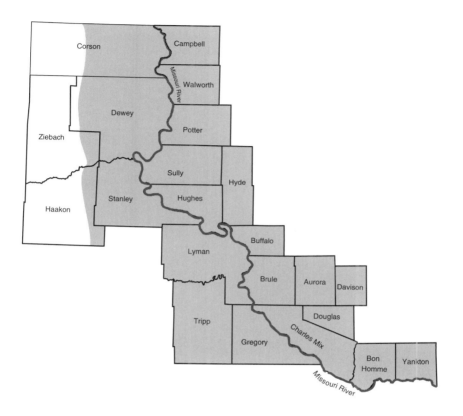

Pheasant Distribution

Great Lakes Region

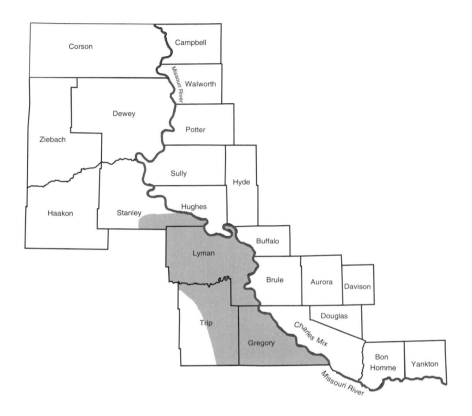

Prairie Chicken Distribution

Great Lakes Region

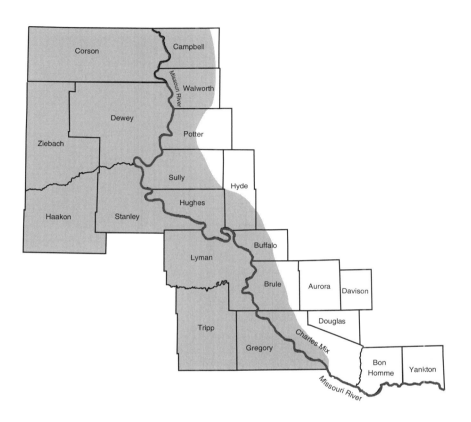

Great Lakes Region

Sharptail Distribution

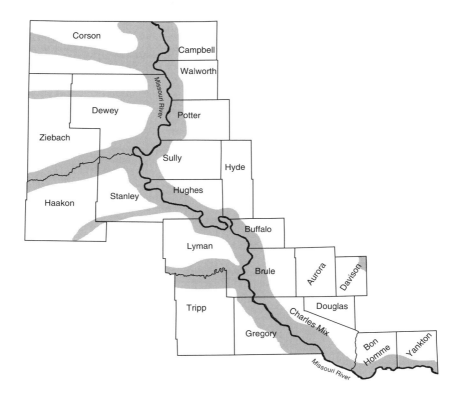

Turkey Distribution

Great Lakes Region

ARMOUR
AND DOUGLAS COUNTY

Population–619	October Temperature–51
Annual Precipitation–23.06"	County Population–3,746
County Area–434 sq. mi.	Acres in CRP–2,604

Armour is a small farming town on the east side of the Missouri River. There is excellent pheasant hunting in Douglas County. Charles Mix County just south of Armour has a good population of bobwhite quail. The area bordering the Missouri River breaks has good turkey hunting. Lake Andes and the Missouri River south and west of Armour provide superb duck hunting for both puddle ducks and divers. There is also good goose hunting during the fall migration.

UPLAND BIRDS
Pheasants, Bobwhite Quail, Turkey, Hungarian Partridge

WATERFOWL
Ducks & Geese

ACCOMMODATIONS
Armour Motel, 281, N. Hwy 281. 605-724-2891. 12 units. Dogs allowed-no extra charge. Bird cleaning area, freezer space. Cable TV. $
Parkway Motel/Corsica, South Dakota, Hwy 281. 605-946-5230. 8 units. Dogs allowed in kennels. Dog exercise area nearby. Cable TV. $$

RESTAURANTS
Armour Steakhouse and Lounge, 614 Braddock. 605-724-2214. Open 12-1pm/5pm-10pm daily.
K's Korner, 701 Braddock 605-724-2593 Open 6am - 11 pm, Mon. - Thurs., 6am - 1am Fri. - Sat.

VETERINARIANS
Armour Veterinarian Service, 627 Main St. 605-724-2457.
John Bakker, DVM, Corsica, SD. 605-946-5471

SPORTING GOODS
Wilson's True Value Hardware, 700 Main St. 605-724-2796
Trustworthy Hardware, Corsica, SD, Main St. 605-946-2796

AUTO RENTAL AND REPAIR
Doug's Repair, 207 Main St. 605-724-2881
T & K Car Care, 408 Braddock Ave. 605-724-2149

MEDICAL ARMOUR
Medical Clinic, 305 Depot. 605-724-2954
Ambulance Service, 605-724-2159

FOR MORE INFORMATION:
Armour Commercial Club
P.O. Box 610
Armour, SD 57313-0610

CHAMBERLAIN AND BRULE COUNTY

Population–2,300	October Temperature–50.9
County Population–5,485	Annual Precipitation–17"
County Area–815 sq. mi.	Acres in CRP–7,048

Chamberlain is nestled on the banks of the Missouri River, surrounded by green rolling hills. Just north of Chamberlain are the Crow Creek and Brule Indian Reservations. Across the river is the small town of Oacoma, home of Al's Oasis with its famous restaurant, gift shop, general store,and marina. Chamberlain is in the heart of some of the best pheasant hunting in the United States. There are also very good hunting opportunities for prairie chickens, sharptails and huns. Numerous outfitters and guides are to be found throughout this area. Lake Sharp and the Missouri River provide outstanding waterfowl hunting. The two Indian reservations have both upland and waterfowl hunting. You can hunt ducks and geese in the morning and get your limit of pheasants in the afternoon.

UPLAND BIRDS
Pheasants, Prairie Chickens, Sharptail Grouse, Hungarian Partridge

WATERFOWL
Ducks and Geese

ACCOMMODATIONS

Hillside Motel, 505 E. King. 605-734-5591. 34 units. Cable TV, bird cleaning facilities & freezer space. Dogs allowed-no extra charge. Dog exercise area nearby. $$

Super 8 Motel, I-90, Exit 263. 605-734-6548. 56 units. Cable TV, bird cleaning facilities, & freezer space. Dogs allowed-$10 deposit per dog. Dog exercise area nearby. $$

Bel Aire Motel, I-90, Exit 265. 605-734-5595. 35 units. Cable TV &, freezer space. Dogs allowed-$10 deposit per dog. Dog exercise area nearby. $$$

Day's Inn, I-90, Exit 260. 605-734-4100. 45 units. Cable TV. Contracts with local guide for freezer space and cleaning. Dogs allowed-$20 deposit per dog. Dog exercise area nearby. Pool & spa. $$$

CAMPGROUNDS AND RV PARKS

Chamberlain KOA Campground, ½ mile south of I-90 at Exit 265. 605-734-5729. Open until October 25th. Heated pool & spa.

Familyland Campground, Box 97, Oacoma 57365. 2 miles west of Chamberlain off I-90, Exit 260. 800-675-6959. 63 RV sites, large tenting area. Hookups, full services.

RESTAURANTS
Al's Oasis, W. Hwy 16. 605-734-6051 Open 6:30am - 10pm, 10:30pm Fri. - Sat.
Rainbow Cafe, 117 S. Main. 605-734-5481 Open at 6:00am
Charly's Steakhouse, 606 E. King. 605-734-6238 4pm-11pm

VETERINARIANS
Mid-River Veterinary Clinic, P.O. Box 98. 605-734-6562. Dr. Julie Williams.

SPORTING GOODS
D&N One Stop, 201 W. King. 605-734-6811.

AUTO RENTAL AND REPAIR
Willrodt Motor Company, 115 S. Courtland. 605-734-5584.
Swanson Service, 314 N. Main. 605-734-6459.
Lakeview Sinclair, Lakeview Heights. 605-734-6396.

AIR SERVICE
Chamberlain Municipal Airport, 3 miles south of town, off I-90. 605-734-5401

Medical
Mid-Dakota Hospital, 300 S. Byron Ave. 605-734-5011.

FOR MORE INFORMATION:
Chamberlain Area Chamber of Commerce
P.O. Box 517
Chamberlain, SD 57325
605-734-6541

GETTYSBURG
AND POTTER COUNTY

Population–1,510	October Temperature–47
County Population–3,190	Annual Precipitation-18.2"
County Area–859 sq. mi.	Acres in CRP–25,295

Gettysburg is located 12 miles east of Lake Oahe in central South Dakota. The area depends on agriculture and ranching. Gettysburg is a progressive and friendly city that welcomes hunters and even provides a free campground for visitors. The agricultural lands provide excellent upland bird hunting. There are several guides and outfitters in the area who provide guided bird hunts. Lake Oahe and the surrounding area provide great waterfowl hunting.

UPLAND BIRDS
Pheasants, Sharptail Grouse
Hungarian Partridge, Mourning Dove

WATERFOWL
Ducks & Geese

ACCOMODATIONS
Trail Motel, 211 E. Garfield. 605-765-2482. 22 units. Dogs allowed-$5.00 per dog extra. Dog exercise area nearby. Freezer space. Cable TV. $$
Super 8, 719 E. Hwy 212. 605-765-2373. 24 units. Dogs allowed-$10.00 extra charge. Dog exercise area nearby. Freezer space. Cable TV. $$

CAMPGROUNDS AND RV PARKS
West Whitlock State Park, 18 mi. west of Gettysburg off US 212. 103 sites (46 elec.) Camping cabins. Dump station. Restrooms and showers. 605-765-9410

RESTAURANTS
Firehouse Bar & Lounge, 109 N. Main. 605-765-2228. 4pm-11pm.
Medicine Rock Cafe, 801 E.Hwy. 605-765-2894. 6am-9pm.

VETERINARIANS
Nold Animal Supply, 101 N. Exene. 605-765-2451. Dr. Martin Nold

SPORTING GOODS
Bohnenkamp's Dakota Supply, W. Hwy 212. 605-765-9400
Coast to Coast, 107 W. Commercial. 605-765-2183

AUTO RENTAL AND REPAIR
  Nagel Motor Service, Jct 83 & Hwy 212. 605-765-9474
  Chase's Ford & Mercury Inc., 210 N. Exene. 605-765-2300 or 800-952-3673

AIR SERVICE
  City Airport, 605-765-9177

MEDICAL
  Gettysburg Memorial Hospital, 606 E. Garfield Ave. 605-765-2488

FOR MORE INFORMATION:
  Gettysburg Chamber of Commerce
  303 South Broadway Street
  Gettysburg, SD 57442
  605-765-9309

GREGORY
AND GREGORY COUNTY

Population–1,384	October Temperature–51.5
County Population–5,359	Annual Precipitation–24.59"
County Area–1,013 sq. mi.	Acres in CRP–5,335

Gregory is a small ranching and farming community located in the heart of out-standing pheasant country. The rolling hills and agricultural land provide ideal habitat for upland birds. This area provides some of the best pheasant hunting in South Dakota.

UPLAND BIRDS
Pheasants, Prairie Chicken, Sharptail, Gray Partridge, Doves, Turkeys

WATERFOWL
Ducks & Geese

ACCOMMODATIONS

Grey House Inn & Motel, 605-835-8479. No dogs. Rates are for two people, two beds. Bruce and Alice. $$

Parkside Motel, 605-835-9696. Continental breakfast, free ice, no dogs, 26 beds. $$

RESTAURANTS

Butch's Steakhouse & Lounge, 605-835-9959. RR5, Dinner.

Doug's Cove Cafe, 605-835-8838. 622 Main Street. Open at 6 a.m.

Stukel's Corner Cafe, 605-835-9970. 601 Main Street. 6 a.m. to 8 p.m.

VETERINARIANS

Gregory Animal Clinic, East Highway 18. 605-835-9237

SPORTING GOODS

Coast to Coast Hardware, 605-835-9601. Main Street.

MEDICAL

Gregory Health Care Center, 400 Park Avenue. 605-835-8394

AIRPORT

Gregory Municipal Airport, 605-835-9978

FOR MORE INFORMATION:
City Hall
P.O. Box 436
Gregory, South Dakota 57533
The City Hall has a list of names, places of hunting facilities, and people who clean birds.

MITCHELL AND DAVISON COUNTY

Population–13,798	October Temperature–49.7
County Population–17,503	Annual Precipitation-22.05"
County Area–436 sq. mi.	Acres in CRP–3,619

Mitchell is located on I-90 in eastern S. Dakota in the center of farm country. It is one hour from Sioux Falls. Pheasant hunting is very good and Hungarian partridge hunting is fair to good in the Mitchell area. Mitchell does not get the intense hunting pressure that central South Dakota does, resulting in a plentiful pheasant population. There is very good field hunting for waterfowl during the fall migration.

UPLAND BIRDS
Pheasants, Hungarian Partridge, Doves

WATERFOWL
Ducks & Geese

ACCOMMODATIONS

Best Western Motor Inn, 1001 S. Burr. 605-996-5536 or 800-528-1234. 81 units. Dogs allowed-no extra charge. Dog exercise area. Cable TV, washers & dryers. $$$
Budget Host Inn, 1313 S. Ohlman. 605-996-6647 or 800-283-4678. 44 units. Dogs allowed-$6 extra. Dog exercise area nearby. Bird cleaning area. Cable TV. $$
Chief Motel, 507 E. Havens. 605-996-7743. 24 units. Dogs allowed-no extra charges. Dog exercise area nearby. Bird cleaning area, freezer space. Laundry, refrigerator in every room, some kitchenettes. Cable TV. $$$
Super 8, 605-996-9678 or 800-800-8000. 107 units. No dogs allowed in rooms. Bird cleaning area & limited freezer space. Cable TV/HBO. $$$

CAMPGROUNDS AND RV PARKS

Dakota Campground, Rt. 2, Box 248. I-90 Exit 330, ½ mile south. 605-996-9432 or 996-5716.
R&R Campground, Box 867. I-90 Exit 332, 1 block north on Hwy 37. 605-996-8895.

RESTAURANTS

Town House Cafe, 101 No. Main. Open 6 A.M.–10 P.M. 7 days a week. 605-996-4615.
Perkins Family Restaurant, 1301 Burr St. Open 24 hrs. a day, 7 days a week. 605-995-1999.
Chef Louie's Steak House, 601 E. Havens. Open 11 A.M.-10 P.M. 605-996-7565. Where steak is king.

The Brig Steakhouse & Lounge, No. Hwy 37. Open Tuesday-Sunday for dinner. 605-996-7444. Specializing in steaks and seafood.

VETERINARIANS
Animal Clinic of Mitchell, 808 N. Sanborn. 605-995-0450
Lakeview Clinic, W. Hwy. 16. 605-996-3242

SPORTING GOODS
Everson Gunsmithing, 2400 N. Main. 605-996-1107
Hooks, Guns, & Ammo, RR 3. 605-996-8384
Leader Hardware and Sporting Goods, 112 E. 2nd Ave. 605-996-0316

AUTO RENTAL AND REPAIR
Harold's Conoco, 600 N. Sanborn. 605-996-1910
Larry's I-90 Texaco, I-90 and Hwy. 37. 605-996-1042
Iverson-Max Motors, 1010 N. Main. Repairs and rental. 605-996-5683

AIR SERVICE
Mitchell Municipal Airport, N. Hwy. 37. 605-996-7281

MEDICAL
Queen of Peace Hospital, 525 N. Foster. 605-995-2000

FOR MORE INFORMATION:
Mitchell Convention-Visitors' Bureau
P.O. Box 1026
Mitchell, SD 57301
605-996-6223, 800-257-CORN

MOBRIDGE
AND WALWORTH COUNTY

Population–3,768
County Population–6,087
County Area–707 sq. mi.

October Temperature–48.3
Annual Precipitation–16.94"
Acres in CRP–27,907

Lake Oahe, a Missouri River impoundment with 2,300 miles of shoreline, borders Mobridge on three sides. Mobridge serves as the trading center in north central South Dakota for a large ranching and agricultural region. It has a modern business district and an abundance of motels and facilities for hunters. The huge Cheyenne River Indian Reservation borders the west side of Lake Oahe. Adjacent farm lands and prairies provide excellent hunting for upland birds. Lake Oahe is also an outstanding waterfowl hunting area. Hunters will find many waterfowl guides and outfitters. Waterfowlers can hunt the lake or over decoys in the adjoining grain fields.

UPLAND BIRDS
Pheasants, Sharptail Grouse, Hungarian Partridge

WATERFOWL
Ducks, Geese, Sandhill Crane

ACCOMMODATIONS

Wrangler Motor Inn, 820 W. Grand Crossing. 605-845-3641. 61 units. Dogs allowed with restrictions-no extra charge for dogs. Dog exercise area nearby. Freezer space, cable TV. Lounge with dining, open 4pm-2am. $$$

Mark Motel, 3rd Ave. E. 605-845-3681. 25 units. Dogs allowed in carrier, must be attended-no extra charge. Dog exercise area nearby. Lg. Kitchenette, freezer. $$/weekly rates.

Super 8, W. Hwy. 12. 605-845-7215. 31 units. Dogs allowed-no extra charge. Freezer space. Cable TV. $$

The Prairie Pillow, RR 1, Box 51. 605-6649-7991. Bed & Breakfast. 4 rooms/9 beds. Group rates. Full breakfast. Dogs allowed-no extra charge. Bird cleaning and freezer space. Satellite TV. Guide service packages available. $

East Side Motel, E. Hwy. 12. 605-845-7867. 15 units. Dogs allowed if well attended-no extra charge. Some cabins, cable TV, kitchenettes, freezer space. $$

CAMPGROUNDS AND RV PARKS

Indian Creek Campground, 2 miles southeast of Mobridge, off Hwy. 12. Open through October. Full facilities.

RESTAURANTS

Wheel Family Restaurant, 820 W. Grand Crossing. 605-845-7474. 6AM-10PM.

Dakota Country Restaurant, 112 W. Grand Crossing. 605-845-7495. 6AM-8:30PM.

The Windjammer Lounge and Captain's Table Restaurant, 820 W. Grand Crossing. 605-845-3641. 5PM-11PM.

VETERINARIANS

Oahe Veterinary Hospital, North Mobridge. 605-845-3634. Dr. Dave Elsom, Dr. Chris Strang, and Dr. Pat Prusha.

SPORTING GOODS

Gibson's Discount Center, W. Hwy. 12. 605-845-3628.

AUTO RENTAL AND REPAIR

Larry Jensen Motors, Inc., W. Hwy. 12. 605-845-7277.

Dave's Auto Clinic, E. Hwy. 12. 605-845-7265.

AIR SERVICE

Mobridge Airport/Oahe Air, 1018 Airport Rd. 605-845-2977

MEDICAL

Mobridge Regional Hospital, 1401 W. 10th Ave. 605-845-3692.

FOR MORE INFORMATION:

Mobridge Chamber of Commerce
212 Main St.
Mobridge, SD 57601
605-845-2387, 605-845-2500

PIERRE
AND HUGHES COUNTY

Population–12,906	October Temperature–50
County Population–14,817	Annual Precipitation–18.67"
County Area–757 sq. mi.	Acres in CRP–9,194

Pierre, the state capital, is located on the eastern banks of the Missouri River. It is a large city with ample services for the hunter. Twenty miles south of town you will find the Fort Pierre National Grasslands, the Crow Creek and the Lower Brule Indian Reservations. The Fort Pierre National Grasslands provide one of the best areas for hunting prairie chickens as well as very good pheasant and sharptail grouse hunting. The Crow Creek and Lower Brule Indian Reservations have very developed upland hunting programs and excellent bird hunting. This area is the heart of incredible waterfowl hunting. There are numerous local outfitters and guides that specialize in waterfowl hunting as well as plenty of public land on Lake Oahe and Lake Sharp for hunters who want to hunt on their own.

UPLAND BIRDS
Pheasants, Prairie Chickens,
Sharptail Grouse, Hungarian Partridge

WATERFOWL
Ducks & Geese

ACCOMMODATIONS

Best Western Ramkota Inn, Rivercentre, 920 W. Sioux. 605-224-6877, 800-528-1234. 151 units. Lounge, restaurant, cable TV, cleaning shed with locked freezer and free ice/paper. Dogs allowed-no charge. Wide range of rates.

Comfort Inn, 410 W. Sioux Ave. 605-224-0377, 800-221-2222. 60 units. Cable TV, free continental breakfast, freezer storage. Dogs allowed in smoking rooms only-no charge. $$.

Fort Pierre Motel, P.O. Box 611, Fort Pierre. 605-223-3111. 21 units. Cable TV, fish and game cleaning available, free freezer space. Dogs allowed-no charge. $

Iron Horse Inn, 205 W. Pleasant. 605-224-5981. 54 units. Cable TV, cleaning shed with freezer. Dogs allowed-$5 fee per dog. $$.

Outpost Lodge, 28229 Cow Creek Rd. 605- 264-5450. 14 units. Steak house, lounge, casino, kitchenettes, ice, freezer space, cleaning facilities. Dogs allowed-no charge. $

Pierre Motel, 914 N. Euclid. 605-224-9266. 18 units. Cable TV, kitchenettes, freezer space. Dogs allowed-no charge. $.

Super 8 Motel, 320 W. Sioux Ave. 605-224-1617, 800-800-8000. 78 units. Cable TV, guide referrals. Dogs allowed-no charge. $$.

CAMPGROUNDS AND RV PARKS

Farm Island State Park and Recreation Area, 1304 Farm Island Rd. 800-710-CAMP. 4 miles east of Pierre on Hwy. 34. 90 camp sites, hookups.

Campgrounds #1, #2, and #3, U.S. Army Corps of Engineers, below Oahe Dam, of Hwy. 1806. 605-224-5862. 200 camp sites, hookups. Campgrounds #1 and #2 accept reservations.

RESTAURANTS

Big R's Steak Emporium, 320 S. Central. 605-224-9720.

Gator's Pizza, Pasta, & Subs, Pierre Mall, 1615 N. Harrison. 605-224-6262.

Town and Country Restaurant, 808 W. Sioux Ave. 605-224-7183. Family dining, open 24 hours.

Point After Sports Bar and Steakhouse, E. Hwy. 34 and truck bypass. 605-224-8326. Lunch and dinner, 7 days a week.

VETERINARIANS

Animal Clinic of Pierre, 115½ E. Dakota Ave. 605-224-1075. Dr. V.B. Sibley.

Oahe Veterinary Clinic, Ft. Pierre. 605-223-2562. Dr. Robert Shay, Dr. James Wolf, Dr. Jeff Ehrenfried.

SPORTING GOODS

Teton River Traders Gun Shop, 101 E. Capitol. 605-224-1371.

Dakotamart, 120 West Sioux Avenue. 605-224-8871. Open 7 am - 10 pm seven days a week.

AUTO RENTAL AND REPAIR

H & H Repair and 24 Hour Towing, E. Hwy. 34. 605-224-6332.

Pro Amoco, 103 E. Pleasant Dr. 605-224-1122, 605-224-2807.

Avis Rent-A-Car, Pierre Airport. 605-224-2911.

Budget Rent-A-Car, 3900 Airport Rd. 605-224-8099.

AIR SERVICE

Pierre Regional Airport, 605-224-2281.

MEDICAL

St. Mary's Healtcare Center, 800 E. Dakota. 605-224-3100.

FOR MORE INFORMATION:

Pierre Area Chamber of Commerce
Box 548
Pierre, SD 57501
800-962-2034, 605-224-7361

PRESHO
AND LYMAN COUNTY

Population–654	October Temperature–51
County Population–3,638	Annual Precipitation–17.43"
County Area–1,679 sq. mi.	Acres in CRP–74,978

Presho is located just north of I-90 in the center of some of the best upland bird hunting in South Dakota. The Fort Pierre National Grasslands is north of town and the Lower Brule Indian Reservation is northeast of town. You will find that Presho is located in the heart of prime pheasant country. Also, the grasslands north of town have one of the best populations of prairie chickens and a good huntable population of sharptail grouse. The Lower Brule Indian Reservation northeast of town has excellent waterfowl hunting and very good upland bird hunting.

UPLAND BIRDS
Pheasants, Prairie Chickens,
Sharptail Grouse, Hungarian Partridge, Doves

WATERFOWL
Ducks & Geese

ACCOMMODATIONS
Coach Light Inn, I-90 exits 225 or 226. 605-895-2383. Dogs allowed-no extra charge, must be well attended. Bird cleaning area, freezer space. Cable TV. $$$
Hutch's Motel, 1/2 mi. west of I-90 exit 226. 605-895-2591. 29 units. Dogs allowed-$5.00 extra. Restaurant/Lounge on premises. Cable TV/free movies. $$

CAMPGROUNDS AND RV PARKS
New Frontier RV Park, I-90 exits 225 & 226. 605-895-2545 or 605-895-2604. Pull-thrus, tenters welcome. Laundry, showers, supplies.

RESTAURANTS
Dakota Cafe & Drive Inn, 918 E. 9th. 605-895-2423. Open 6am - 8pm daily.
Hutch's Cafe & Lounge, 924 E.9th. 605-895-2641. Open 7am - 11pm daily.

VETERINARIANS
Willis Veterinary Supply, 900 E. 9th St. 605-895-2438. Dr. Willis

SPORTING GOODS
Coast To Coast Stores, 113 Main. 605-895-2461

Auto Rental and Repair
New Frontier Truck & Auto Station, 922 E. 9th St. 605-895-2545
Cenex, 161 Main Ave. 605-895-2682
Car Care Center, 221 Fir Ave. 605-895-2612

Air Service
Presho City Airport 605-895-9650

Medical
Stanley Jones Memorial Clinic, 121 Main Ave. 605-895-2589
Ambulance 605-895-2422

For more information:
Presho Chamber of Commerce
P.O. Box 415
Presho, SD 57568-0415
605-895-9650

WINNER
AND TRIPP COUNTY

Population–3,354	October Temperature–52.7
County Population–6,924	Annual Precipitation–23.55"
County Area–1,618 sq. mi.	Acres in CRP–33,771

Winner is a service center for ranchers & farmers in South Dakota's very best pheasant country. This is one of the friendliest towns in America. The folks of Winner go out of their way to make hunters feel welcome. The chamber of commerce produces the Tripp County Hunting Guide, a comprehensive list of places to stay and hunt in this area. Farm and ranch land in Tripp county and the surrounding area has unsurpassed pheasant hunting. Hunting is also very good for sharptail grouse and prairie chicken. In order to insure a place to hunt you should book your hunt as early as possible. The Missouri River east of Winner has memorable hunting for waterfowl

UPLAND BIRDS
Pheasants, Sharptail Grouse
Prairie Chicken, Hungarian Partridge

WATERFOWL
Ducks & Geese

ACCOMMODATIONS
Super 8, 902 Hwy. 44 E. 605-842-0991. 25 units. Cable TV. Dogs allowed-no extra charge. Dog exercise area nearby. Bird cleaning facilities. $$$

Dakota Inn, 501 S. Hwy. 18. 605-842-1440. 24 units. Cable TV. Dogs allowed-no extra charge. Dog exercise area nearby. Bird cleaning facilities, limited freezer space. $$$

Buffalo Trail Motel, 950 W. 1st St. 605-842-2212. 31 units. Cable TV. Dogs allowed-no extra charge. Dog exercise area nearby. Bird cleaning facilities. $$$

Warrior Inn, 845 E. Hwy. 44. 605-842-3121. 39 units. Cable TV. Dogs allowed—must not be left unattended-no extra charge. Dog exercise area nearby. Bird cleaning facilities. $$$

RESTAURANTS
H-K Steak House, E. Hwy. 44. 605-842-3055. 5:30AM–11:00PM.

Out-West Bar, Grill, Cafe, 865 W. 2nd St. 605-842-2324. 6:00AM–11:00PM.

Sargent's Cafe, 317 Main St. 605-842-3788. 5:30AM–8:00PM, Mon.–Sat. 5:30AM–2:00PM, Sundays.

VETERINARIANS
Animal Clinic, 660 W. 2nd St. 605-842-1854. Dr. Al Pravecek. Dr. C.A. Owen.
Winner Veterinary Hospital, RR 3, Box 34. 605-842-3711. Dr. William Nielsen.

SPORTING GOODS
Outlaw Trading Post, P.O. Box 191. 605-842-3623.
Pamida, P.O. Box 70. 605-842-2288.

AUTO RENTAL AND REPAIR
Frontier Motors, P.O. Box 350. 605-842-1880. Repairs and rental.
Harry K. Ford Store, P.O. Box 391. 605-842-2505. Repairs and rental.

AIR SERVICE
Winner Regional Airport, north of Winner. Call Western Aviation, 605-842-0740, for more information. No commercial service.

MEDICAL
Winner Regional Healthcare Center, 745 E. 8th. 605-842-2110.

FOR MORE INFORMATION:
Winner Chamber of Commerce
Winner, SD 57580
605-842-1533, 800-658-3079

YANKTON
AND YANKTON COUNTY

Population–12,703
County Population–19,252
County Area–518

October Temperature–50.6
Annual Precipitation–23.46"
Area in CRP–3,668

Yankton is located on the banks of the Missouri River and Lewis and Clark Lake. It is a short drive from the Sioux City, Iowa, commercial airport. The farmlands and the Missouri breaks provide excellent hunting for all of the upland birds. The Missouri River and Lewis and Clark Lake have outstanding waterfowl hunting. You can hunt the water with a johnboat or from a blind. The grain fields also provide unsurpassed hunting for both ducks and geese over decoys.

UPLAND BIRDS
Pheasants, Bobwhite Quail, Hungarian Partridge, Doves

WATERFOWL
Ducks & Geese

ACCOMMODATIONS

Lewis and Clark Resort and Marina, West Hwy. 52. 605-665-2680. Park sticker required. 24 motel rooms, $$ 10 cabins, $(3 night minimum stay). Dogs allowed, must be well attended, not allowed on beach-no extra charges. Bird cleaning area, freezer space. Restaurant on premises. Cable TV. $

Comfort Inn, 2118 Broadway. 605-665-8053. 45 units. Dogs allowed if carefully attended-no extra charges for dogs. Dog exercise area nearby. Cable TV, free continental breakfast, hot tub. $$

Star-Lite Inn, 500 Park (Hwy 52 & 4th). 605-665-7828 or 800-658-5570. Dogs allowed-$3.00 extra per day. Dog exercise area nearby. Bird cleaning area, freezer space, microwave & refrigerators available in some rooms. Cable TV. $$

Colonial Inn, 1509 Broadway. 605-665-3647. 20 units Dogs allowed-$3.00 per dog per day. Dog exercise area nearby. Bird cleaning area, ice machine for coolers. Cable TV. $$

CAMPGROUNDS AND RV PARKS

Lewis & Clark Recreation Area State Park, 6 mi. west of Yankton. 800-710-2267. 384 sites, 10 cabins. RV dump station. Lake, marina, boat rentals.

Vacation Village, Hwy 52 1 mi. west of Yankton. 26 pads w/ all hookups. Phone, Cable TV. 605-665-3265 or 605-665-7095.

Lewis & Clark Resort & Marina, W. Hwy 52. 605-665-2680. Full hook-ups, reservations must be paid in full in advance.

RESTAURANTS

The Black Steer Restaurant & Lounge, 300 E. 3rd. 605-665-5771. Open 5pm to midnight, Mon-Sat., 5pm-10pm, Sundays. Steak, ribs, seafood.

Chateau Restaurant & Lounge, 1210 Broadway. 605-665-1438. Open 6am to 10pm, 7 days a week. Steak, seafood, pasta.

Fryin' Pan Family Restaurant, 21st & Broadway. 605-665-6230. Open 24 hours.

VETERINARIANS

Veterinary Medical Clinic, 1603 Broadway. 605-665-9441. Dr. Jamea N. Pajl.

Animal Health Clinic, 801 Whiting Dr. 605-665-4291. Dr. Donald Lepp, Dr. Bruce Teachout, Dr. Cynthia Franklin. 24 hour emergency service.

SPORTING GOODS

Dakota Archery and Outdoor Sports, 2301 E. Hwy. 50. 665-8340.

AUTO RENTAL AND REPAIR

Falcon Aviation/Rentals, Yankton airport. 605-665-3473.

Rent-A-Wreck/Rentals, 1019 Broadway Ave. 605-665-2782.

Groseth Motors Inc./Repairs, 3100 Broadway. 605-665-3618.

Rasmussen Motors Inc./ Repairs, 209 Cherry. 605-624-4438.

AIR SERVICE

Chan Gurney Airport. 605-665-3473. Commercial service; United Airlines @ 800-241-6522, Great Lakes Airlines @ 605-665-1042

MEDICAL

Sacred Heart Hospital, 501 Summit. 665-9371.

Yankton Medical Clinic, 1104 W. 8th St. 605-665-7841

FOR MORE INFORMATION:

Yankton Chamber of Commerce
218 W .4th Street
Yankton, SD 57078
605-665-3636

REGIONAL GUIDES AND OUTFITTERS

PHEASANT HUNTING COUNTRY
HC69, Box 36, Chamberlain, SD 57325
605-734-6153
Contact: Bob Priebe
Land - 1,000 acres
Game - native pheasants
Personal Guides - available, all must hunt with same group
Dogs - hunter's dogs welcome
Extras - daily gun fee for guided group hunts

CIRCLE CE RANCH
RR5, Box 98, Dixon, SD 57533
605-835-8281
Contact: Dick Shaffer
Land - 3,000 acres
Game - native pheasants
Personal Guides - available, 1 group of up to 8 only, can hunt independently
Dogs - hunter's dogs welcome
Extras - lodging, meals available

STUKEL'S BIRDS & BUCKS
Rt.1, Box 112, Gregory, SD 57533
605-835-8941
Contact: Frank or Ray Stukel
Land - 10,000 acres
Game - native pheasants, sharptail, prairie chickens
Personal Guides - available, can hunt independently
Dogs - hunter's dogs welcome
Extras - lodging, meals, clays

CIRCLE H RANCH
P.O Box 88038, Sioux Falls, SD 57105 (Hunts 8 mi. South of Gregory, SD)
605-336-2111
Contact: Peter Hegg
Land - 3,000 acres
Game - native pheasant, doves, ducks, geese
Personal Guides - available, can hunt independently
Dogs - hunter's dogs welcome
Extras - lodging, meals, clays

LUBBER'S FARMS HUNTING SERVICE

Rt.1, Box 119, Gregory, SD 57533
605-835-9134
Contact: Jim Lubbers
Land - public
Game - native pheasants, sharptails, turkey, prairie chicken
Personal Guides - available, no independent hunting
Dogs - available, hunter's dogs welcome
Extras - lodging, meals

BIGGIN'S HUNTING SERVICE

RR3, Box 1, Gregory, SD 57533
605-835-8518
Contact: Gregory Biggins
Land - 12,000 acres
Game - native pheasants, doves, ruffed grouse, sharptail, turkey, prairie chicken, geese.
Personal Guides - available, can hunt independently
Dogs - hunter's dogs welcome
Extras - lodge, meals

ROOSTER ROOST RANCH

RR 2, Box 221, Mitchell, SD 57301
605-996-4676
Contact: Dean Strand, 7 - 10 pm
Land - 2,500 acres
Game - native pheasants, Huns, ducks
Personal guides - available, can hunt independently
Dogs - available, hunter's dogs welcome
Extras - lodge, meals

THE PRAIRIE PILLOW

RR 1, Box 51, Selby, SD 57472 near Lake Oahe
605-649-7991
Contact: Angie Marin
Land - private
Game - native pheasants, sharptails, Huns
Personal Guides - no
Dogs - hunter's dogs welcome
Extras - bird cleaning, freezers, lodging, meals, laundry

OUTRAGEOUS ADVENTURES
RR1, Box 6, Selby, SD 57472
605-649-6363
Contact: Kerry or Dawn Konold
Game - native pheasant, sharptail, geese
Personal Guides - available, can hunt independently
Dogs - available,hunter's dogs welcome
Extras - bird processing, transportation

OUTPOST LODGE
28229 Cow Creek Rd., Pierre, SD 57501
605-264-5450
Contact: Tom Olson
Land - seven private ranches
Game - native pheasants, grouse
Personal Guides - available, can hunt independently
Dogs - hunter's dogs welcome
Extras - package rates, lodging, meals

BUSH'S GOOSE CAMP
18279 283 Ave., Pierre, SD 57501
605-264-5496
Contact: Jeff Bush
Land - 5,000 acres
Game - preserve and native pheasants, sharptail, Huns, geese, ducks
Personal Guides - available, can hunt independently
Dogs - available, hunter's dogs welcome
Extras - lodging, meals, clays

BALL GUIDE SERVICE
2016 Antelope, Pierre, SD 57501
605-224-7530
Contact Judd Ball or Bruce Lyon
Land - 2,200 acres
Game - native pheasants, sharptail, prairie chicken, geese, ducks
Dogs - hunter's dogs welcome
Extras - package rates, local motel lodging and meals

TAIL FEATHER GUIDE SERVICE
3521 Regent Place, Pierre, SD 57501
605-224-0397
Contact: Brian Thompson
Land - 10,000 + acres
Game - native pheasant, sharptail, prairie chicken
Personal Guides - available

Dogs - hunter's dogs welcome
Extras - lodging, meals, package rates

SPRING CREEK RESORT

610 N. Jackson, Pierre, SD 57501
605-224-8336
Contact John or Marlene Brakss

Land - 8,000 acres
Game - native pheasants, geese
Personal Guides - available, can hunt independently
Dogs - hunters dogs welcome, kennels available
Extras - lodging, meals, package rates, bird processing

TINKER KENNELS

3031 Sussex Place, Pierre, SD 57501
605-224-5414
Contact: Bob Tinker

Land - 50,000 acres
Game - native pheasants, sharptail, prairie chickens, Huns,bobwhite, ducks, geese
Personal Guides - available, no independent hunting
Dogs - available, hunter's dogs welcome
Extras - lodging, meals

MEDICINE CREEK PHEASANT RANCH, INC.

Box 63, Vivian, SD 57533
605-683-6411
Contact: Mike Authier

Land - 10,000 acres
Game - native pheasants, geese
Personal Guides - available, can hunt independently
Dogs - available, hunter's dogs welcome
Extras - lodging, meals, clays, bird processing, package rates

DICK SMITH

Box 56, Vivian, SD 57576
605-683-4836
Contact: Dick Smith

Land - 3,000+ acres
Game - native pheasant, sharptail, prairie chicken
Personal Guides - yes, no independent hunting
Dogs - hunter's dogs welcome
Extras - only one party at a time, owns land

P & R Hunting Lodge
Rt. 5, Box 117, Dallas, SD 57529
605-835-8050
Contact: Paul or Ruth Taggart
Land - 20,000 acres
Game - native pheasants
Personal Guides - guided hunts only
Dogs - available, hunter's dogs welcome
Extras - lodging, meals, bird processing, package rates

S & S Hunting Service
RR1, Box 64, Burke, SD 57523
605-775-2262
Contact: Gary or Mary Ann Shaffer, evenings
Land - 1,000 acres
Game - native pheasants, sharptails, bobwhite, dove, prairie chicken
Personal Guides - available, can hunt independently
Dogs - available, hunter's dogs welcome
Extras - lodging, meals, clays

Doom's Guide Service
541 West 11th, Winner, SD 57580-0266
605-842-0746
Contact: Chuck Doom
Game - native pheasants, sharptails, prairie chicken, turkey
Personal Guides - available, can hunt independently
Dogs - hunter's dogs welcome

Missouri River Adventures
151 Hwy 281, P.O. Box 169, Pickstown, SD 57567
605-487-7262
Contact: Bill Dillon
Land - 6,000 acres
Game - native pheasants
Personal Guides - available, can hunt independently
Dogs - hunter's dogs welcome
Extras - lodging, meals, package rates

GLACIAL LAKES AND PRAIRIES REGION

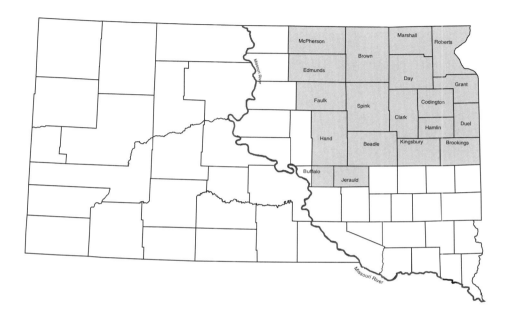

Once covered with massive glaciers, this region has numerous clear-blue glacial lakes. The glaciers also created miles of prairies. and rolling hills. Waterfowl abounds in the region. The more than 120 natural lakes and over 10,000 sloughs and potholes encompass one of the largest prairie pothole regions in the U.S. Each fall approximately 350,000 ducks and over one million geese migrate through the region.

The prairies support an abundance of pheasants, sharptail grouse and Hungarian partridge. Hunting for all of these species is very good to excellent.

Gray Partridge Distribution

Glacial Lakes & Prairies Region

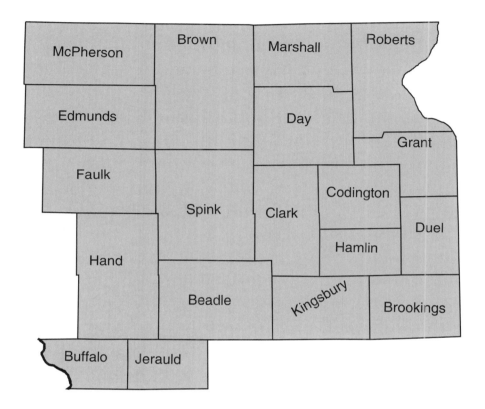

Mourning Dove Distribution

Glacial Lakes & Prairies Region

Pheasant Distribution

Glacial Lakes & Prairies Region

Glacial Lakes & Prairies

Sharptail Distribution

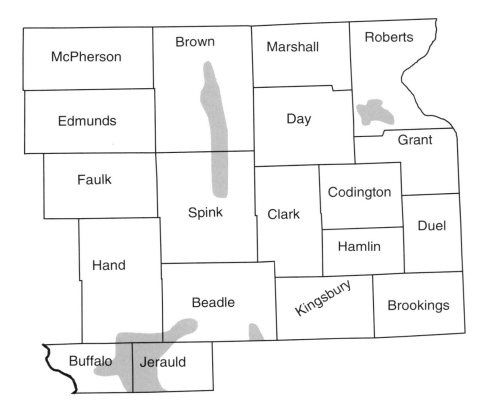

Turkey Distribution

Glacial Lakes & Prairies Region

ABERDEEN
AND BROWN COUNTY

Population–24,995	October Temperature–47.3
County Population–35,580	Annual Precipitation–18.55"
County Area–1,722 sq. mi.	Acres in CRP–42,070

Aberdeen is a large regional shopping center with many fine motels, restaurants and retail services. It has a commercial airport with daily flights to both Minneapolis, and Denver. The Chamber of Commerce maintains a list of landowners who allow hunting. The farm lands provide excellent hunting for upland birds. The Sand Lake National Wildlife Refuge is located just 30 miles north east of town. The refuge and its many waterfowl production areas over 20,000 acres provide outstanding waterfowl hunting.

UPLAND BIRDS
Pheasants, Hungarian Partridge, Doves

WATERFOWL
Canada Geese, Snow Geese,
Dabbling and Diving Ducks

ACCOMMODATIONS

Holiday Inn, 2727 SE 6th Ave. 605-225-3600 or 800-465-4329. 153 units. Dogs allowed-no extra charge for dogs. Dog exercise area nearby. Bird cleaning service, freezer space. Cable TV. **BB's Cafe** on premises. $$$.

Super 8 North, 770 NW Hwy. 281. 605-226-2288. 25 units. Dogs allowed-no extra charge for dogs. Dog exercise area nearby. Cable TV $$.

Super 8 East, 2405 SE 6th Ave. 605-229-5005. Dogs allowed-no extra charge for dogs. Dog exercise area nearby. Bird cleaning facilities, freezer space. Cable TV Restaurant on premises, open 24 hours. $$

Ramkota Inn–Best Western, 1400 NW 8th Ave. 605-229-4040 or 800-528-1234. 154 units. Dogs allowed-no extra charge for dogs. Dog exercise area nearby. Bird cleaning service, freezer space. Restaurant on premises, 6:30AM–10PM. Cable TV. $$$.

Comfort Inn, 2923 SE 6th Ave. 605-226-0097. 40 units. Dogs allowed-$20 deposit per dog. Dog exercise area nearby. Shuttle service to airport. Cable TV. $$.

Breeze Inn, 1216 SW 6th Ave. 605-225-4222 or800-288-4248. Dogs allowed-$50 deposit per room, Dog exercise area nearby. Cable TV. $$.

CAMPGROUNDS AND RV PARKS

Mina Lake State Park Campground, 11 mi west of Aberdeen off US 12. 605-225-5325 36 sites, 19 w/elec. Restrooms, showers.

Wylie Park, 1 mi. north of Aberdeen, on US 281. 605-622-7015/Mon.-Fri, 8am-5pm. 48 sites, water, electrical, sewer hookups. RV dump station. Restrooms, showers. Pull-thru pads. Recreational theme park.

Richmond Lake State Park Campground, 10 mi. northwest of Aberdeen, off US 12. 605-225-5325. 24 sites-12 w/ elec. Restrooms.

RESTAURANTS

BB's Cafe, 2727 SE 6th Ave. 605-225-3600. 6AM–2PM, 5PM–11PM.

The Bar-N, NE 8th Ave. 605-229-1997. 11AM–11:30PM, prime rib at night.

The Coffee Shop/Ward Hotel, 104 S. Main. 605-225-6100. 7AM–5PM.

Millstone Family Restaurant, 2210 SE 6th Ave. 605-229-4105. 24 hours.

Perkin's,1401 SW 6th Ave. 605-225-9050. 24 hours.

The Place at the Lake, 6000 S. Shore Dr. 605-225-0271. 4pm–9pm, steaks and prime rib.

VETERINARIANS

Animal Health Clinic, 704 S. Melgaard Rd. 605-229-1691. Dr. William Svensen and Dr. Mark Stenstrom.

Dan's Veterinary Clinic, 304 6th Ave., SE. 605-226-2038. Dr. Dan Tarver.

Holman Veterinary Clinic, 1210 2nd Ave., NW. 605-225-2045.

SPORTING GOODS

Sodak Sport & Bait, 850 S. Hwy. 281. 605-225-2737.

B.S. Sports Exchange, 727 6th Ave., SW. 605-226-1501.

Outdoors Unlimited, Inc., 214 S. Main St. 605-225-7661.

AUTO RENTAL AND REPAIR

Avis Rent-A-Car, Aberdeen Airport. 605-225-9153.

Hertz Rent-A-Car, Aberdeen Airport. 605-225-4163.

National Car Rental, Aberdeen Airport. 605-225-1384.

B & N Auto Repair, 711 S. Applewood St. 605-229-2647.

Parcel-Erickson Texaco, 204 N. 2nd St. 605-229-0111.

AIR SERVICE

Aberdeen Regional Airport, 4400 East Hwy. 12. 605-622-7020.

Northwest Airlink/Mesaba, 605-226-0008 or 800-692-2746

BROOKINGS
AND BROOKINGS COUNTY

Population–16,270	October Temperature–46.2
County Population–25,207	Annual Precipitation–22.89"
County Area–795 sq. mi.	Acres in CRP–16,276

Brookings is the home of South Dakota State University. Like most college towns, it has an abundance of motels, restaurants, and retail facilities. There is very good pheasant and Hungarian partridge hunting in the agricultural areas surrounding Brookings. The city is conveniently located in the Madison Wetland Management District. There are numerous pot holes and small lakes to be found nearby which provide outstanding hunting opportunities. Each fall there is a large migration of Snow geese that pass through the area.

UPLAND BIRDS
Pheasants, Hungarian Partridge, Doves

WATERFOWL
Ducks and Geese

ACCOMMODATIONS
Star Motel, 108 6th St. 800-884-2518. 32 units. dogs allowed-no extra charge. Cable TV. $$

Super 8, 3034 LeFevre Drive. 605-692-6920. 46 units. Dogs allowed in kennels-$25.00 deposit for dogs. Cable TV. $$

Wayside Motel, 1430 6th St. 800-658-4577. 20 units. Dogs allowed. Your hosts Gary and Bette Watts welcome hunters. $$

RESTAURANTS
Perkin's, 2205 6th St. 605-692-4400. Open 24 hrs.
Cook's Kitchen, 403 Main Ave. 605-692-1303. Open 6am - 6pm.
Ram Pub, 327 Main Ave. 605-692-2485. Open evenings for dinner.
Steak & Buffet, 1815 6th St. 605-692-1740. Open for lunch and dinner.

VETERINARIANS
Brookings Animal Clinic, 420 12th St. South. 605-692-2815.

SPORTING GOODS
WalMart, 2421 6th St. 605-692-6332
K-Mart, 808 25th Ave. 605-692-9898
Bob's Sport Shop, 306 Main. 605-692-2431

212 — WINGSHOOTER'S GUIDE TO SOUTH DAKOTA

Auto Rental and Repair
Dakota Service, 214 Front St. 605-692-7545

Air Service
Brookings Municipal Airport. 605-692-9359. Commercial service by United.

Medical
Brookings Hospital, 300 22nd Ave. 605-692-6351

For more information:
Brookings Chamber of Commerce
P.O. Box 431
Brookings, SD 57006-0431

HURON
AND BEADLE COUNTY

Population–12,448	October Temperature–48.5
County Population–18,253	Annual Precipitation–20.08"
County Area–1,259 sq. mi.	Acres in CRP–34,142

Huron is a growth center and major shopping area for a seven county region. Beadle county is also a sportsman's dream. The Huron area chamber of commerce has an annual hunting and land use guide that is available for no charge (call *1-800-Huron SD* for the guide and information). Pheasant hunting is excellent and sharptail grouse country starts in Beadle county. There is also good hunting for doves in the early season and you can find a fair to plentiful population of Hungarian partridge. The James River, and Lake Byron, located 15 miles northeast of town, provide memorable waterfowl hunting. Huron lies in the center of the Huron Wetland Management District. This is part of the prairie pothole region and there are thousands of acres of wetland open for hunting. See section on refuges, page 245.

UPLAND BIRDS
Pheasants, Sharptail Grouse, Doves, Hungarian Partridge

WATERFOWL
Ducks & Geese

ACCOMMODATIONS

Crossroads, 100 4th St. SW. 352-3204 or 800-876-5858. Dogs allowed-no extra charges-free dog biscuits. Bird cleaning services and freezers. Restaurant and bar on premises. Whirlpool, sauna, indoor pool. $$$

Fair City Bed & Breakfast, 1080 Iowa Ave.,SE. 352-1470. Reasonable rates. 3 rooms w/ private bath. Well trained dogs welcomed. Dog exercise area nearby. Cable TV. Full breakfast $$

Super 8, South Hwy. 37. 352-0740 or 800-800-8000. Dogs allowed-no extra charges. Bird cleaning area. Cable TV. $$$

Travelers Motel, 241 Lincoln Ave.,NW. 352-6703. Reasonable Rates. Dogs allowed-no extra charge. Dog exercise area nearby. Bird cleaning area. Cable TV. $$

CAMPGROUNDS AND RV PARKS

Huron Overnight Camping Area, Waibel Dr. & Jersey Ave. SE. 605-352-9197. 24 hook-ups. Shower, restrooms, golf course.

South Dakota State Fairgrounds, 890 3rd St. SW., 1 block south of US 14 Truck By-pass. 605-353-7340 or 800 529-0900. 1162 sites. All sites w/ elec., 52 with water, sewer, & electrical. RV dump station,showers, restrooms, picnic areas available. Open all year, water left on for bird season / shut off for remainder of the winter.

RESTAURANTS

Happy Chef, 2101 Dakota Ave. 605-352-8779 Open 24 hours.

The Barn Family Restaurant, Hwy 37 S. 605-352-9238 Open 9am - 9pm.

Tailgate Dining, 455 Dakota Ave. S. 605-352-8432. Open 11am - 2pm, 5pm - 10pm, Mon.-Sat., closed Sunday

Festivals Restaurant, 100 4th St. SW. 605-352-3204. Open 6:30am - 10pm.

VETERINARIANS

Huron Veterinary Hospital, 340 4th St., NW. 352-6063. Dr. William Will.

SPORTING GOODS

K Mart, 1000 18th St. SW. 605-352-7110.

Pamida, 100 Dakota Ave. N. 605-352-1406

Coast to Coast, 900 21st St. SW. 605-352-2132

Mahowald Hardware, 259 Dakota Ave. S. 605-352-2132.

AUTO RENTAL AND REPAIR

Jim & Tim's Auto Center, 2075 Dakota Ave., S. Ste 2. 353-1181.

R & R Amoco, Hwy. 14, W. 352-5242.

AIR SERVICE

Huron Regional Airport

Flight Services/Info. 605-352-3806

Skyway, services & info. 605-352-4609

United Express, 605-352-6559.

MEDICAL

Huron Regional Medical Center, 172 4th St., SE. 353-6200, emergency–353-6226.

Huron Clinic, 111 4th St. SE. 605-352-8691

FOR MORE INFORMATION:

Huron Area Chamber of Commerce and Convention and Visitors' Bureau
15 4th Street SW
Huron, SD 57350.
352-8775, 800-HURON SD

MILLER
AND HAND COUNTY

Population–1,678	October Temperature–48.6
County Population–4,272	Annual Precipitation–18.24"
County Area–1,437 sq. mi.	Acres in CRP–14,263

Miller is a small, friendly, farming community located in east central South Dakota. The surrounding farm lands provide excellent hunting for upland birds. Miller is located within the Huron Wetlands Management area. The numerous potholes and waterfowl production areas provide good hunting for ducks and geese.

UPLAND BIRDS
Pheasants, Hungarian Partridge, Doves

WATERFOWL
Ducks & Geese

ACCOMMODATIONS
Dew Drop Inn, Jct. Hwy 14W & 45 North. 605-853-2431. 17 units. Dogs allowed-no extra charge. Cable TV. $$
Super 8, Jct Hwy 14W & Hwy 45 North. 605-853-2721. 21 units. No dogs allowed. Cable TV. $$

CAMPGROUNDS AND RV PARKS
Miller Municipal Park. 3 day limit. Restroom,electrical hookup.

RESTAURANTS
Ranch Cafe, Hwy 14 East. 605-853-3441. Open 6am - evening
Prairie Gardens, Main St. 605-853-2811. Open for Breakfast, lunch, dinner.

VETERINARIANS
Meriweather Veterinary Supply, 132 N. Broadway. 605-853-3632.

AUTO RENTAL AND REPAIR
JJ Auto Service, 104 West 1st. 605-853-3691.

AIR SERVICE
Contact Aero Spray Service, East Hwy 14. 605-853-2777

MEDICAL
Hand County Memorial Hospital, 300 W. 5th St. 605-853-2421.

FOR MORE INFORMATION:
Miller Civic and Commerce Assoc.
P.O. Box 152
Miller, SD 57362-0152

REDFIELD
AND SPINK COUNTY

Population–2,770	October Temperature–46.9
County Population– 7,981	Annual Precipitation– 19.13"
County Area–1,505 sq. mi.	Acres in CRP–30,129

Redfield lies in the James River basin and has some of the best pheasant hunting in South Dakota. This is a rich agricultural area with corn, soybean, wheat, sunflowers and other grain crop which make for excellent pheasant habitat. Redfield has accommodations ranging from motels to free camping. The Chamber of Commerce has a list of places to hunt and stay. Redfield bills itself as the "Pheasant Capital of the World." They have outstanding pheasant hunting and very good hunting for Hungarian partridge and doves. The James River and the Huron Wetland Management District, with its numerous potholes and small lakes, provide excellent hunting for ducks and geese.

UPLAND BIRDS
Pheasants, Hungarian Partridge, Doves

WATERFOWL
Ducks and Geese

ACCOMMODATIONS

Super 8, Jct W. Hwy 212 & 281. 605-472-0720. 27 units. No dogs allowed. Restaurant on premises. Cable TV. $$

Wilson Motor Inn, E .Hwy 212. 605-472-0550. 21 units. No dogs allowed. Bird cleaning area, freezer space, cable TV. $$

Randy & Carol Maddox, 501 E.4th St. 605-472-3339. Can sleep up to 8. Dogs allowed. Private entrance. $

Terry Hansen, RR2 Box 81A. 605-472-1355. Can sleep up to 10, 1500 acres available. Dogs allowed. Meals provided if needed. $

Kathy Anderson, 822 W. 5th St. 605-472-3349. Dogs allowed. Can sleep up to 7. Kitchenette. Hunting land available. $

Julie Becker, HC61, Box 14A, Rockham, SD 57470. 605-472-0351. Can sleep 9. Dogs allowed-no extra charge. 3 meals with room. Bird cleaning area, freezer space available.

In addition to these spots, the Chamber of Commerce will be able to provide a list of other locals willing to accommodate hunters. 605-472-0965.

CAMPGROUNDS AND RV PARKS
Fisher Grove State Park, 7 mi E of Redfield, off US 12. 605-472-1212 28 sites, 12 w/ elec. Restrooms, showers, RV dump station. Open

Hav-A-Rest City Park, W. Hwy 212. 10 pads, 4 w/ elec. No charge/No reservation.

RESTAURANTS
Coachman Supper Club & Lounge, Jct. of Hwy. 212 and Hwy. 281. 605-472-0790. 5pm–2am, Tues.–Sat.

Leo's Good Food, 602 N. Main. 605-472-3540. 6am–8pm, Mon.–Sat. 7am–1:30pm, Sun.

Saks, Jct. of Hwy. 212 and Hwy. 281. 605-472-1626. 6:30am–8pm.

Terry's Bar and Steakhouse, 616 N. Main. 605-472-2091. 8am–2am.

VETERINARIANS
Animal Health Services, 912 E. 7th Ave. 605-472-2423. Dr. R.W. Baus and Dr. W.R. Baus.

SPORTING GOODS
Coast to Coast Hardware, 525 Main St. 605-472-1131.

Butch's Gun and Bait Shop, 629 E. 3rd St.

Alco Discount Store, 614 W. 3rd St.

AUTO RENTAL AND REPAIR
Reinbold Service Center, 1217 W. 3rd. 605-472-2753.

Schilling Auto Clinic, E. Hwy. 212. 605-472-0985.

AIR SERVICE
Air Strip, 605-472-0660

MEDICAL
Community Memorial Hospital and Clinic, 605-472-1110.

FOR MORE INFORMATION:
Redfield Area Chamber of Commerce
517 Main Street
Redfield, SD 57469
605-472-0965

SISSETON AND ROBERTS COUNTY

Population–3000
County Population–9,914
County Area–1,102 sq. mi.

October Temperature–49
Annual Precipitation–21.12"
Acres in CRP–26,261

This friendly prairie town is located in the northeastern part of South Dakota, at the base of the "Coteau des Prairies" (hills of the prairies) region. These open prairies and rolling hills provide excellent cover and very good hunting for both pheasants and Hungarian partridge. The Waubay National Wildlife Refuge and the numerous waterfowl production areas nearby provide great hunting for giant Canada geese, snow geese, and both dabbling and diving ducks.

UPLAND BIRDS
Pheasants, Hungarian Partridge, Doves

WATERFOWL
Ducks & Geese

ACCOMMODATIONS

Viking Motel, Box 99, 3 1/2 mi. west of I-29 on Hwy 10. 605-698-7663. 24 units. Dogs allowed in rooms-no extra charge. Cable TV. Your Hosts; Atley & Dee Holmquist $
Holiday Motel, E. Hwy 10. 605-698-7644. 19 units. Dogs allowed in room-no extra charge. $
I-29 Motel, E. Hwy 10. 605-698-4314. 29 units. Dogs allowed-$3.00 per dog. $$

RESTAURANTS

Billy's Cafe, 407 Veteran's Ave. 605-698-3241 Open 6:30am-9pm,closed Sunday.
Country Kitchen, W. Hwy 10. 605-698-3077. Open 6am - 10pm, daily.
Lakeland Lanes Restaurant, 614 W. Hickory. 605-698-7407. Open 5pm - 11pm, closed Sunday
Terry's Bar & Steakhouse, 616 N. Main. 605-472-2091. Open 11am - 2pm, 5pm - 11pm, closed Sunday.

VETERINARIANS
Sisseton Veterinary Clinic, Route 1. 605-698-3311

SPORTING GOODS
Stavig Dept. Store, 410 Veterans Ave.. 605-698-7531

Auto Rental and Repair
Brooks Motors, 120 Veterans Ave. 605-698-7633

Air Service
Sisseton Airport, 605-698-9083

Medical
Coteau Des Prairies Hospital, Cedar Heights. 605-698-7647

For more information:
Chamber of Commerce
Box 121
Sisseton, SD 57262
605-698-7261

WATERTOWN
AND CODINGTON COUNTY

Population–17,632	October Temperature–47.6
County Population–22,698	Annual Precipitation–22.23"
County Area–694 sq. mi.	Acres in CRP–10,038

Watertown is the trade center for thousands of people and owes its existence to the rich grain fields and grass lands that surround it. The agricultural lands provide very good hunting for both pheasants and Hungarian partridge. You will find Watertown located in the heart of pothole country. To the north of town is the Waubay National Wildlife refuge. This refuge and its many waterfowl production areas provide excellent hunting for waterfowl. There is a large population of giant Canada geese, snow geese and both dabbling and diving ducks.

UPLAND BIRDS
Pheasants, Hungarian Partridge, Doves

WATERFOWL
Ducks & Geese

ACCOMMODATIONS

Days Inn, E. Hwy 212. 605-886-3500 56 units. No Dogs allowed-private kennels adjacent. Pool, sauna. Cable TV. Restaurant/Bar on premises. $$$

Super 8, South Hwy 87. 605-882-1900. 58 units. No dogs allowed. Dog exercise area nearby. Pool, sauna, laundry, movie rentals. Cable TV. $$

Travel Host, West Hwy 212. 605-886-6120. 29 units. No dogs allowed. Bird cleaning area and freezers available. Cable TV. $$

Stone's Inn, Jct 1-29 & US 212. 605-882-3630. 34 units. No dogs allowed. Adjacent to 24 hr. cafe. Freezer space. Cable TV. $$

CAMPGROUNDS AND RV PARKS

Sandy Shores State Park Campground, 5 mi. west off US12. 605-886-4769. 20 sites, 12 w/elec. Showers, restrooms.

RESTAURANTS

BJ's Steak House, Pizzeria, and Bar, W. Hwy. 212. 605-882-4947. 4pm–11pm, Tues.–Sat.

Country Kitchen, Jct. 212 and 81. 24 hours, 7 days.

The Grainery, E. Hwy. 212 and I-29 Jct. 605-882-3950. 24 hours, 7 days.

Lakeshore, N. Hwy. 20. 605-882-3422. 5pm–11pm, Tues.–Sat. Res. suggested.

Office Bar and Restaurant, E. Hwy. 212. 605-886-2996. 11am–10pm, Mon.–Sat.

2nd Street Station Steak House, 15 2nd St., SW. 605-886-8304. 3pm–2am, Mon.–Sat.

VETERINARIANS

Care Small Animal Hospital, 320 4th St., NE. 605-886-0898. Dr. Mark Rieb.

Lake Area Veterinary Clinic, 601 SW 10th St. 605-886-5002.

Howard Veterinary Clinic, N. Hwy. 20. 605-882-4188. Dr. William J. Howard.

Watertown Animal Clinic, N. Hwy. 20. 605-886-2011. Dr. James D. Rokusek and Dr. Bruce W. Hutton.

SPORTING GOODS

Lester's Gunshop, 1902 5th St., SE. 605-882-4687.

AUTO RENTAL AND REPAIR

Ford Rent-A-Car, 1600 9th Ave., SE. 605-886-5844.

Hertz Rent-A-Car, 800-654-3131.

Sensible Car Rental, 1904 9th Ave., SE. 605-882-0060.

Dale's Auto Repair, 1016 3rd Ave., NW. 605-886-5175.

Gus's Towing and Repair, 317 W. Kemp Ave. 605-886-4776.

AIR SERVICE

Watertown Municipal Airport.

Mesaba Airline, 605-886-9300.

MEDICAL

Prairie Lakes Hospital, 400 10th Ave., NW. 605-882-7000.

FOR MORE INFORMATION:

Convention and Visitors' Bureau
P.O. Box 1113
Watertown, SD 57201
605-886-5814, or 800-658-450

REGIONAL GUIDES AND OUTFITTERS

UNLIMITED RINGNECKS
HCR 1, Box 67A, Cresbard, SD 57435 (Aberdeen - Redfield area)
605-324-3282
Contact: Jon Batteen or Cindy Nielsen
Land - 3,000+ acres
Game - native pheasants
Personal Guide - available, can hunt independently.
Dogs - hunter's dogs welcome
Extras - package rates, lodging, meals, bird processing, transport

DAKOTA DREAM HUNTS
RR2, Box 17, Arlington, SD 57212
605-983-3291 or 605-983-5058 for Rich Converse
605-983-5033 for Doug Converse
Land - 3,000 acres
Game - native pheasants, Huns, geese, ducks
Personal Guide - available, can hunt independently
Dogs - available,hunter's dogs welcome
Extras - lodging, meals

ALP HUNTING
20922 485th Ave., Elkton, SD 57026-9335
605-542-5461
Contact: Adolph Petersen
Land - 2000 acres/640 acres preserve
Game - native and preserve pheasants
Personal Guide - available, can hunt independently in small groups
Dogs - available,hunter's dogs welcome
Extras - lodging, meals, camping hookups, kennels

WELLS SHOOTING PRESERVE
RR1, Box 44, Oldham, SD 57051-9724
605-854-3284
Contact: Dale E. Wells
Game - preserve pheasants
Personal Guides - available, can hunt independently
Dogs - hunter's dogs welcome
Extras - lodging, bird processing

LAKE'S BYRON LODGE
RR 2, Box 216, Huron, SD 57350
605-352-3241 or 605-224-0569
Contact: Doug Lake

224 — WINGSHOOTER'S GUIDE TO SOUTH DAKOTA

Land - 3,000 + acres
Game - preserve pheasants, native pheasants, doves, geese, ducks
Personal Guides - available, can hunt independently
Dogs - hunter's dogs welcome
Extras - lodging, meals, bird processing, package rates, specializes in small parties.

DAKOTA EXPEDITIONS
HC 64, Box 109, Miller, SD 57362-9542
605-853-2545
Contact: Clint or Vicki Smith
Land - 20,000 acres/ 600 preserve
Game - native & preserve, pheasants, sharptail, Huns, prairie chickens, ducks, geese
Personal Guides - available, can hunt independently
Dogs - available,(we raise & train gun dogs), hunter's dogs welcome
Extras - lodging, meals, bird processing.

INGALLS PRAIRIE
RR 1, Box 111, Bryant, SD 57221
605-628-2327
Contact: Jim Ingalls
Game - preserve & native pheasants, sharptails, doves, Huns, geese, ducks
Personal Guides - available, can hunt independently
Dogs - available, hunter's dogs welcome
Extras - lodging, meals, package rates

WILD FLUSH INC.
RR2, Box 75, Waubay, SD 57273
800-599-2393
Contact: Mike Frederick
Land - 1,100 acres
Game - preserve & native pheasants, sharptails, Huns, ducks, geese
Personal Guides - available, can hunt independently
Dogs - available, hunter's dogs welcome
Extras - lodging, meals, kennels, bird processing, package rates

GREAT PLAINS HUNTING
RR 2, Box 33, Wessington, SD 57381
800-892-9528 or 605-883-4526
Contact: Clyde or Dottie Zepp
Land - 5,000/350 preserve
Game - preserve & native, pheasants, sharptails, prairie chickens
Personal Guides - available, can hunt independently
Dogs - hunter's dogs welcome
Extras - lodging, meals, small groups.

DAKOTA HERITAGE REGION

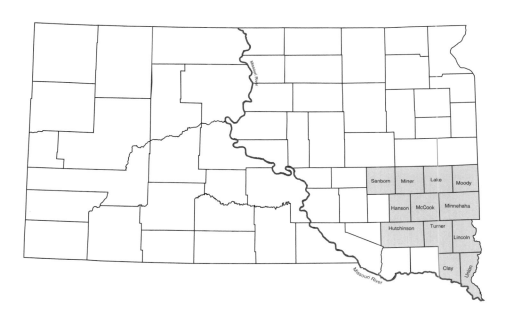

This region includes 14 counties and is located in the southeastern part of the state. Sioux Falls, South Dakota's largest city, is located in this region. This is prime farm land and has excellent habitat for upland birds. The Missouri River forms the southern border of the region where the sandbars and small islands create a duck and goose hunting paradise. Along the river you can find excellent hunting for pheasants and waterfowl. This area is also the best bet for good bobwhite quail. The Dakota Heritage region doesn't get the hunting pressure of some of the other regions, making it a good place to find birds without running into too many other hunters.

Bobwhite Quail Distribution

Dakota Heritage Region

Mourning Dove Distribution

Dakota Heritage Region

Gray Partridge Distribution

Dakota Heritage Region

Pheasant Distribution

Dakota Heritage Region

Turkey Distribution

Dakota Heritage Region

MADISON
AND LAKE COUNTY

Population–6,257	October Temperature–49.3
County Population–10,550	Annual Precipitation–23.64"
County Area–560 sq. mi.	Acres in CRP–5,050

Madison is a farming community located in eastern South Dakota. There is very good hunting for pheasants and fair hunting for Hungarian partridge on the agricultural lands around Madison. The numerous lakes and the Madison Wetland Management Area provide excellent hunting for waterfowl. In the fall, thousands of snow geese migrate through this area.

UPLAND BIRDS
Pheasants, Hungarian Partridge, Doves

WATERFOWL
Ducks & Geese

ACCOMMODATIONS

Lake Park Motel, West Hwy. 34, 605-256-3524, 40 units. Dogs allowed-no extra charge, dog exercise area nearby. Bird cleaning area, freezers. Cable TV $$

Super 8, Junction Hwy. 34 & 87, 34 units. Dogs must be restrained and attended-no extra charge, dog exercise area nearby. Bird cleaning area. Cable TV $$

CAMPGROUNDS AND RV PARKS

Madison Mobile Acres, 602 NW 9th. 605-256-2126

RESTAURANTS

Downtown Cafe, 105 SW 1st. 605-256-9735 5:30am-1:20pm/Mon.-Fri. 6am-12:30pm/Saturdays.

Nicky's Restaurant & Lounge, W. Hwy 34. 605-256-3791. 11am-5pm Mon.-Sat. Steaks and seafood.

Country Cafe, 119 1/2 S. Egan. 605-256-3730. 6am-4pm/Mon.-Fri. 6am-1pm/Sat.

VETERINARIANS

Lake Veterinary Clinic, 231 S. Highland. 605-256-3547.

SPORTING GOODS

Pamida, S. Washington and 8 SE. 605-256-6641.

AUTO RENTAL AND REPAIR
F & M Coop, Hwy. 34. 605-256-4516.
Jack's Service, 209 S. Highland. 605-256-4347.
Lake Herman Auto, W. Hwy. 34. 605-256-6339.

AIR SERVICE
Madison Municipal Airport, 107 N. Union Ave. 605-256-7524. Small craft.

MEDICAL
Madison Community Hospital, 917 N. Washington. 605-256-6551.

FOR MORE INFORMATION:
Greater Madison Area Chamber of Commerce
P.O. Box 467
Madison, SD 57042-0467
605 256-2454

SIOUX FALLS
AND MINNEHAHA COUNTY

Population–100,836	October Temperature–48.6
County Population–123,809	Annual Precipitation–23.86"
County Area–810	Area in CRP–7,449

Sioux Falls is the largest city in South Dakota and is located in the southeastern part of the state, just south of I-90 The city has a large commercial airport and plenty of retail services and accommodations for the hunter. The area around Sioux Falls has very good hunting for pheasants. Most of the outfitters in the area hunt wild birds, along with running a game preserve. For the hunter with limited time Sioux Falls is an ideal location to fly into and hunt for several days.

UPLAND BIRDS
Pheasants, Hungarian Partridge, Doves

ACCOMMODATIONS

Fairfield Inn, 4501 W Empire Place. 361-2211. 63 units Dogs allowed in smoking rooms only-no extra charges. Dog exercise area nearby. Cable TV. $$

Select Inn, I-29 & 41st St. 361-1864. Reasonable rates. Dogs allowed-$25.00 deposit. Dog exercise area nearby. Cable TV. $$

Super 8, 1508 W. Russell St. 339-9330. Dogs allowed in smoking rooms only-no extra charges. Dog exercise area nearby. Cable TV. $$$

CAMPGROUNDS AND RV PARKS

KOA, Jct I-90 & North Cliff. 605-332-9987

Sioux Falls Kamp Dakota/Goos RV's, I-90 Exit 390. 605-528-3983.

RESTAURANTS

Baxter Cafe, 4001 E. 10th St. 605-331-3615. 11am–9pm, Mon.–Thurs. 11am–10pm, Fri.–Sat. 8am–3pm, Sun.

Casa del Rey, 901 W. Russell St. 605-338-6078. 11am–10pm, Sun.–Thurs. 11am–11pm, Fri.–Sat.

Denny's, 4510 W. 41st St. 605-361-0093. 24 hours, 7 days.

Doc & Eddy's, 3501 W. 41st St. 605-361-8700. 7am–10pm, Mon.–Thurs. 7am–11pm, Fri.–Sat. 9am–9pm, Sun.

Lone Star Steakhouse and Saloon, 1801 W. 41st St. 605-331-3648. 11am–10pm, Sun.–Thurs. 11am–11pm, Fri.–Sat.

Louie's Italian Grill and Bar, 408 S. Main. 605-336-3100. 11am–2pm and 5pm–10pm, Mon.–Thurs. 5pm–11pm, Fri.–Sat.

Perkin's, 3 locations in Sioux Falls. 5304 N. Cliff Ave., 3400 Gateway Blvd., 2604 W. 41st St. 24 hours, 7 days.

Village Inn Pancake House, 108 Minnesota Ave. 605-334-5911. 6am–3am, Mon.–Sat. 6am–1am, Sun.

VETERINARIANS

All City Pet Care, 2 locations. 43rd St. and Minnesota Ave. 605-335-4004. 26th St. and Sycamore Ave. 371-2100.

Animal Medical Clinic, 1102 E. 10th St. 605-338-3223, Emergency, 605-338-2861. Dr. Douglas Brost and Dr. Dawn I. Dale.

Sioux Valley Veterinary Clinic, 4600 E. 10th St. 605-334-0559. Dr. Sophie O'Neill, Dr. Bill Lias, Dr. Teresa Haugen.

East Acres Animal Hospital, 3001 E. 10th St. 605-332-0066. Dr. David C. Rola.

SPORTING GOODS

Gary's Gunshop, 905 W. 41st St. 605-332-6119.

Scheel's All Sports, 4001 W. 41st St. 605-361-6839.

Ron's Gun Shop & Repair, Inc., 1212 E. Benson Rd. 605-338-7398.

Ace Hardware, 41st St. and Minnesota Ave. 605-336-6474.

J & B Waterfowl Specialties, 5609 Thrush Pl. 605-339-2479.

AUTO RENTAL AND REPAIR

T & A Service and Supply, 3412 S. Minnesota Ave. 605-339-9717, 800-658-3423.

Midtown Service, 1401 S. Minnesota Ave. 605-335-2719.

Gus's Amoco, 41st St. and S. Western Ave. 605-335-0306.

Jim's Service, 1601 E. 10th St. 605-332-0000.

Hertz Rent-A-Car, Sioux Falls Regional Airport. 605-336-8790.

Avis Rent-A-Car, Sioux Falls Regional Airport. 605-336-1184.

Budget Rent-A-Car, Sioux Falls Regional Airport. 605-334-4211.

AIR SERVICE

Sioux Falls Regional Airport, 2801 Jaycee Lane. 605-336-0762. Northwest, Delta.

MEDICAL

McKennan Hospital, 800 E. 21st St. 605-339-8000, 800-658-3030.

Sioux Valley Hospital, 1100 S. Euclid Ave. 605-333-1000.

FOR MORE INFORMATION:

Sioux Falls Convention and Visitors' Bureau
200 N. Phillips, Suite 102
Sioux Falls, SD 57102
605-336-1620, 800-333-2072

VERMILLION AND CLAY COUNTY

Population–10,034	October Temperature–52.1
County Population–13,186	Annual Precipitation–24.72"
County Area–409	Area in CRP–6,458

Vermillion is located in southeastern South Dakota on the banks of the Missouri River. Pheasant hunting is very good to excellent. The area around Vermillion is one of the best in the state for bobwhite quail and is also fair hunting for Hungarian partridge. The Missouri River has outstanding waterfowl hunting. You can hunt from a johnboat, water blind, or in the nearby fields over decoys. This is a great area to combine a morning duck hunt with an afternoon pheasant shoot.

UPLAND BIRDS
Pheasants, Bobwhite Quail, Hungarian Partridge, Doves

WATERFOWL
Ducks & Geese

ACCOMMODATIONS

Budget Host Tomahawk Motel, 1313 W. Cherry St.,(Hwy. 19 & Bus. 50). 20 units. 605-624-2601or 800-283-4678. Dogs allowed-no extra charge for dogs. $$

Comfort Inn, 701 W. Cherry (Bus.50). 605-624-8333. 46 units. Dogs allowed-$5.00 per dog. Dog exercise area nearby. Freezer space. Cable TV. $$

Super 8, 1208 E. Cherry,(Bus.50). 605-624-8005. 39 units. Reasonable rates. Dogs allowed-$5.00 per dog. Dog exercise area nearby. Cable TV. $

Coyote Motel, 701 W. Cherry St.,(Bus 50). 605-624-2616. 20 units. Dogs allowed with permission. Sauna, some kitchenettes. Cable TV. $

Lamplighter Motel, 112 E. Cherry St.,(Bus 50). 605-624-4451. 31 units. Dogs allowed with permission. Cable TV. $

CAMPGROUNDS AND RV PARKS

Lions Park, between Princeton & High Streets. Camping facilities, RV dump, electricity hook-ups, 3 days & 2 night free with additional day/night charge of $5.00 per.

RESTAURANTS

Silver Dollar Saloon & Restaurant, 1216 E. Cherry. 605-624-4830. Open 7 days a week, 11am to midnight. Steaks, chicken, seafood.

Recuerdo de Mexico, 112 E. Main. 605-624-6445. Open 7 days a week, 11am to 10 pm. Mexican food, steaks, margaritas.

The Cowboy Family Restaurant, 1122 E. Cherry. 605-624-8879. Open 6am to 11pm Mon./Sat., 6am to 10pm Sundays.

VETERINARIANS
Dakota Animal Clinic, 115 E. Main. 605-624-2344.

SPORTING GOODS
Pamida, Cherry & Princeton St. 605-624-8651
Coast to Coast, 9 Court St. 605-624-6725

AUTO RENTAL AND REPAIR
Brunick Service, 901 W. Main. 605-624-9909.
Mart Auto Body, 1123 W. Main. 605-624-3814.
Rasmussen Motors, 209 W. Cherry. 605-624-4438.

AIR SERVICE
Harold Davidson Municipal Airport, Small craft. Charter service available. 605-624-7734

MEDICAL
Dakota Medical Center, 801 E. Main. 605-624-2611

FOR MORE INFORMATION:
Vermillion Area Chamber of Commerce
906 E. Cherry Street
Vermillion, SD 57069
605-624-5571

REGIONAL GUIDES AND OUTFITTERS

VALLEY WEST HUNTING PRESERVE,
809 w. 10th St., Sioux, Falls, SD 57104
800-424-2047
Contact: Daniel Stock
Land - 700 acres
Game - pheasants - preserve birds only
Personal Guides - Yes
Dogs - Available / hunter's dogs welcome
Extras - meals available, lodge, clays

MORRIS GAME FARM
Box 126, Artesian, SD 57314
605-527-2424
Contact: Thomas Morris
Land - 900 acres
Game - native pheasants, Hungarian partridge, ducks, geese
Personal Guides - available, not required
Dogs - hunter's dogs welcome
Extras - lodging available, lunch, continental breakfast

RALPH ERICKSON HUNTING PRESERVE
RR1, Box 50, Humboldt, SD 57035
605-297-3561
Contact: Ralph Erickson, evenings
Land - 1,000 acres
Game - pheasant
Personal Guides - available
Dogs - Available / hunter's dogs welcome
Extras - meals available

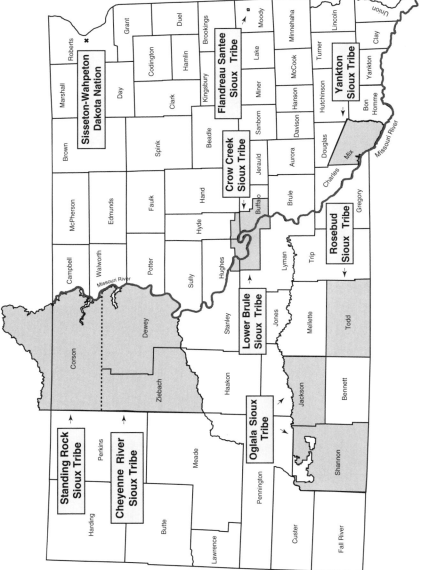

Indian Reservations

SOUTH DAKOTA INDIAN RESERVATIONS

South Dakota is home to the great Sioux Nation. There are nine reservations ranging in size from 2,356 acres to 1.7 million acres. Together the reservations provide excellent hunting for upland birds, ducks, geese and big game hunting on 4.9 million acres.

Each reservation has its own fish and game department and its own license fees, seasons, and limits. You do not need a state license to hunt on the reservation. However, if you are hunting waterfowl you will need a federal duck stamp, and you must use nontoxic shot. Waterfowl hunting on reservations bordering the Missouri River system is outstanding, and licenses are easy to obtain.

Most of the reservations have hunting partners. These are Indians who provide guide services for a daily fee. You can obtain a list of hunting partners when you write the fish and game department of the reservation on which you wish to hunt. I recommend that you use a guide for at least one day. I have found that guides are very helpful in showing you the areas where good bird hunting is located. They can save you a great deal of time and walking to find birds.

Most of the reservations have full-scale, Las Vegas style casinos and resorts. They also have motels and RV parks. You can combine a hunting trip with some fun and gambling.

When visiting and traveling on the reservations, be particularly respectful of the people you meet. Many tribes work to attract visitors, but some Indians feel that tourists invade their privacy and compromise the integrity of their culture and traditions.

In order to make your visit pleasant for everyone, be sensitive to your surroundings and obey all tribal laws and regulations.

Standing Rock Indian Reservation

522,000 acres in South Dakota
Yanktonai, Hunkpapa tribes
Standing Rock Fish & Wildlife
P.O. Box D
Fort Yates, ND 58538
701-854-7236

Home of Sitting Bulls' Hunkpapa tribe along with the Yanktonai, this reservation is located in north-central South Dakota and south-central North Dakota. The eastern part of the reservation borders the Missouri River and provides excellent hunting for Canada and Snow geese and ducks. The rest of the land is shortgrass prairie and provides excellent hunting for sharptail grouse and pheasant. Hungarian partridge hunting is fair. There is also a fall turkey season for both hens and gobblers and a spring season for gobblers only.

Deer and antelope hunting is excellent and can be combined with a bird hunt. Hunting partners (guides) are available.

The nearest major town is Mobridge, located on Route 12 just east of the Missouri River and the reservation. See page 185 for Mobridge accommodations and services.

Standing Rock has the Prairie Knights Casino & Lodge located in Fort Yates, North Dakota.

For more information on the Casino, call 1-800-425-8277

Cheyenne River Sioux Tribe

1.4 Million acres
Minnecoujou, Two Kettle, Sans Arc and Blackfoot Sioux reside on this reservation
Cheyenne River Game Fish and Parks
P.O. Box 590
Eagle Butte, S. D. 57625
605-964-7812

This reservation is located in north central South Dakota. Its eastern edge borders the Missouri River, and its topography consists of rolling plains, prairies, wooded areas, croplands, and marshes.

Faith is the largest town and is located on the reservation's western edge (see page 149). Pierre is the largest town on the eastern edge of the reservation (see page 187).

There is excellent hunting for sharptail grouse and prairie chicken. Hungarian partridge hunting is also good. Dove hunting is very good during the early part of the season. Currently, nonresidents of the reservation are not allowed to hunt pheasants. Fall turkey hunting for either sex is also available. The current fee for upland birds is a real bargain at $15.00 for a season license. Goose and duck hunting is excellent along the Missouri River. You can combine your bird hunt with a hunt for whitetail deer as well as antelope. Trophy bison hunts are also available.

Oglala Sioux Tribe

1.7 million acres
Oglala tribe
P.O. Box 570
Kyle SD 57752
605-455-2584
Species available include turkey, sharptail, and grouse.

The Pine Ridge Reservation is located in the southwestern part of South Dakota. Approximately 120,000 acres of reservation is in the Badlands, which joins Badlands National Park.The two closest towns are Kadoka, located on I-90 to the north (see page 153), and Martin, located on the southern border of the reservation (see page 157).

Rosebud Sioux Tribe

882,000 acres
Brule Sioux
Rosebud Sioux Tribe
Department of Natural Resources
Box 430
Rosebud, SD 57570
605-747-2289

The Rosebud Reservation is located in south central South Dakota, and its southern boundary borders the state of Nebraska. The closest towns are Murdo on the northern edge (see page 159) and Winner on the eastern edge of the reservation (see page 191). The terrain consists of plains, prairie, grasslands, rolling hills, farmland, and brushy draws. Excellent hunting is available for sharptail grouse, prairie chicken, dove, and pheasant. There is excellent turkey hunting, with a fall season for one turkey of either sex. Some good waterfowl hunting can be found along the rivers and potholes for ducks. The Rosebud also offers big game hunts for elk, buffalo, antelope, and deer.

Lower Brule Sioux Tribe

132,601 acres
Great lakes
Lower Brule Wildlife Department
Box 246
Lower Brule, SD 57548
605-473-5666

This reservation is located in the central part of South Dakota in Lyman and Stanley counties. Its eastern part borders Lake Sharpe, located on the Missouri River. The two closest towns are Presho, located on the southwest corner of the reservation on I-90 (see page 189), and Chamberlain, located 12 miles sout east on route I-90 (see page 177).

The tribe operates the Golden Buffalo Casino and Resort Hotel, and an RV park is located on the reservation. You can make reservations by calling 1-800-658-4554.

The Lower Brule has an extensive hunting program for upland birds, waterfowl, and trophy big game. Their wildlife department has actively pursued modern biological techniques and is managing its birds and animals to provide outstanding hunting. The terrain consists of prairies, rolling grasslands, farmland, and marshes.

Upland Birds — Excellent hunting can be found for pheasants, sharptail grouse, prairie chickens, and doves. The reservation has a special unit called the Grassrope that is intensively managed for crop and wildlife production. This unique, 7,000-acre river bend area provides outstanding hunting for pheasants. A daily license, currently $30, is required to hunt the grassrange area in addition to the regular hunting permit. Bird hunting is restricted to only a few people per day on the Grassrope unit, so if you want a quality hunt in a beautiful area, try out Grassrope.

Waterfowl — The reservation's eastern border is located on Lake Sharpe and is one of the best areas in the state for waterfowl hunting. Snow and Canada goose hunting are excellent. The Lower Brule has two special goose camps: the 2,500-acre Min-Sho Sho Ranch and 500-acre Iron Nation Camp attract thousands of geese daily from their nearby resting areas on the refuges of the Missouri River. You need a special permit and a reservation to hunt these camps. Transportation to and from the fields is provided. You will hunt from shooting pits, and pass shooting is allowed as the geese fly overhead on the way to the grain fields. The Medicine Creek Wetland, new in 1995, is managed for quality duck hunting. It is located on the shores of Lake Sharpe. Hunting is from designated blinds. A limited number of hunters are allowed on a first-come, first-served basis.

There are extensive walk-in hunting areas open for hunting without permission for upland birds. You can also hunt Lake Sharpe and the Missouri River for ducks and geese with either a reservation waterfowl permit or a state waterfowl permit. You will need a federal waterfowl stamp. Only nontoxic shot is allowed for waterfowl hunting.

The Lower Brule has trophy big game hunting for elk, buffalo, and deer. Permits for these hunts are limited. Hunting is done on 3,000 acres of rolling river breaks specifically managed to produce trophy animals.

Crow Creek Sioux Tribe

125,591 acres
Department of Natural Resources
Crow Creek Tribe
P.O. Box 50
Ft Thompson, SD 57339
605-245-2221
**Species allowed: pheasant, sharptail grouse, prairie chicken,
doves, ducks, and geese**

The Crow Creek Reservation is located in south-central South Dakota on the eastern bank of the Missouri River, on what is now Lake Sharpe and Lake Francis Case. The terrain consists of vast areas of grassland prairies and agricultural lands, intersected by lush riparian zones of oak, ash, cottonwood, and river bluffs. The reservation offers exceptional upland game bird and waterfowl hunting as well as deer, antelope, and varmint hunting. Being centered in the Central Waterfowl Flyway, the fall season brings massive numbers of migrating Snow and Canada geese and ducks. The result is outstanding waterfowl hunting.

The reservation has the Lode Star Casino. The closest town is Chamberlain, located 8 miles south of the reservation on I-90 (see page 177).

Yankton Sioux Tribe

40,000 acres
Yankton Sioux Tribe
P.O. Box 248
Marty, SD 57361
605-384-3651
**Species available: pheasant, sharptail grouse, prairie chicken,
bobwhite quail, ducks, and geese**

The reservation is located in the eastern two-thirds of Charles Mix County and is bordered on the south and southwest by the Missouri River and the Fort Randall Dam (Lake Francis Case). The terrain consists of agricultural lands, grasslands, riparian areas, and high river bluffs. This area is in the heart of prime pheasant country. The Missouri River provides outstanding hunting for ducks and very good hunting for geese. Charles Mix county is one of the few areas where you can find fair to good hunting for bobwhite quail.

The tribe operates the Fort Randall Casino and Hotel, 605-487-7871. The closest town is Lake Andes, just north of the reservation on Route 50.

Sisseton-Wahpeton Sioux Tribe

106,000 acres
Sisseton-Wahpeton Game & Fish
Box 509
Agency Village, SD 57262
605-698-3911
Species available: pheasant, Hungarian partridge, dove, turkey, ducks, and geese

This reservation is located in northeastern South Dakota. The terrain consists of over 1,000 small lakes and wetlands, providing some of the best waterfowl hunting in the state. The western part of the reservation lies on the Coteau Des Prairies. There are many wooded coulees running from the western plateau east to the Minnesota River lowlands. The nearest major towns are Aberdeen to the southwest (see page 207) and Watertown on its southern border (see page 219).

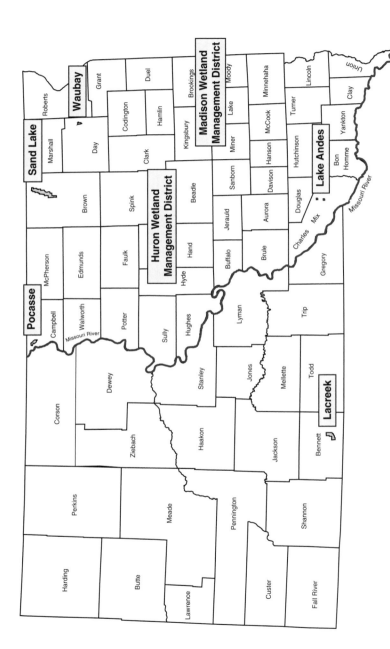

Wildlife Refuge Areas

NATIONAL WILDLIFE REFUGES AND WATERFOWL PRODUCTION AREAS

There are two Wetland Management Districts, five Wildlife Refuges and several hundred Waterfowl Production Areas in South Dakota, for a total of 144,000 acres.

The National Wildlife Refuges were established primarily to protect and enhance wetlands for the conservation of migratory birds. The Wetland Management Districts were set up for the same purpose. A Wetland Management District may contain a Wildlife Refuge. Waterfowl Production Areas are smaller bodies of water, potholes and wetlands that are established for the production of waterfowl. Think of the Waterfowl Production areas as mini refuges. The WPAs are open to the public for hunting.

Both the Wildlife Refuges and the Wetland Management Districts have waterfowl production areas. These areas are public lands that provide outstanding hunting opportunities for waterfowl and upland birds. Pheasants and sharptail grouse are the most abundant upland birds.

Each refuge has its own set of hunting regulations and seasons. Steel shot is required to hunt both waterfowl and upland birds on any refuge. Currently, you can use lead shot when hunting upland birds in the Waterfowl Production Areas. However, proposed regulations call for steel shot only in the WPAs starting in 1998.

Both a federal and state duck stamp are required when hunting waterfowl in addition to a state hunting license.

The *South Dakota Sportsman's Atlas* contains maps of each South Dakota county with all the state Game Production Areas, State Recreation Areas and Federal Waterfowl Production Areas marked in color. It is a very useful guide. It is available for $5.00 from:

South Dakota Game, Fish and Parks
523 East Capitol
Pierre, South Dakota 57501

Sand Lake National Wildlife Refuge and Waterfowl Management Area

Rural Route 1, Box 25
Columbia, South Dakota 57433-9761
605-885-6320

43,500 acres
Central Flyway
Glacial Lakes and Prairies Region

Sand Lake is located in northeastern South Dakota in Brown County. The closest town is Aberdeen. The refuge consists of 21,451 acres. Waterfowl hunting on Sand Lake is open during the regular South Dakota season. Hunters are restricted to hunting in the 300 spaced blinds located along the various sections of the refuge boundary. The blinds are occupied on a first-come, first-served basis. The blinds hold 2 hunters each, and hunters must shoot from within the blind. There is a 60-yard retrieval zone associated with each blind for unarmed retrievals only. A wheelchair accessible blind is available with an associated parking space is located at the Goose corner blind area. Mallards, teal, and pintails are the major duck species on the refuge. There are also Canada and snow geese. You may also hunt tundra swan on the refuge, for which you will need a special permit. Permits are issued at the refuge headquarters and are free.

The only upland hunting permitted on the refuge is for pheasants. The season begins the day after the last firearm deer season ends each year, which is usually around December 10-12, and lasts until December 31. No vehicles are allowed on the refuge during the pheasant hunt, so hunters must walk into the refuge from the boundary. Nontoxic shot is required during this hunt.

Sand Lake National Wildlife Refuge complex administers approximately 155 Waterfowl Production Areas (WPA) comprising 43,500 acres in the eight north central counties of Brown, Campbell, Edmunds, Faulk, McPherson, Potter, Spink, and Walworth. Hunting for both upland birds and waterfowl is permitted on the WPAs. Each WPA is clearly marked on the boundaries with this sign:

The WPAs range in size from less than 100 acres to several thousand acres. The *South Dakota Sportsman's Atlas* contains the locations of all of the WPAs. Hunting for both waterfowl and upland birds is allowed. Hunters must abide by all applicable state and federal regulations while hunting on WPAs.

Pocasse Wildlife Refuge
Administered by the Sand Lake Office

Sand Lake National Wildlife Refuge
Rural Route 1, Box 25
Columbia, South Dakota 57433
605-885-6320

Waterfowl hunting is not permitted on the refuge. The refuge is located in north central South Dakota in Campbell county, and the closest town is Mobridge.

Hunting is permitted for pheasant on the 2,200 acres around the refuge. The season opens after the end of the deer season around the middle of December and normally runs till the end of the year.

Waubay National Wildlife Refuge

RR 1, P.O. Box 79
Waubay, South Dakota 57273

Hunting allowed
39,000 acres of WPA
Central Flyway
Glacial and Prairie Region

Waubay National Wildlife Refuge is located in northeastern South Dakota. Over 39,000 acres of waterfowl production areas are managed in a six-county area. These areas range from less than a hundred acres to several thousand acres. *The Sportsman's Atlas* will show the location of all the WPAs in this region. Excellent hunting can be found for both waterfowl and upland game on the WPAs. Mallard, teal and gadwall are the major ducks. This is also a major area for both Canada and snow geese. You can also hunt tundra swan, however, you will need a special permit that can be obtained at the refuge headquarters or South Dakota Fish and Game. There is no charge for the permit.

Madison Wetland Management District

P.O. Box 48
Madison South Dakota 57042
605-256-2974

36,000 acres
Central Flyway
Glacial and Prairie Region

The Madison Wetlands comprise nine counties in east central South Dakota. The towns of Brookings, Madison and Watertown are the major centers. There are over 230 Waterfowl Production Areas in the Madison district. These are prairie potholes ranging from several acres to 20 acres.

The potholes provide excellent hunting for waterfowl. Puddle ducks are predominant. The major species are mallards, teal, widgeon, and gadwall. Most years there is a spectacular migration of snow geese through the area. Canada geese hunting is also excellent. Upland hunting is available on most of the areas.

Huron Wetland Management District

Room 317 Federal Building
200 4th Street SW
Huron, SD 57350
605-352-5894

11,000 acres
Central Flyway
Glacial and Prairie Region

The Huron district is an eight-county area in central South Dakota east of the Missouri River. The town of Huron is located in the center of this district. The 65 WPAs are like mini refuges. These are small prairie potholes. Waterfowl hunting is excellent. Major duck species are mallards, bluewing teal, and widgeon. They have excellent hunting for both Canada and snow geese. Hunting is also very good for upland birds.

Lake Andes National Wildlife Refuge and Wetland Management District

R.R. 1, Box 77
Lake Andes, South Dakota 57356
605-487-7603

Refuge 4,700 acres
WPA 40–19,000 acres
Central flyway
Heritage region

This district comprises 13 counties in the southeastern part of the state. The Lake Andes refuge is north of the Missouri River in Charles Mix county. Mitchell and Corsica are the nearest major towns. Waterfowl hunting is permitted in the central unit of the refuge, and you may use a boat or hunt from the dike. Major duck species are mallards, teal, and redheads. Hunting for both Canada and snow geese is excellent. This WPA provides excellent hunting for both waterfowl and upland game. The western part of this district is known for its outstanding pheasant hunting.

LaCreek National Wildlife Refuge and Little White River Recreation Area

HWC 3, Box 14
Martin, South Dakota 57551

7,000 acre refuge
Central flyway
Black Hills region

LaCreek refuge is located in southwestern South Dakota, with Martin being its major town. This refuge does not allow hunting for waterfowl, however, they do allow hunting for upland birds. The major birds are pheasants and sharptail grouse. Steel shot is required. The Little White River Recreation Area north of the refuge has hunting for both waterfowl and upland birds.

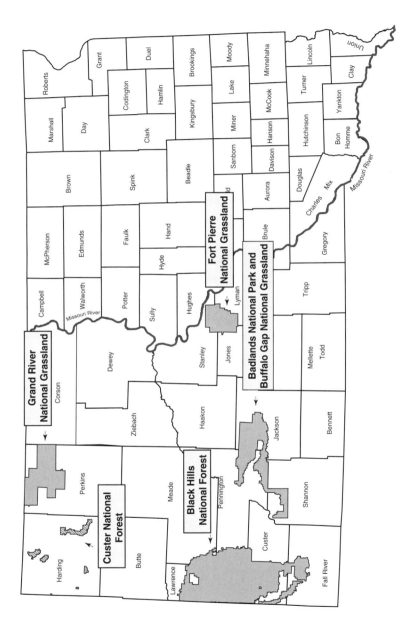

National Forests and Grasslands

SOUTH DAKOTA NATIONAL GRASSLANDS

South Dakota has three national grasslands containing a total of 866,000 acres. These are publicly owned lands administered by the USDA Forest Service. These grasslands consist of mixed and tall grass prairie. They are home to and provide ideal habitat for many mammals and birds. There are a great number of game birds, deer and antelope that inhabit the grasslands. Hunting possibilities are great, and there is only mild hunting pressure on the grasslands.

History of the Grasslands

These lands were once home to many Indian tribes, including Kiowa, Cheyenne, Crow, and Sioux, as well as huge buffalo herds that were their main source of food and clothing. By the end of the 1870s, Indians had lost their use of the lands. Late in the 19th century, under the Homestead Act of 1862, settlers, primarily farmers and cattleman, made their homes on the grasslands. However, due to low amounts of rainfall, less than 20" a year, the land was not well suited to farming. The drought and dust bowl of the 1930s saw thousands of homesteaders leave the area and abandon their farms.

From 1933 to 1943, nearly 10 million acres of drought-stricken land were purchased by the federal government. During this period, hundreds of thousands of acres were reclaimed, shelter belts were planted and erosion controls installed. By 1945 the lands were once again supporting soil-stabilizing grasses.

On June 23, 1960, nearly 4 million acres of Land Utilization Projects, located in the Great Plains region, became national grasslands to be managed by the National Forest Service as part of the National Forest system. These lands, unsuitable for cultivation, were now managed for wildlife, habitat, forage, prairie woodlands, water and outdoor recreation to the benefit of both land and people. Hunting is one of the primary purposes and uses of the grasslands.

Habitat Types in the National Grasslands

Trees: Cottonwoods, green ash, boxelder, elm, and juniper are located in woody draws, riparian areas, and shelter belts.

Upland Shrubs: Silver sagebrush, big sagebrush, and yucca

Other Shrubs: Buffaloberry, chokecherry, plum, and willow found primarily in woody draws, riparian areas, and shelter belts.

Short Grass: Primarily buffalograss and bluegrass.

Mid and Tall Grasses: Mid grasses include western wheatgrass and needle grasses. Tall grasses include prairie sandreed, prairie cordgrass, and big bluestem.

Aquatic Habitats: open water, including streams, stock ponds and reservoirs.

All of the grasslands are a mixture of public and private land. It is important that you obtain a map of the grassland that you intend to hunt so that you can identify the public land. It is illegal to hunt on private land without permission.

Maps and information of all of the three grasslands can be obtained at:

National Grasslands Visitor Center
708 Main Street
P.O. Box 425
Wall, South Dakota 57790
605-279-2125

Hunting Regulations and Seasons

National grasslands seasons are the same as the state of South Dakota. You do not need any additional licenses to hunt the grasslands. You will need a resident or nonresident South Dakota license. Buffalo Gap National Grassland does have an entrance fee for part of the area.

Buffalo Gap National Grassland

600,000 acres
Black Hills Region
Species Available: sharptail grouse, pheasants, Hungarian partridge

Buffalo Gap National Grassland is located in scattered tracts within Pennington, Jackson, Custer, and Fall River counties in the Black Hills Region of southwest South Dakota. The town of Wall on I-90 is located at the north entrance of the grasslands. There is a very nice and informative visitor center in Wall that has maps, books, and film programs about the grasslands. Rapid City is on the western edge of the grasslands. They have a commercial airport and would be the closest city to fly into for hunters.

This grassland offers a rich diversity of prairie habitats, including riparian areas, wooded draws, shrublands, juniper breaks, and open grasslands.

Sharptail grouse is the most abundant bird. Hunting sharptail is good to excellent depending on the spring hatch and weather. Sharptails roost in woody draws and can be found feeding in the grasslands or adjunct crop fields.

There is a fair to good population of pheasants. They roost in grasslands and draws and feed on croplands and grasslands.

Some hunting can be found for Hungarian partridge. They roost in draws and grasslands and can be found in wheat and alfalfa fields as well as grasslands.

Excellent deer and good antelope hunting is available on the grasslands.

Fort Pierre National Grasslands

116,000 acres
Great Lakes Region
Species Available: greater prairie chicken, sharptail grouse, pheasants

These grasslands are located in south central South Dakota in the Great Lakes Region and include the counties of Hughes, Sully, Stanley, Jones and Lyman. The nearest town is Pierre, the state capital.

Habitat is comprised of a patchwork of farms and ranches. There are croplands, tame pastures, and native rangeland, along with grasslands and brushy draws.

This is a prime habitat for the greater prairie chicken, and hunting is good to excellent. Prairie chicken feed in the alfalfa and grain fields and on the insects and plants of the grasslands.

Sharptail grouse hunting is good to excellent. Sharptails feed in the grain fields and grasslands and roost in grasslands or draws.

Pheasant hunting is fair to good. Pheasants feed in the grain fields and roost in the grasslands.

Grand River National Grassland

155,000 acres
Black Hills Region
Species Available: sharptail grouse, Hungarian partridge, pheasants

This grassland is located in north central South Dakota in the Black Hills Region and Perkins County. Lemmon, the closest town, is located on the northern edge of the grasslands and the border of North Dakota.

The area is comprised of a mixture of rangeland and grassland.

Sharptail grouse and Hungarian partridge are the main game birds. They feed on both croplands and grasslands.

Some pheasant hunting is available, and they can be found feeding in the croplands and grasslands.

SOUTH DAKOTA WALK-IN AREA PROGRAM

The Walk-In Area Program was designed to put hunters in contact with landowners and give them increased hunting possibilities on private land.

This program was created in 1987 by the Wildlife Division after a careful study of the "Where do I find a place to hunt?" question and in light of the opportunities created by CRP. It also provides hunters with hunting destinations that are certain, and provides landowners with liability assurances and a fee for allowing unlimited public hunting. Funding for the program is provided by your license fee and Federal Aid to Wildlife Restoration funds.

This is the eighth year of the program, and there are now approximately 500,000 acres, most of which is CRP, enrolled in the program. Virtually every county in South Dakota has some land in the program. Each property enrolled is clearly marked with a Walk-In Area Sign:

Walk-In Areas are not open to pheasant hunting during the special extended season in late December.

A directory of Walk-In Areas is available from South Dakota Game Fish and Parks. There is no charge for this publication. Ask for the *Walk-In Areas Atlas*. You can order it in the summer from:

> South Dakota Game Fish and Parks
> 523 East Capitol
> Pierre, South Dakota 57501
> 605-773-3485

This directory has maps showing all the areas and lists each area by county and total acreage. Map reproductions are very small, so we recommend that you carry a magnifying glass in order to read and identify the areas.

GAME PRODUCTION AREAS

The department of Game Fish and Parks owns, leases, and manages over 500 Game Production Areas, totaling more than 173,000 areas. These areas are identified by yellow and black signs and are managed by the Wildlife Division for wildlife production as well as public hunting. Statewide, 44% of GPAs are grasslands, 38% are wetlands, 11% cropland, and 7% trees and shrubs.

You can obtain a free listing of the Game Production Areas by writing for the booklet, *South Dakota Public Hunting Areas*. GPAs are marked with this sign:

There is also a *South Dakota Sportsman's Atlas*. This is a spiral-bound book containing maps of each South Dakota county, with all State Production Areas, State Parks and Recreation Areas, and Federal Waterfowl Production Areas marked in color. Cost of the atlas is $5.00.

For either or both of these publications write to:

South Dakota Game Fish and Parks
523 East Capitol
Pierre, South Dakota 57501
Phone 605-773-3485

Managing Wildlife on Game Production Areas

A variety of habitat management techniques are used to improve wildlife habitat. For example, controlled grazing and burning are used to rejuvenate upland nesting cover and stimulate vegetation growth. Winter cover is improved by planting wide shelter belts (most often over 20 rows wide), forage sorghum and cane, and stands of native grasses or sweet clover. Wetlands are enhanced by installing water-control structures and constructing pond-island complexes and level ditches. Waterfowl nesting structures and predator-proof fences are constructed to help the nesting success of waterfowl and other upland nesting birds. It is also important to restrict vehicular travel to designated roads, trail, and parking lots to maintain the quality of wildlife habitat on these areas. Consequently, boundary fence, access road and parking lot maintenance are also important tools used by wildlife managers to maintain and improve habitat.

In many instances, Game, Fish and Parks enters into lease agreements with area landowners to accomplish some of these habitat improvements on Game Production Areas. Game, Fish and Parks is also cooperating with Ducks Unlimited, Pheasants Forever, and the Rocky Mountain Elk Foundation to accomplish many of the habitat improvements and new acquisitions. In addition, sportsman's groups have become involved in improving wildlife habitat and access on Game Production Areas through a new Conservation Partners Program.

Each year over 300 acres of dense nesting cover, 5,550 acres of food plots, and 250 acres of trees are planted in an effort to maintain and improve various types of wildlife habitat on GPAs. In addition, 30 miles of boundary fence and posting main-tenance, 10,000 acres of noxious weed control, over 100 parking lots, and over 75 miles of access roads are maintained annually.

In all, the Game, Fish and Parks Wildlife Division spends over $2 million each year to maintain and improve wildlife habitat, access and public hunting opportu-nity on Game Production Areas.

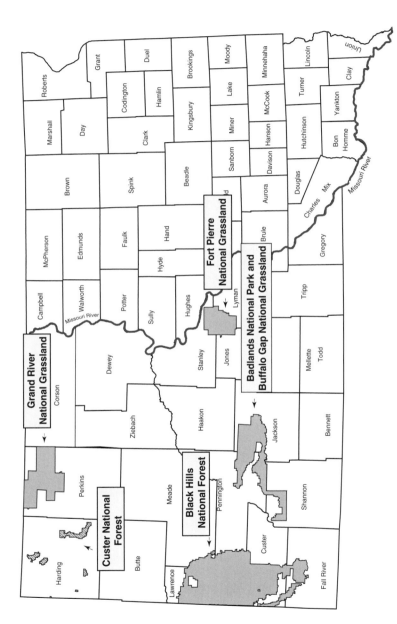

National Forests and Grasslands

NATIONAL FOREST AND STATE PARKS

BLACK HILLS NATIONAL FOREST

Black Hills National Forest is part of Custer National Forest. It comprises 1,250,000 acres and is located in the southwest part of the state. Elevations range from 3,000 to 7,200 feet. Open to hunting, it provides excellent wild turkey and ruffed grouse hunting. Trophy whitetail deer hunting is also excellent, making it a good choice for combining deer and bird hunting. Deadwood, the historic town where Wild Bill Hickok was shot, is in the center of this national forest. Rapid City is located on its eastern border and has a large commercial airport.

For information and maps of the Black Hills National Forest, contact:

> Black Hills National Forest
> RR2, Box 200
> Custer, South Dakota 57730
> Phone 605-673-2251

CUSTER STATE PARK

Located at the southern end of the Black Hills, Custer State Park comprises 73,000 acres. It is open to hunting and has excellent possibilities for wild turkey, ruffed grouse, and trophy whitetail.

For information and maps of Custer State Park:

> Custer State Park
> HC83, Box 70
> Custer, South Dakota 57730
> Phone 605-255-4515

CUSTER NATIONAL FOREST

Custer National Forest is located in southeastern Montana and northwestern South Dakota. The Cave Hills, Slim Buttes, Long Pines, and Short Pines areas in northwestern South Dakota provide excellent hunting for Merriam's wild turkey. Both a fall and spring gobbler season are offered with a permit system for both residents and nonresidents.

For information and maps ($3) of the national forest, write:

Custer National Forest
U.S. Forest Service
Box 2556
Billings, MT 59103

APPENDIX I
Traveling with Dog and Gun

Regulations for taking dogs and firearms on a plane vary from airline to airline. Listed below are some basic guidelines, but it will be necessary for you to ask about specific policies when you make your reservation.

Insurance is available for both animals and firearms. Check with your airline for costs and limits.

Dogs

1. Your dog will have to be checked as baggage. Most airlines charge an extra fee per dog (usually around $50).
2. You will need a travel kennel for each dog accompanying you. Kennels are available at most pet supply stores and sometimes at the airport. It is best to familiarize your dog with the kennel 2-3 weeks prior to the trip so that he will be comfortable. Your dog must be able to stand up, turn around, and lie in a comfortable position. There must be absorbent material in the bottom of the kennel (a towel or black-and-white newspaper is acceptable). Two empty dishes for food and water must be accessible from the outside. Also, don't forget to label your dog's kennel with your name, address, phone number, and final destination. It is necessary to attach certification that the animal has been fed and watered within four hours of departure time. Label the kennel with signs stating "Live Animal" and "This Side Up" with letters at least one inch high.
3. You will need a certificate of health from your veterinarian, including proof of rabies vaccination. Tranquilizers are not recommended because high altitude can cause dangerous effects. If you must sedate your dog, be sure to discuss it with your vet first.
4. Federal regulations exist regarding safe temperatures for transport of your dog.
   - Animals will not be accepted if the temperature is below 10°F at any point in transit.
   - If the temperature at your destination is below 45°F, a certificate of acclimation stating that your dog is used to low temperatures will be necessary. This is available from your vet.
   - Temperatures above 85°F can be dangerous for animals in transit. Many airlines will not accept dogs if the temperature at any transit point is more than 85°.

Temperatures in South Dakota during fall may vary widely. It is a good idea to check with the reservation desk regarding current temperatures and make your reservations accordingly. If you run into difficulty transporting your dog, remember these regulations are for your dog's safety.

Guns and Ammunition

1. Firearms and ammunition must be checked as baggage and declared by the passenger. You will be required to fill out a declaration form stating that you are aware of the federal penalties for traveling with a loaded firearm and that your gun is unloaded.

2. Guns must be packed, unloaded, in a hard-sided crushproof container with a lock specifically designed for firearm air transport. If you do not already have a case, they are usually available at the airport. Call your airline for details about dimensions. If your gun does not arrive on the baggage carousel, you may be required to claim it at a special counter in the baggage claim area.

3. Ammunition must be left in the manufacturer's original packaging and securely packed in a wood or metal container separate from the firearm. Most cities in South Dakota have sporting goods stores that carry a large variety of ammunition. It might be easier to purchase shells at your destination rather than traveling with them. If you use a rare or special type of ammo, you can pre-ship it through a service like UPS.

APPENDIX II
Hunter Conditioning and Equipment

Hunting the western prairies is dramatically different than hunting your favorite grouse or woodcock cover back east. You can drive for miles between ranches and towns without spotting any evidence of civilization. Prairies are characterized by dry, open spaces. Water is scarce.

A normal hunt for Huns, sharptails, and sage grouse starts in early morning when the temperature will be in the 20s. Early in the season (September-October), the temperature may climb into the 60s or even as high as the 90s by noon. Coveys of birds, while numerous, are spread over great distances. I usually leave the truck quite early and return in the late afternoon or evening. In the course of the day I cover 10-16 miles of open prairie. In order to enjoy your hunt, you need to be well conditioned and properly equipped.

Conditioning

I recommend that you start a walking or running program at least four months before you plan to hunt. You should be able to walk about three miles an hour on level ground. Try walking with a weighted pack. Remember, you will be walking with a shotgun, vest, and shells when hunting. Walk in the boots you intend to wear hunting. You don't have to be a marathon runner to have a productive hunt, however, if you are in good shape you can cover more ground.

Clothes

I wear lightweight ankle-high hunting boots. Unless you are hunting for waterfowl or are near a high stream, waterproof boots are not necessary. I wear two pairs of socks—an inner polypropylene sock to wick away moisture and a heavy wool outer sock for support.

I like to wear a light pair of canvas pants during the early part of the season and double-faced pants during the late season.

It is important to layer clothing on your upper body because of the wide range of temperatures you might encounter. Wear two or more layers of lightweight clothing that can be easily removed as temperatures climb, such as a polypropylene undershirt and a canvas or wool overshirt.

Sunburn is a common problem in the West. Always wear sunscreen and a billed hat while hunting. A bandana provides protection from the sun and can be used as a tourniquet for emergency purposes.

In the early season use a hunting shell bag and a hunting vest during the late season. If the weather is cold and snowy, wear an oilcloth coat and a vest big enough to fit over all your outer garments.

It's a good idea to carry a pair of light leather shooting gloves. Finally, take a good pair of shooting glasses for sun and eye protection and earplugs to protect your hearing.

Equipment

I carry a small folding knife in a sheath on my belt, along with a 24-inch dog lead. I also have a wristwatch that has a compass on the band and carry a whistle and a hemostat around my neck (it's great for picking out cactus needles). I always carry at least one quart of water for my dogs. When it is especially hot and water is scarce, I carry several quarts because I have come close to losing dogs to heat prostration. I normally wear a small fanny pack that holds water, lunch, camera, and other miscellaneous items. Finally, I carry a small amount of honey for my dogs, which can rejuvenate an exhausted dog.

Following is an equipment list for clothes, dogs, and supplies. Make copies and use it as a checklist when packing for your trip.

EQUIPMENT CHECKLIST

CLOTHING

_____ polypropylene underwear

_____ inner socks

_____ wool socks

_____ long sleeve canvas/chamois shirts

_____ pants, double-faced

_____ hunting boots

_____ billed hat

_____ bandana

_____ shooting gloves

_____ shooting glasses

_____ ear protectors

_____ hunting vest/coat

_____ down vest/coat

_____ raingear

_____ hip boots/waders for waterfowl hunting

_____ chaps

DOG SUPPLIES

_____ food, bowls

_____ beeper collar

_____ lead

_____ dog boots, pad toughener

_____ hemostat

_____ whistle

_____ water bottles

_____ *Field Guide to Dog 1st Aid*

_____ dog first aid kit

_____ record of dog vaccinations

_____ scissors

_____ toenail clippers

HUNTING SUPPLIES

_____ *Wingshooter's Guide to SD*

_____ shotgun/shells

_____ cleaning kit

_____ maps

_____ knife

_____ fanny pack

_____ water bottle

_____ camera, film

_____ binoculars

_____ game shears

_____ ice chest

_____ notebook, pen

_____ license

_____ matches

_____ axe, shovel

_____ sunscreen

_____ twine

_____ decoys, decoy anchor

_____ compass

_____ flashlight

_____ bird calls

_____ spare choke tubes

_____ magnifying glass for maps

APPENDIX III
Conditioning of Hunting Dogs

Dogs, like people, must be in top physical condition to hunt day after day. As for any athlete, proper food and exercise is the key to good health. The best performing dogs are those that are in training year-round.

Many hunting dog owners are not willing or able to devote enough time to exercising their dog throughout the year. Even if you are pressed for time, you should start working your dog regularly at least four or five weeks before hunting season. You and your dog will start getting into shape and have more stamina throughout the season.

Proper feeding of a hunting dog is important and a good grade of dog food certainly helps. Feeding once a day is sufficient, but I feed my dogs smaller amounts of moistened food twice a day. If they are working hard, animals should be given all the moistened food they want.

A dog should not be fed just prior to a workout, so feed them early in the morning before going hunting. I don't subscribe to the old adage, "A hungry dog fights best." I believe I hunt better and harder after having a good breakfast and so do my dogs. I recommend that red meat be added to the dog's diet during hunting season. It increases the palatability of the food and encourages the dog to eat more, which in turn will increase nutritional intake and energy reserves.

The benefits of a well-trained dog for bird hunting are many. Considerable time and money is required to maintain hunting dogs, but in the long run, it will add a new dimension to your life. Keep your dogs in good physical condition; they expect it of you.

Bob Tinker puts rubber boots on his dog.

- Exercise your dog all year long if possible.

- Exercise your dog at least one month before hunting season.

- Feed a good grade of dog food that is high in protein.

- Do not let your dog get overweight (an obese dog in the field can collapse quickly due to lack of conditioning).

- When transporting dogs, make sure your vehicle is well ventilated. Don't smoke around your dog in close quarters.

- Carry ample supplies of water in the field and in the vehicle.

- Dogs should be watered often which helps with stamina and scenting ability.

- Dog boots and tummy savers are useful when hunting in prickly pear country or stubble fields.

- Let dogs rest occasionally.

- Give your dogs a small nutritional treat from time to time (they deserve it).

- In the field, dogs come first. See to any needs immediately (thorns, burrs, cuts, etc.).

- Feed, care for, and make your dogs comfortable before you take care of yourself.

Charles F. Waterman waters Shoe.

APPENDIX IV
The Prairie Wagon

Almost any vehicle can be used for upland gamebird or waterfowl, but a four-wheel drive rig does give you an advantage in rough country. I have a 4x4 pickup truck with an extra cab and a fiberglass topper (white to keep the dogs cool), designed with six dog compartments that can hold up to a dozen dogs. It has a fan and a drain system that allows for dry storage beneath the topper with ample room for hunting needs.

These are the things I keep in my hunting rig at all times:

shovel, axe
come-along
jumper cables
tow rope
paper towels

flashlight
small air compressor
fencing tool (for fixing fence only)
extra key taped under the chassis

For the dogs:
5 gallons of water
several 1-gallon water jugs
lead
beeper collars
whistles

two different sizes of hemostats
duct tape
water bottle
first aid kit
Seven 5™ dust for use against ticks

For the hunter:
water bottle
first aid kit
cooler
knife
toilet paper

extra socks
soap, towel
binoculars
extra warm fleece pullover
extra set of keys for a partner

APPENDIX V
Preparing a Bird for Mounting in the Field

by Web Parton, Taxidermist

The art of taxidermy has made considerable advances in recent years. This is especially true in the realm of bird taxidermy. How you take care of your birds in the field determines the finished quality of your mounts. This crucial step is out of the control of the taxidermist. However, with a modicum of preparation, you can proceed confidently when you are holding a freshly taken bird destined for the book shelf.

Start by putting together a small kit to be carried with you in the field. Use a small plastic container, such as a plastic traveler's soap box. Throw in some cotton balls, a few wooden toothpicks, a dozen or so folded sheets of toilet paper, and a pair of panty hose.

After shooting a bird, examine it closely. First, look for pin feathers. If there are any present, you will notice them on the head directly behind the beak or bill and on the main side coverts below the bird's wing. If there are even a few pinfeathers, the specimen may not be worth mounting. By all means, save it and let your taxidermist make the decision. However, it wouldn't hurt to examine additional birds to find one with better plumage. The taxidermist can always use extra birds for spare parts.

The next step is to check for any bleeding wounds in order to prevent the taxidermist from having to wash the bird before mounting. Plug any visible wounds with cotton. Use a toothpick as a probe to push the cotton into the holes. Now pack the mouth and nostrils, remembering that the body is a reservoir of fluids that can drain down the neck. Make a note or take a photo of any brightly colored soft tissue parts (unfeathered areas) for the taxidermist's reference later. Fold several sheets of toilet paper and lay them between the wings and the body. Should the body bleed, this will protect the undersides of the wings from being soiled. Slide the bird head first into the nylon stocking. Remember that the feathers lay like shingles: they slide forward into the stocking smoothly, but will ruffle if you pull the bird back out the same end. The taxidermist will remove it by cutting a hole in the material at the toe and sliding the bird forward. When the specimen is all the way down, knot the nylon behind its tail. Now you are ready to slide the next one in behind it.

Place the wrapped bird in an empty game vest pocket, allow it to cool, and protect it from getting wet. When you return to your vehicle, place the bird in a cool spot. At home, put it in a plastic bag to prevent freezer burn, and freeze it solid. You can safely wait several months before dropping it off at the taxidermist.

For the traveling hunter, there is the option of next-day air shipping. Provided that you can find a place to freeze the birds overnight, even a hunter on the other side of the nation can get birds to his taxidermist in good shape. Wrap the frozen birds, nylons and all, in disposable diapers. Line a shipping box with wadded newspapers. Place the birds in the middle with dry ice. Dry ice is available in some major supermarkets. Call your taxidermist to be sure someone will be there, and then ship the parcel next-day air. Be sure to contact them the next day so that a search can be instituted in the event that the parcel did not arrive.

Mounted birds are a beautiful memory of your days in the field. With just a little bit of advance preparation, you can be assured of a top-quality mount.

APPENDIX VI
Field Preparation of Game Birds for the Table

The two most important tools for preparing birds in the field for the table are game sheers and a knife with a gut hook.

During early season, when temperatures are in the 70° to 90° mark, I draw my birds immediately or shortly after I leave the field. You can draw your birds by several methods.

I make a cut with my sheers at the end of the breast, making a small entry hole into the body cavity. I then take my gut hook, insert it into the cavity and pull out the intestines and other body parts.

The other method I use is to take my sheers and cut up the center of the bird's back, splitting the bird in two. Then you can use your gut hook and knife to clean out the intestines and other body parts.

I like to place my birds in a cooler during the hot early season. When the temperatures are cooler (below 55°), I store my birds in either a burlap or net bag. This type of bag allows air to circulate around the birds.

I like to hang my birds before cleaning and freezing. I hang my birds in a room where the temperature is less than 60° F. I have found that two to three days hanging time is best for the smaller birds (i.e., huns, grouse, woodcock). I hang my larger birds (pheasants, ducks) from four to five days. Hanging birds is a matter of individual preference. My friend, Datus Proper, hangs his birds for a much longer period of time than I do. I suggest that you experiment and then pick a hanging time that suits your tastes.

When the temperature is over 60°F, I clean my birds and freeze them immediately. We wrap our birds in cling wrap, place them in a ziplock bag, and then mark the bag with the type of bird and the date.

APPENDIX VII
Information on Hunting and Maps

LICENSES

South Dakota Department of Game, Fish and Parks
312 West Missouri
Pierre, SD 57501-4521
Phone 605-773-3485

PROFESSIONAL GUIDES AND OUTFITTERS

South Dakota Professional Guides and Outfitters Association
P.O. Box 703
Pierre, SD 57501
Phone 605-224-9270

The association has a booklet listing all of its members and the services they offer.

VACATION INFORMATION

South Dakota Department of Tourism
711 East Wells Avenue
Pierre, SD 57501-3369
Phone 1-800-732-5682
Fax 605-773-3256

MAPS AND PUBLICATIONS

There are several maps and publications designed to aid the hunter. Following is a list of those maps, their publishers and their cost.

South Dakota Sportsman's Atlas
Game, Fish and Parks
523 East Capitol
Pierre, SD 57501 $5.00
    Contains maps of each South Dakota county with all state Game Production Areas, state parks and recreation areas, and federal Waterfowl Production Areas marked in color.

National Forests and Grasslands

Buffalo Gap National Grassland
U.S. Forest Service
125 North Main
Chardon, NE 69337 $3.00

Grand River and Cedar River
    National Grasslands
U.S. Forest Service
Box 2556
Billings, MT 59102 $3.00

Fort Pierre National Grasslands
U.S. Forest Service
Box 417
Pierre, SD 57501 $3.00

Custer National Forest
U.S. Forest Service
Box 2556
Billings, MT 59103
Color map including Cave Hills, Slim
Buttes, Long Pines, and Short Pines in
northwestern SD as well as Custer
National Forest in Montana $3.00

Other Agencies

BLM Surface Management Quads
Bureau of Land Management, R.A.H.
310 Roundup Street
Belle Fourche, SD 57717
Phone 605-892-2526

Shows public land in extreme western and northwestern South Dakota. Free index, map costs vary.

Missouri River Boating and Recreation Guide Maps
Department of Army, Corps of Engineers Omaha District
Operations Division
215 North 17th Street
Omaha, NE 68102
Phone 402-221-4139

Includes water area and government lands on the mainstem reservoirs of the Missouri River. Maps for Lakes Lewis and Clark, Francis Case, Sharpe, and Oahe can be ordered. Check with the Corps for map costs and postage.

South Dakota Game, Fish and Parks Publications

523 East Capitol
Pierre, SD 57501
605-773-3485

South Dakota Public Hunting Areas — free booklet listing all hunting areas
    and locations.
Walk-In Area Atlas — annual publication mapping private and leased land
    for public hunting

South Dakota Fishing and Hunting Handbooks — synopsis of regulations for the current season, free

Missour River Reservoir Access Maps — separate color maps of each lake showing locations of access

Other Sources

Campground Guide
Department of Tourism
711 East Wells Avenue
Pierre, SD 57501

Free booklet listing private as well as public campgrounds with descriptions and location maps.

South Dakota Conservation Digest
Game, Fish and Parks
412 West Missouri
Pierre, SD 57501

Full color, 32-page magazine published six times a year. Articles on fishing, hunting, camping, and other outdoor activities, $5 per year.

Recommended Reading

American Game Birds of Field and Forest. Frank C. Edminster. New York: Castle Books, 1954.

American Wildlife & Plants: A Guide to Wildlife Food Habits. Alexander C. Martin, Herbert S. Zim, Arnold L. Nelson. New York: Dover Publishing, Inc., 1951.

•*Autumn Passages: A Ducks Unlimited Treasury of Waterfowling Classics.* Ducks Unlimited & Willow Creek Press, 1995. $27.50

•*Best Way to Train Your Gun Dog: The Delmar Smith Method.* Bill Tarrant. New York: David McKay Company, Inc., 1977. $20.00

•*Bill Tarrant's Gun Dog Book: A Treasury of Happy Tails.* Bill Tarrant. Honolulu: Sun Trails Publishing, 1980. A great collection of fireside dog stories. $25.00

•*Ducks, Geese & Swans of North America.* Frank C. Bellrose. Harrisburg, PA: Stackpole Books, 1976. $49.95

•*A Field Guide to Dog First Aid.* Randy Acker, D.V.M., and Jim Fergus. Bozeman, MT: Wilderness Adventures Press, 1994. An indispensible pocket guide. It could save your dog's life. $15.00

•*Fool Hen Blues: Retrievers, Shotguns, & the American West.* E. Donnall Thomas, Jr. Bozeman, MT: Wilderness Adventures Press, 1995. Don hunts sharptails, Huns, sage grouse, mountain grouse, pheasants, and waterfowl against the wild Montana sky. $29.00

Game Birds of North America. Leonard Lee Rue, III. New York: Harper & Row, 1973.

Game Management. Aldo Leopold. Madison, WI: University of Wisconsin Press, 1933.

•*Good Guns Again.* Steve Bodio. Bozeman, MT: Wilderness Adventures Press, 1994. A survey of fine shotguns by an avid gun collector and trader. $29.00

Grasslands. Lauren Brown. New York: Alfred A. Knopf, 1985.

Grouse and Quails of North America. Paul A. Johnsgard. Lincoln, NE: University of Nebraska Press, 1973.

•*Gun Dogs and Bird Guns: A Charlie Waterman Reader.* Charles F. Waterman. South Hamilton, MA: Gray's Sporting Journal Press, 1986. To be reprinted in the fall of 1995.

•*Hey Pup, Fetch It Up: The Complete Retriever Training Book.* Bill Tarrant. Mechanicsburg, PA: Stackpole Books, 1979. $25.00

•*How to Hunt Birds with Gun Dogs.* Bill Tarrant, Mechanicsburg, PA: Stackpole Books, 1994. Bill covers all the birds, what dogs to use and how to hunt each game bird. $21.00

•*A Hunter's Road.* Jim Fergus. New York: Henry Holt and Co., 1992. A joyous journey with gun and dog across the American Uplands. A hunter's *Travels with Charlie*. $25.00

•*Hunting Ducks and Geese.* Steve Smith. Harrisburg, PA: Stackpole Books, 1984. A bit dated, but still the best how-to book on hunting waterfowl. $20.00

Hunting Upland Birds. Charles F. Waterman. New York: Winchester Press, 1972.

•*Kicking Up Trouble*. John Holt. Bozeman, MT: Wilderness Adventures Press, 1994. John takes you on a delightful bird hunting trip through Montana. $29.00

Life Histories of North American Gallinaceous Birds. Arthur Cleveland Bent. New York: Dover Publishing, Inc. 1963.

•*Meditations on Hunting*. José Ortega y Gasset. Bozeman, MT: Wilderness Adventures Press, 1995. The classic book on hunting. Special edition. $60.00

Peterson Field Guides: Western Birds. Roger Tory Peterson. Boston: Houghton Mifflin, 1990.

•*Pheasants of the Mind*. Datus C. Proper. Bozeman, MT: Wilderness Adventures Press, 1994. Simply the best book ever written on pheasants. $25.00

•*Problem Gun Dogs*. Bill Tarrant. Mechanicsburg, PA: Stackpole Books, 1995. $20.00

Prairie Ducks. Lyle K. Sowls. Lincoln, NE: University of Nebraska Press, 1978.

A Sand County Almanac. Aldo Leopold. New York: Oxford University Press, 1949.

•*Training the Versatile Retriever to Hunt Upland Birds*. Bill Tarrant. Bozeman, MT: Wilderness Adventures Press, 1996. $29.95

Waterfowl: An Identification Guide to the Ducks, Geese and Swans of the World. Houghton Mifflin Co. $29.95

Western Forests. Stephen Whitney. New York: Alfred K. Knopf, 1985.

•Available from Wilderness Adventures

INDEX

NOTES

NOTES

A WINGSHOOTER'S GUIDE TO SOUTH DAKOTA

If you would like to order additional copies of this book or any other Wilderness Adventures Press publication, please fill out the order form below or call **1-800-925-3339** or **fax 406-763-4911.**

Mail to:
Wilderness Adventures Press, P.O. Box 627, Gallatin Gateway, MT 59730

Ship to:
Name _____

Address _____

City _____ State _____ Zip _____

Home Phone _____ Work Phone _____

Payment: ☐ Check   ☐ Visa   ☐ Mastercard   ☐ Discover   ☐ American Express

Card Number _____ Expiration Date _____

Signature _____

Quantity	Title of Book and Author	Price	Total
	Total Order + shipping & handling		

Please add $3.00 per book for shipping and handling.

Coming in 1996 from Wilderness Adventures Press

Wingshooter's Guide to Arizona

Reserve Your Copy Now!